Global Sport

Global Sport

Identities, Societies, Civilizations

JOSEPH MAGUIRE

Polity Press

First published in 1999 by Polity Press in association with Blackwell Publishers Ltd.

Editorial office:
Polity Press
65 Bridge Street
Cambridge CB2 1UR, UK

Marketing and production:
Blackwell Publishers Ltd
108 Cowley Road
Oxford OX4 1JF, UK

Published in the USA by
Blackwell Publishers Inc.
Commerce Place
350 Main Street
Malden, MA 02148, USA

A catalogue record for this book is available from the British Library.

Library of Congress Cataloging-in-Publication Data

Maguire, Joseph A., 1956–
    Global sport : identities, societies, civilizations / Joseph Maguire.
        p.   cm.
    Includes bibliographical references (p.   ) and index.
    ISBN 0-7456-1531-7 (hardback). — ISBN 0-7456-1532-5 (pbk)
        1. Sports—Sociological aspects.   2. Nationalism and sports.
    3. Sports—Cross-cultural studies.   I. Title.
    GV706.5.M34   1999
    306.4'83—dc21   98-52191
                                                                                    CIP

Typeset in $10^1/_2$ on 12 pt Palatino by Wearset, Boldon, Tyne & Wear.
Printed in Great Britain by TJ International, Padstow, Cornwall.

This book is printed on acid-free paper.

Contents

Preface

This book reflects the work I have been involved in throughout the 1990s. In many ways it should have been completed sooner. A range of challenges, personal and professional, have, however, got in the way. At times, I felt that the book would not be completed. With the enduring help of friends and colleagues I have finally managed to complete it and, with some difficulty, 'let it go'. Yet, despite the unforeseen delays, perhaps it has been for the best. As a consequence of these delays my own position has changed and I have had the opportunity to reflect on recent work, include new material and engage with others in lectures and debates. I hope my visits to places such as Australia, Canada, Denmark, Ireland, Japan, South Korea, Sweden, Switzerland and the USA had some positive impact on the local audience – the feedback received certainly sharpened my own thinking. I thank my colleagues in these places.

Since beginning my doctoral work in 1979 I have always felt that figurational sociology has been misrepresented in certain quarters; I am not sure if I could ever convince some of its potential value. Nevertheless, this book is a contribution towards sustaining the idea that figurational sociology has something distinctive to offer the sociology of sport. I hope, in some small way, that it adds to the work undertaken by Norbert Elias and Eric Dunning. More generally, however, I also hope that this book will be seen as a contribution to the globalization debate and how figurational sociology can assist in understanding globalization processes. Ironically, figurational sociologists have themselves been somewhat slow to grasp how their perspective can contribute to the ongoing debate about globalization. I have tried to combine theoretical insights with empirical enquiries and have drawn on work published over the past five years. It will be for others to judge the worth of what has been accomplished.

Joseph Maguire
Loughborough
August 1998

Acknowledgements

Readers of academic books sometimes forget that writers have their own lives to live, just like them. In developing my own life and along the way, my sociological thinking, I have met many people who have helped shape my thoughts and feelings. My early lecturing experience was ably and generously supported by Anita White when we both taught at West Sussex Institute of Higher Education. My first experience of NASSS was via the wisdom and kindness of Jay Coakley. I will be forever grateful. Over the years friends and colleagues such as David Andrews, Cheryl Cole, Alan Klein, Bruce Kidd, John Loy, Jim McKay, Bill McTeer, Geneviève Rail, Kim Schimmel and Phil White have always made my visits to North America both enriching and bound up in wonderful memories. These people, and many more, have helped in so many ways. Similarly, my colleagues in ISSA, notably Kari Fasting and Bart Vanreusel, have provided stimulation and support when I have needed it over the past decade. British colleagues and friends such as Grant Jarvie, Jennifer Hargreaves, Garry Whannel and Louise Mansfield have always been there for me. I thank them all. Nearer home, my colleagues at Leicester University, Pat Murphy, Ivan Waddington and Ken Sheard, repeatedly remind me of my doctoral roots! Similarly, colleagues like Stephen Mennell at University College, Dublin, and Ian Henry and David Kerwin at Loughborough University, have provided encouragement when needed. I should also thank my sociology of sport colleagues David Stead, Emma Poulton, Cath Possamai and Jason Tuck – each in their own way knows how they have helped in this project.

My thanks are also due to Gill Motley and Jennifer Speake at Polity Press for their kindness, understanding and expert eye.

In closing these remarks there are other friends and colleagues whom I wish to thank. Going back over twenty years Bob Pearton has provided support and advice on many occasions – I wish I had taken the advice more frequently. Similarly, of late, Alan Ingham has shared insights with me that go beyond the call of a 'friend in need'. I would also like to thank Peter Donnelly for giving me support and friendship when first developing my ideas on American football and for being my most stern, but also most constructive critic over the years. In addition, Kevin Young and I have shared time together and conducted in-depth research across the globe; long may this continue! Finally, but not least, let me also acknowledge my immense gratitude to Eric Dunning: he has got me into, but mostly out of more conceptual and other scrapes than I dare to mention. The lesson I learnt early on from Eric was to 'think until it hurts'! This book is not the fault of my friends and colleagues but they have helped me along the way and I could not have done it without them.

In the process of writing a book life does not stand still. During this period I have encountered joys yet also sadness and loss of different kinds. Throughout all these experiences I have had the privilege to be the father of my wonderful son, Thomas. I thank him for being Thomas and reminding me of the important moments in life.

I would like to thank the Norbert Elias Stichtung for granting permission to reproduce a number of passages from the works of Norbert Elias. I would also like to thank: The Guardian/Observer News Service, London, for permission to reproduce material © *The Guardian; The Observer* (London) for permission to reproduce material © *The Observer; The Independent* for permission to quote from leading articles (12 March 1993 and 12 June 1993) and from articles by Andrew Marr and Mark Lawson; Ewan MacNaughton Associates for permission to use material © *The Daily Telegraph*; News International for permission to quote material © Patricia Finney, *The Sunday Times* (18 January 1987), © William Rees-Mogg, *The Times* (12 August 1993) and © Simon Barnes, *The Times* (20 January 1984). The extract on p. 123 is reprinted with the permission of *The Globe and Mail* (Toronto).

Every effort has been made to trace all the copyright holders in respect to the data in this book; should any others have been inadvertently overlooked the author and publisher will be pleased to make the necessary arrangements at the first opportunity.

Introduction:
Sports, Local Cultures and Global Processes

A product of modern European civilization, studying any problem of universal history, is bound to ask himself [*sic*] to what combination of circumstances the fact should be attributed that in Western civilization, and in Western civilization only, cultural phenomena have appeared which (as we like to think) lie in a line of development having universal significance and value.

Weber, *The Protestant Ethic and the Spirit of Capitalism*, 1920

As humankind approaches the third millennium it is impossible to overlook the pervasive influence of modern sport on the lives of people from different parts of the globe. Scaling the highest mountains, traversing the most difficult terrain, exploring the depths of the sea and skimming across the oceans, soaring through the skies and descending into deep valley gorges, tunnelling far into the interior of the earth and shaping its exterior with both 'natural' and 'artificial' surfaces and structures, sportsmen and sportswomen straddle the globe, and the sportization of the planet seemingly knows no bounds. To say this is not to praise the present state of affairs. Nor is it to suggest that all human beings are involved in and affected by modern sports in the same way. How then is this very long-term process to be understood? How has this present global sport formation emerged out of the past? What are the main 'structured processes' involved? What functions, meanings and significance has the existing global sport-system in people's lives across the world? What possible tendencies can be detected as we approach the end of the twentieth century? These are some of the central questions that this book seeks to address through empirically grounded theoretical research but also, at times, by some preliminary and speculative insights.

Given that the term 'globalization' has itself become global in its usage, and subject, as chapter 1 explores, to intense academic scrutiny and debate, perhaps it is unsurprising that an English newspaper would connect this process to sport. In an editorial in the *Guardian*, written in 1994, it was observed:

> Compared with this summer's continuing – and, since Monday evening, somewhat deflated – attempt to sell football to the Americans, today's arrival of the Tour de France in England is only a small step in the globalisation of sport. But there can be little doubt that both are part of the same process. Sport may be the quintessence of nationalism on many occasions, but it is also one of the most effective means yet devised of uniting the global village.
>
> (*Guardian*, 6 July 1994: p. 23)

While these comments may well overstate and romanticize its unifying effects, the writer is correct to observe that sport has diffused on a global scale. The connections between sport and globalization are, however, as chapter 2 demonstrates, more complex than the writer suggests, though it is not without significance that a newspaper editorial would make such a connection. Sport, in all its forms and guises, does have a remarkable appeal to contemporary human beings. Consider the vast audiences who watch media coverage of the Olympic Games and other world championship events. In global sports contests people invest a great deal of their self, communal and national identities. Sport has tremendous symbolic value. As players, officials, administrators or spectators at the live event or as consumers of mediated sport, people express, for better or worse, a range of embodied emotions.

Emotions, expressed 'locally', are constructed in the context of a global sport process. Representatives of government departments, private organizations and multinational corporations, show a significant interest and play an important part in this global cultural interchange. Sport, therefore *matters* (Dunning, in press). It moves people emotionally; as a multi-billion-pound enterprise it employs, directly or indirectly, large numbers of people; in so doing it uses significant amounts of scarce resources and leaves its footprint on the environment. It also has a major political impact in terms of national prestige, and also through education, health and the voluntary sector, it plays a part in the internal socialization and the external migration of citizens and is viewed, by some, as potentially developing international fellowship.

The Globalization Perspective

Issues of this kind, and the questions raised at the outset about modern sport, are more usually painted on a narrower natio-centric canvas. The frame of reference adopted here is global in perspective and, as such, is in keeping with the observations that Roland Robertson (1995) and Mike Featherstone and Scott Lash (1995) have made regarding globalization. That is, we must 'move away from social change conceived as the internal development of societies to focusing on change as the outcome of struggles between the members of a figuration of interdependent and competing nation-states', and then, 'add to this an understanding of the intensification of trans-societal flows which are pushing towards a borderless global economy' (Featherstone & Lash, 1995: p. 2). Globalization processes are viewed here as being long-term processes that have occurred unevenly across all areas of the planet. These processes – involving an increasing intensification of global interconnectedness – appear to be gathering momentum and despite their 'unevenness', it is more difficult to understand local or national experiences without reference to these global flows. Every aspect of social reality – people's living conditions, beliefs, knowledge and actions – is intertwined with unfolding globalization processes. These processes include the emergence of a global economy, a transnational cosmopolitan culture and a range of international social movements. Considered in this manner, and as Roudometof and Robertson conclude, globalization:

> constitutes a process of mutual interaction among different power networks over a long period of time. Globalization theory concerns itself with the multidimensional interrogation of these interciviliza-tional 'encounters' or interactions ... [and] represents an attempt toward a more holistic understanding of the phenomena in question by incorporating cultural-ideological factors as autonomous or relatively autonomous forces in the making of the modern 'global' system.
>
> (Roudometof & Robertson, 1995: p. 287)

Viewed from this vantage point, globalization, as Robertson himself observed, refers 'in its most general sense, to the process whereby the world becomes a single place' (Robertson, 1992: p. 135). He is keen to avoid the suggestion that this notion of a 'single place' entails a crystallization of a cohesive system. Yet, he maintains, globalization does involve the development of a global culture. This culture, he argues, is not a homogeneous, binding whole, but refers to a 'general mode of discourse about the world as a whole and its variety' (Robertson, 1992: p. 133). Concerned to trace the way in which the world is ordered, Robertson also maps out the 'global field'. In tracing the pattern of this global field, that results from an interweaving of societies, individuals, international relations and humankind as a whole, Robertson maintains that a reference to a single causal process must be avoided. In mapping out the global condition, Robertson identifies five main phases in this long-term process. The details need not detain us at this point, though it is important to add that this pattern of phasing, combined with the work done by Elias and Dunning (1986) on the early sportization phases, underpins the structure of chapters 3 and 4.

The Figurational/Process-Sociological Perspective

The perspective adopted here is in sympathy with the sentiments expressed by Robertson and is underpinned by a figurational/ process-sociological approach to the study of globalization processes (Dunning, 1992b; Elias, 1987/1991; Maguire, 1995b; Mennell, 1990, 1994). As Norbert Elias observed:

> as a sociologist one can no longer close one's eyes to the fact that in our time, in place of the individual states, humanity split up into states is increasingly becoming the framework of reference, as a social unit, of many developmental processes and structural changes. Without *global frames of reference* such processes and structural changes cannot be either adequately diagnosed or adequately explained. The incipient breakthrough to a new level of integration that can be observed on all sides demands a breakthrough to a new level of synthesis in sociology.
>
> (Elias, 1987/1991: p. 163; italics added)

Throughout this text, then, I will make the case that process-sociological thinking and research can assist in establishing this breakthrough. One feature of my argument, developed at some length in chapter 2, is that the present global sport formation has arisen out of an interweaving between the intentional acts of individuals and social groups that are grounded in the relatively unplanned features of inter-civilizational processes. Considered in this way, I want to stress the impact that sports have on the embodied identities of people and how this is embedded in wider 'local' and national cultural processes. These processes are, in turn, interconnected with broader global changes. A process-sociological perspective can also assist in addressing the other questions identified at the outset as being crucial to understanding the global sport formation. I will also argue that this perspective enables the researcher to avoid certain conceptual snares in which some sociological accounts of global processes are entrapped. One such trap is the seemingly non-resolvable debate concerning whether globalization leads to homogeneity or heterogeneity (Robertson, 1995; Nederveen Pieterse, 1995).

In highlighting issues of homogeneity, and the mutual contest of *sameness* and *difference* in global cultural flows, the analysis can be developed with reference to the figurational concepts of diminishing contrasts and increasing varieties, commingling and established-outsider relations (Elias, 1939/1994; Mennell, 1985). This has several benefits. These concepts arguably enable the analyst to steer a path between the excesses of the homogeneity thesis and the simplicities of the voluntarist position that assumes that individuals freely choose and cultures freely contribute, in equal measure, to global cultural diversity. These concepts also ensure that we conduct a serious comparison of contemporary civilizations in the context of the debate surrounding resurgent nationalism and globalization processes.

These concepts also help in making sense of the global diffusion, patterning and differential popularization of sports. Indeed, by focusing attention on these concepts, aspects of the figurational/process-sociological approach to sport can be refined and extended. These concepts have been relatively neglected and not given due prominence in previous figurational accounts. This may explain, in part, some of the misunderstandings and misinterpretations that have arisen over the past three decades. By highlighting these concepts, my hope is that it can be shown that there is greater common ground with other approaches than is perhaps realized or accepted.

One area of common ground identified in chapter 1 is with those analyses that emphasize the multifaceted, multidirectional and complex sets of power balances that characterize the global sport process. The essential point of departure is that an understanding of the global sportization formation is bound up in an inter-civilizational analysis. While the development of modern sport can be clearly associated with the West, both the interconnections with already existing non-occidental body cultures and the degree to which contemporary sport has been permeated by oriental forms and values must be assessed. These issues are central to the debate concerning globalization, inter-civilizational analysis and the role sport plays within global processes.

Structure of the Book: Main Themes and Issues

This book is divided into two main parts. In part I my concern is to map out the broad conceptual and historical context in which to place the global sport process. Chapter 1 reviews a range of competing approaches to the study of globalization more generally and sport in the global process in particular. Certain key findings and common ground between these approaches are identified. In chapter 2 a figurational or process-sociological approach to globalization is outlined. Emphasis is placed both on the distinctiveness of its inter-civilizational analysis but also on how this approach complements research conducted from other perspectives examining global sport. Chapter 3 applies this approach to sport more broadly and a greater stress is placed on the notion of civilizing offensives than is usually the case in other figurational work. Chapter 4 outlines, in preliminary form, five main phases in what is termed the global sportization process. Building on the work of Elias and Dunning, the approach also draws on the model of globalization processes proposed by Robertson (1992). The main features of the sport system are also identified.

Sportization processes arguably involve the multilayered flow of sports, capital, personnel, technologies/landscapes and ideologies and part II of this book focuses on an examination of the interconnected patterns that these flows form (Appadurai, 1990). A series of substantively based case studies probes the intensification of global flows that characterize the global sport formation. A sociological model of labour migration is presented in chapter 5. This provides the base both for the construction of a typology of sport labour migration and the substantive case studies that probe the movement of basketball and ice hockey players. Chapter 6 examines the global sports industry and consideration is given to the role of transnational corporations, exploitative practices and environmental issues. The media–sport production complex that contours and shapes the worldwide consumption of sport is the main focus of chapter 7. Attention is given to the network of interdependency chains that tie sports organizations, media conglomerates, corporate businesses, marketing firms and franchise/merchandising operations together. Particular consideration is given in this connection to the global diffusion of American football. In chapter 8 the role that sport plays in identity testing and formation at the personal, civic, national and global levels is examined. Consideration is given to the contradictory role that global sport plays in binding people to habitus memories and 'invented traditions', yet also exposing them to the values, feelings and images of the 'other'. The Conclusion draws together several conceptual and empirical strands and makes the case that the study of global sport can illuminate globalization processes more broadly.

Conclusion

Remarkably, very little attention has been paid to sport by those studying global cultural processes. Yet, investigations of this kind allow for a detailed exploration of the multidirectional interweaving of global cultural flows. There are, however, other reasons why this task needs to be conducted. More important than simply the global movement of cultural wares, this shift towards the competitive, regularized, rationalized and gendered bodily exertions of achievement sport involves changes at the level of personality, body deportment and social interaction. A more rationalized young, male and able-bodied habitus was and is evident that affects people and groups in different societies in fairly fundamental ways. Sport, in specific respects, is a globalized 'male preserve' (Dunning & Maguire, 1996). Tracing the global sportization process also reveals that this dominance has not gone unchallenged. Studies of these sportization processes can thus be understood, as Elias noted, 'as contributions to knowledge of changes in the social habitus of people and of the societies they form with each other' (Elias, 1986: p. 23).

Tackling the phenomena in this way also allows scope for the investigation of links between occidental and non-occidental societies over time and in the present day. Such an approach also recognizes that the 'local' was and is never hermetically sealed from the 'other'. Though it perhaps jars on our hearing, it is more correct to say that we are dealing with 'glocalization' processes (Robertson, 1995). Furthermore, while the present global sport formation has emerged out of past figurational sequences, its present form was neither planned nor inevitable. Indeed, while humankind is faced with differing blends of constraints and possibilities in their lives, people are not 'locked' into an unfolding global sport formation that acts as a type of rationalized 'iron cage'. Sporting futures are there to be made.

By more adequately understanding the power dynamics and interdependency chains within which they are located, citizens and their representatives, empowered by the efforts of themselves and, dare one say, social scientists, may construct and develop a global sport formation that is less wasteful of lives and resources (Elias, 1978). In reaching this 'optimistic' conclusion I should not disguise or underestimate that what is at stake is the character and form of inter-civilizational relations. In the sports world, as elsewhere, there is an ongoing cultural contest, of sameness, difference, selective elimination, selective emulation and commingling. Citizens of the West may well have to get used to the idea that their forms of sport, and 'civilization', are but part of a long-term process and that, in the third millennium, different notions of body culture and 'civilized' behaviour will be rekindled from within the West or emerge from non-occidental peoples. We shall see.

Part I

Conceptual and Theoretical Issues

1

Theorizing Sport in the Global Process

Let us export our oarsmen, our fencers, our runners into other
lands. That is the true free trade of the future; and the day it is
introduced into Europe the cause of Peace will have received a
new and strong ally.
Pierre de Coubertin, paper presented at the Union des Sports
Athlétiques, Sorbonne, 25 November 1892

That the representatives of cultures communicate, compete,
emulate and/or distinguish themselves from others across a range
of global networks has seemingly become so much part of the lives
of late twentieth-century Westerners that it is viewed as 'second
nature' and treated in an unproblematic way. Clearly, the export of
the Olympics, that de Coubertin called for, has proved to be so
successful that people do not question its history, though George
Orwell's comments about international sport being, 'war minus
the shooting', should make people more circumspect about
whether the Olympics add to global peace and harmony.

Several issues arise when examining cross-cultural processes.
Though there was a range of contacts between peoples in the so-
called 'ancient worlds', the games at Olympia being one example,
the frequency, form and depth of interaction has, over time, intensified. Though people have become more aware of making comparisons between 'others', they show little sensitivity to how this
process has emerged out of the past and is structured in the
present. A high degree of hodiecentric or 'today-centred' thinking
is evident (Goudsblom, 1977: p. 7). In addition, when people make

comparisons, they do so on the basis of a taken-for-granted international rank order of worth and a valorization of identities,
values, customs and cultural forms. The meaning, experience and
consumption of global sport are no exception to this general
process. How then are we to make sense of this global cultural
interchange? Here, I will examine the broad debate concerning
globalization processes and then consider how the study of global
sport reflects the general issues and questions that characterize this
debate. In doing so, a broad review of the existing pool of social
scientific knowledge regarding the global sport process will be
provided.

Making Sense of the Globalization Debate

Use of the term *globalization* has become, as noted, widespread in
academic and media discourse over the past two decades. The
meaning and usage of the term has been, however, marked by con-
fusion, misinterpretation and contentious debate. Perhaps because
the term diffused so rapidly into 'everyday' use, commentators,
politicians and academics have taken fairly rigid positions over its
precise meaning. In addition, the term appears to provoke a degree
of moral judgement, as if its use, in itself, implies support for or
criticism of the existing world order. The following remarks
offered by Tony Mason, a historian, are symptomatic of this
kind of thinking when applied to the study of sport. Comparing
Brazilian and European soccer, Mason observes:

> In 1994 it could be argued that this footballing dichotomy of styles
> no longer exists. All teams now play in a similar fashion with team-
> work and organization paramount ... Caution is the watchword;
> the game is not to lose. Perhaps this is an aspect of that globalization
> or homogenization of the sporting world about which sociologists
> excitedly chatter ... But if the homogenization theory is true some-
> thing which made football vital and attractive will have been lost.
>   (Mason, 1995: pp. 156–7)

In these observations, globalization is unequivocally equated with
homogenization and is seen as a 'threat' to some idealized notion
of what football was or is. Yet, as subsequent chapters will show,
the local meanings and patterning of sport in general and of football in particular, were influenced by global diffusion processes in
quite complex ways. The contrasts between playing styles may
have diminished but new varieties of playing formations have

emerged. Equally, the perspective offered by sociologists on globalization is, ironically, not as homogeneous as Mason's observations suggest.

Indeed, several traditions have sought to compare and contrast the development of different societies. These traditions include: the modernization perspective, theories of imperialism, dependency theory, world-system theory, hegemony theory and 'globalization' research. Each finds expression in the current debate surrounding globalization. I do not intend simply to review the degree to which these traditions – or specific pieces of work within them – have variously advanced our collective fund of relatively adequate social scientific knowledge. Rather, I want to identify several key issues and themes that characterize the debates, within and between these traditions, regarding globalization. In turn, when consideration is given to the emergence and diffusion of sport cultures, a number of these issues and themes are also evident.

Several key features associated with the term globalization can be detected in the literature. Reference is repeatedly made to the idea that globalization involves some form of greater interdependence between the local and the global.[1] A series of local–global nexuses can be identified. These include: local responses to economic practices; local resistance to ideological processes; local revivals of traditional customs; local celebrations of diversity and local initiatives to combat global pollution. I will return to these local–global nexuses in Part II. It is clear that every aspect of social reality, our activities, conditions of living, belief systems, knowledge base and responses, is affected by interconnections with other groups, both 'near' and 'far' away. For Anthony Giddens, globalization entails 'the intensification of world-wide social relations which link distinct localities in such a way that local happenings are shaped by events occurring miles and miles away and vice versa' (Giddens, 1990: p. 64).

These interconnections are seen to have deepened and also to have stretched across the globe. The world becomes 'compressed' as the scope and intensity of global interconnectedness has increased. Central in this regard have been the emergence of a world economy, an international nation-state system, a global

---

[1] Globalization research has taken various forms and has been subjected to extensive debate. For further discussion, see Beyer, 1994; Chase Dunn, 1989; Featherstone, 1990, 1991a, 1991b; Featherstone, Lash & Robertson, 1995; Friedman, 1994; Giddens, 1990; Gilpin, 1987; Hall, 1991; Hall et al., 1992; King, 1991; McGrew, 1992; Robertson, 1990a; Rosenau, 1980; Sanderson, 1995; Sklair, 1991; Waters, 1995; Wolfe, 1991.

diffusion of technology and division of labour, and a system of military alliances and treaties (Giddens, 1990: pp. 63–77). Hand in hand with these interconnections, the scale, velocity and volume of globalization processes gathered momentum.

This much is clear. Understood in this light, we can see that a series of interconnections also characterize global sport. Consider the example of basketball. Citizens of countries spread across the globe regularly tune in by satellite broadcasts to National Basketball Association (NBA) games. In these games perform the best male players drawn from North America and Europe. The players use equipment – balls, shoes, uniform, etc. – that is designed in a range of European and North American locations, financed in the USA and assembled in the Pacific Rim. This equipment is then sold on to a mass market across the globe. This equipment, basketball boots for example, is made out of raw materials from 'developing countries', the molecular structure of which was researched and patented, in the case of Nike, in Washington State (USA) and fabricated in Taiwan. Several other transnational corporations are also involved in the production and consumption phases of this global cultural product. The product is itself provided by a global media sport production complex and is viewed on a television that was itself manufactured as part of a global telecommunications network. The beguiling appeal of the slogan 'Just Do It', and of the transnational cultural icon Michael Jordan, hides the stark reality of the global sports industry complex.

Several writers have sought to discern a pattern, or structure, to these interconnections. Appadurai (1990), for example, refers to a series of diverse, fluid and unpredictable global flows. These 'scapes' include the movement of capital, technologies, people and mediated images. As a consequence of the diverse and unpredictable nature of these movements, a series of 'disjunctures' marks these 'scapes'. Hannerz (1990) also views globalization in terms of 'cultural flows'. These flows include: cultural commodities, the actions of the state in organizing and managing meanings, the dissemination of habitual perspectives and dispositions and the activities of social movements. Though he emphasizes diversity as opposed to uniformity, Hannerz observes that, 'the world has become one network of social relationships, and between its different regions there is a flow of meanings as well as of people and goods' (Hannerz, 1990: p. 237).

The idea that the world 'has become one network' has been taken up by several writers (Giddens, 1990; Robertson, 1992; Wallerstein, 1974). In this connection it is useful to highlight Robertson's notion of a global field. In mapping what he terms the 'global human condition', Robertson stresses four aspects of the global field. These are: nations/societies; individuals or selves; relations between nations/societies; and humankind as a whole. The pattern of this global field stems from the interweaving of these aspects (Robertson, 1992). People have become aware of the global condition, and of the 'finitude and boundedness of the planet and humanity' (Featherstone, 1991a). For Featherstone and Lash, an understanding of this 'global human condition' requires new types of thinking, and for them, 'the global *problematique* represents the *spatialization* of social theory' (1995: p. 1). In this endeavour, sociologists have been joined by geographers who examine the geography of global change, focusing on place, space, 'power geometry' and identity politics; the local/global scales of economic processes and the interconnections between human activities and ecological sustainability (Dickens, 1992; Harvey, 1989; Johnson et al., 1995; Massey, 1994; Yearley, 1996). Some of these concerns, as will be noted later, have also surfaced in the geography of sport (Bale, 1994).

   If these are some of the broad themes and issues where a degree of consensus is evident, when it comes to understanding the periodization of globalization, the main dynamics involved, and the impact that such processes have, then what emerges is a sharp division of opinion and position. Let me try to illustrate some of the tensions and major fault lines that characterize these debates. A series of binary oppositions can be detected. Are globalization processes unidimensional or multidimensional? Are monocausal or multicausal factors the main dynamic of global processes? Do globalization processes lead to a form of 'unity', or perception of 'unity' or of fragmentation? Are globalization processes the intended or the unintended result of intended social actions? Do globalization processes lead to homogenization or heterogenization? At this stage, it is appropriate to examine the claims of the various contributors to these debates.

Making Sense of Cross-cultural Processes: Competing Traditions

Several traditions of sociological thought have, as noted, sought to examine trans-societal development. The modernization approach, closely linked to functionalism, was the dominant paradigm in this research area until the early 1970s. Essentially concerned with how traditional societies reach modernity, this approach has focused on the political, cultural, economic and social aspects of this process.

Consideration is given to the development of political institutions that support participatory decision-making. The growth and development of secular and nationalist ideologies is also examined. The emergence of a division of labour, the use of management techniques, technological innovations and commercial activities have been the subject of attention. These changes are seen to be accompanied by urbanization and the decline of traditional authorities. The modernization approach also tends to assert that the 'effects' of these trends leads to homogenization. Societies in different parts of the globe 'eventually' follow the Western model of development.[2]

Some or all of these themes have surfaced in 'comparative' studies of sport where a 'critical' approach has failed to take hold (Baker, 1982; Jokl & Simon, 1964; Pooley, 1981; Seppanen, 1970). This, of course, relates to a major criticism that other traditions have of the modernization approach: issues of conflict, exploitation and underdevelopment are ignored (Hettne, 1990). Cultural imperialist analyses have proved more popular in accounts provided by sport historians and sociologists of sport (Klein, 1989; Mangan, 1986). Ironically, though cultural imperialist accounts stress issues of conflict and exploitation, they share an important feature in common with the modernization approach, that is, an emphasis on the alleged homogenizing impact of these processes. Equally, these approaches tend to stress the unidirectional character of these global developments – from the West to the 'rest' – and deploy a monocausal explanation, technological or economic, to explain these changes.

In cultural imperialism accounts, terms such as 'Westernization' or 'Americanization' are used to capture the homogenizing tendencies said to be involved in cross-cultural processes. Cultural flows are identified with the activities of representatives of nation-states and/or multinational corporations. These activities entail a form of domination of one culture over another. Issues of power, control and the ability of 'indigenous' people to interpret, understand and/or resist cultural manipulation and domination arise in evaluating these types of studies. The idea of the 'invasion' of an indigenous culture by a foreign one is the usual way of understanding the processes involved (Tomlinson, 1991).

Two main emphases in cultural imperialism accounts of global cultural flows can be identified. In one, the focus is placed on a

---

[2] For further discussion of this, see Blomstrom & Hettne, 1984; Frank, 1967; Hettne, 1990; Larrain, 1989. For consideration of how this approach has been applied to the development of sport, see Gruneau, 1988.

'world' made up of a collection of nation-states in competition with each other. One manifestation of this is 'Yankee imperialism'. The 'hearts and minds' of foreign people are said to be at stake. Another approach views the 'world' as an integrated political-economic system of global capitalism. Here the focus is on the activities of multi- or transnational corporations. Whether attention focuses on the imperatives of multinational capitalism, or on the spread of a specific nation's 'value-system', an alleged homogenizing trend is identified. While the scale and pace of the process are disputed, the general drift towards the convergence of cultures is accepted.

Studies within this Marxist tradition explain the colonialism of specific nation-states, especially Western nation-states, in terms of the necessity for capitalist expansion. At least three dimensions of these colonial ventures have been noted. These include the search for new markets in which to sell products, the search for new sources of raw materials and the search for new sources of 'cheap' or 'skilled' labour power. This process is seen to help Western economic development while impoverishing the rest of the world. Large business corporations, as well as state organizations, have played and continue to play a leading role in these developments. While the formal possession of empires has largely disappeared, with the concomitant rise in self-governing countries a form of economic neo-imperialism has developed. Western countries are thus able to maintain their position of ascendancy by ensuring control over the terms upon which world trade is conducted. Ideas of this kind have surfaced, as will be developed shortly, in the literature on sport.

In several respects dependency theory links with neo-imperialist accounts. Dependency theorists argue that the global economy cannot be conceived as a system of equal trading partners and relations (Frank, 1967; Larrain, 1989). The superior military, economic and political power of the 'centre' imposes conditions of unequal exchange on the 'periphery'. Former colonial countries remain dependent on the West. Concerned with the uneven manner and form of global development, advocates of dependency theory also stress the integrated and systematic nature of modern global capitalism. Though the origins and nature of the dependency of specific nations vary according to how far a country was colonized, and by whom, those countries located at the 'periphery' experience unequal access to markets and unequal exchange for their raw materials. These materials include cash crops, such as sugar, or 'human crops', such as athletes.

There are, however, several strands, including dependent

underdevelopment, dependent development and dependency reversal, that are evident in this tradition. In the first strand, it is argued that the global capitalist system operates actively to under-develop the 'third world'. This is done largely, but not exclusively, through multinational corporate activity. The impoverishment of third world countries is the direct result of their subordinate position compared with the industrialized countries. The wealth of the industrialized countries is at the expense of third world countries, the latter being economically dependent on the former. Exponents of this strand argue that no genuine development is possible if this system is in place. Western ownership and control of the major governing bodies, the media–sport complex and the sports equipment manufacturing and services nexus ensure that this is also the case in world sport.

Yet, this dependent underdevelopment strand appears unable to account for the growth of some 'third world' countries. Hence, advocates of this approach coined the idea of dependent development. That is, the growth of some third world countries is acknowledged, but this is viewed as limited in nature. Examples include South Korea and Taiwan – both nations which have become bases for the manufacture of sports goods such as tennis racquets and shoes. While dependent development is conceived of as possible, such an approach still does not appear to grasp that certain countries can break out of the 'double bind' of dependent development. In this context, a further revision of the basic approach is evident in which reference is made to dependency reversal. In this approach, it is viewed as possible that certain third world countries, and/or institutional sectors of third world countries, can escape and reverse the previous disadvantageous relations with developed countries. Successful individual or team performances by representatives of third world countries could be considered as evidence of such an 'escape', but these countries remain locked into a structure of world sport controlled by the West. Despite the fruitfulness of the dependency perspective, attention has increasingly been given, if not in the study of sport, then certainly in other fields of social science, to 'world-system theory'.

Associated with the work of Wallerstein (1974), the main theme of world-system theory centres on the historical dynamics of capitalism. The logic of capitalism permeates global processes. Several key elements of this approach can be identified. Dating from the sixteenth century onwards, a 'world system' of commerce and communication has developed. Based on the expansion of a capitalist world economy, this world system has produced a series of economic and political connections. For Wallerstein, the world capitalist economy is orientated around four sectors. The core states dominate and control the exploitation of resources and production. Their wealth derives from their control over manufacturing and agriculture, and is characterized by centralized forms of government. Those states that are linked in various kinds of dependent trading are referred to by Wallerstein as being semi-peripheral to the core. Peripheral states are those that depend on selling cash crops directly to the core states, and are seen as at the outer edge of the world economy. For Wallerstein, however, there were states that were, until colonial expansion, relatively untouched by commercial development. Their dependency, and indeed that of those states at the periphery of the world economy, has been established and maintained by the legacy of colonialism. These nations are enmeshed in a set of economic relations that enrich the industrial areas and impoverish the periphery. The driving force of globalization is seen to be located in the logic of the capitalist world economy. As yet, this latter approach has not been taken up extensively by scholars studying global sports and leisure development. It is not difficult, however, to view the trade of sports talent from 'peripheral' countries to 'core' countries from this perspective. Think of the recruitment of African athletes to American college sport programmes (Bale & Sang, 1996).

This approach alerts us to the extent to which hegemonic powers exploit other nations in their search for new markets to sell sport forms, leisure products, equipment and cultural merchandise. Further, in the context of sports and arts labour migration, the activities of hegemonic states centre on the search for new sources of 'skilled' labour whose early development was resourced by these former colonial countries. From this perspective, the global sports and leisure system can be seen to operate largely but not exclusively through multinationals or organizations dominated by first world nations. This system operates actively to underdevelop the third world by excluding third world countries from the centre of the global political decision-making process and from the economic rewards derived from the world sports/leisure economy.

Indeed, it could be argued that the core states dominate and control the exploitation of resources and production. A deskilling of semi-peripheral and peripheral states occurs on the terms and conditions set by core states. The most talented workers, in which peripheral or semi-peripheral states have invested time and resources, are lured away to the core states whose wealth derives from their control over athletic and artistic labour and the media–sport/leisure production complex. Non-core states are thus in a position of dependent trading, their athletic or artistic labour being the equivalent of the cash crops that they sell in other sectors of the world economy.

While the existence of these relatively autonomous transnational practices must be recognized, it is also important not to overlook another key feature of the global media–sport complex. In seeking to avoid slipping into a homogenization thesis, the analysis must not overlook how transnational practices are subject to control and manipulation. This can involve the actions of transnational agencies or individuals from the 'transnational capitalist class' (Sklair, 1991). Transnational agencies such as the International Olympic Committee (IOC), the International Amateur Athletic Federation (IAAF), the International Marketing Group (IMG) or International Sport and Leisure (ISL) seek to regulate access to cultural flows. Individuals who belong to the 'transnational capitalist class' (such as, Juan Antonio Samaranch, Primo Nebiolo, Mark McCormack and the late Horst Dassler) are also centrally involved as these are some of the key players whose plans and actions interweave in attempting to develop a global media–sport complex. Such interventions cause cultural struggles of various kinds and at different levels.[3]

Several of these themes, as will be emphasized later in this chapter, have been fruitfully employed by scholars in sport history and the sociology of sport. Any account of global sport that does not consider the issues of power, exploitation and cultural control that such work highlights would be deficient. Yet, it has also to be noted that there are several problems associated with cultural imperialist and world-system theory accounts. These can best be summarized as several 'sensitizing' questions that need to be asked about these accounts. What constitutes Westernization and/or Americanization? Is it simply a question of the presence of a cultural product from a 'foreign' culture or does it involve a shift in the conscious and subconscious make-up of people? How 'intended' is the process described? How complete does the process have to be for domination to be said to have occurred? What ability have people to understand, embrace and/or resist these processes? What constitutes the 'indigenous/authentic' culture that the foreign culture threatens? The problems associated with a modernization account of convergence have already been noted. Ironically, by emphasizing a unidirectional and monocausal

---

[3] For examples of how this cultural imperialism approach has been applied to the media more generally, see Emanuel, 1992; Mattelart, 1977; Rollin, 1989; Schiller, 1969; Tunstall, 1977.

explanation, evident in some cultural imperialism accounts, the contested and contradictory nature of global change is overlooked.

Writers such as Featherstone (1991a), Nederveen Pieterse (1995), Robertson (1990b) and Tomlinson (1991) have concluded that this is a non-productive line of thinking, and have sought to reconceptualize the debate, suggesting that the globalization concept helps reorientate the analysis. Several objections to variants of dependency theory are thus raised by exponents of globalization research. Whereas dependency theories use monocausal explanations, for example Americanization, to explain the global condition, some globalization research emphasizes the need for a multicausal analysis. Globalization research also disputes whether there is a trend towards homogenization. In contrast, Robertson and Featherstone maintain that the unity of nation-states is being dissolved, identity pluralized and a partial mixing of global cultures is occurring. Indeed, in some globalization accounts, emphasis is placed on the emergence of global diversity (Nederveen Pieterse, 1995). Citizens of different nations are becoming aware of 'otherness' and recognizing difference. Polyculturalism, not homogenization, is said to be one of the main features of global processes.

A feature that reinforces these processes is the reassertiveness of 'local' identities. Global cultural products are also seen to be actively interpreted and used by those who consume them. From this, some observers have concluded that the dynamics of globalization are powered by an 'infinitely varied mutual contest of sameness and difference' (Appadurai, 1990: p. 308). Globalization is viewed as a far less coherent or culturally directed process and occurs as a result of the complex dynamics of political, economic and cultural practices. These do not, of themselves, aim at global integration, but nonetheless produce it. The effects, then, of globalization are to weaken the cultural coherence of nation-states. This includes those nations who are more powerful within the interdependent world order (Tomlinson, 1991).

In stressing the formation of a global culture, the danger is thus to overstate the case for homogeneity and integration (Featherstone, 1990). This tendency is due to associating the idea of a global culture with the culture of any one nation-state. The tendency towards dichotomous thinking regarding global culture reinforces this weakness. Instead of endlessly arguing about whether homogeneity or heterogeneity, integration or disintegration, unity or diversity are evident, it is more adequate to see these processes as interwoven (Nederveen Pieterse, 1995; Robertson, 1992). Moving the analysis to an examination of what Sklair (1991) describes as transnational practices, the observer is better placed to note that there is something more at work than solely flows between nation-states. Transnational practices, which take a variety of cultural forms, gain a degree of *relative autonomy* on a global level.

Referring to what he terms trans-societal processes, Robertson (1990) maintains that it is these that sustain the exchange and flow of goods, people, information, knowledge and images. By utilizing terms such as *transnational* and *trans-societal*, both Sklair and Robertson are seeking to move beyond the nation-state as the sole reference point for understanding the 'integration' of the world. It is not difficult to conceive how, as chapter 7 demonstrates, the media–sport production complex is an integral part of this general process. Think of the technological advances involved in the media coverage of the modern Olympics and how satellites now relay powerful images across the globe in an instant. For Real (1989b), these images, however briefly and superficially, reflect and help sustain the emergence of a global culture.

How then to navigate a route round or through these competing explanations? Robertson tries to steer a middle course. Others, as will be noted, seek to move away from a homogeneity thesis altogether. Though Robertson sees globalization as referring, 'in its most general sense, to the process whereby the world becomes a single place' (Robertson, 1992: p. 135), he is also keen to avoid the suggestion that this notion of a 'single place' entails a crystallization of a cohesive system. Yet, he maintains, globalization does involve the development of a global culture. This culture, he argues, is not a homogeneous, binding whole, but refers to a 'general mode of discourse about the world as a whole and its variety' (Robertson, 1992: p. 133). Concerned to trace the way in which the world is ordered, Robertson maps out, as noted earlier, what he refers to as the 'global field'. In tracing the pattern of this global field, Robertson maintains that reference to a single causal process must be avoided. Globalization is not the direct outcome of inter-state processes. Rather, these processes need to be understood as operating relatively independently of conventionally designated societal and socio-cultural processes. He stresses the relative autonomy and 'logic', and the long-term nature of the processes involved. While he refers to the development of a global culture, Robertson also stresses, as noted, that globalization processes do not lead to homogeneity. For Robertson, global processes involve both the particularization of universalism and the universalization of particularism (Robertson, 1992: p. 130). That is, these processes are marked by heterogeneous tendencies and characteristics. In sum, 'globalization is ... best understood as indicating the problem of the form in terms of which the world becomes "united" but by no means integrated' (Robertson, 1992: p. 51).

The process by which people have come to understand the world-system as a whole has a long history. In mapping out the global condition, Robertson identifies five main phases (germinal, incipient, take-off, struggle for hegemony and uncertainty phase) in this long process (Robertson, 1992). Lasting from around the 1870s until the mid-1920s, the third phase involves the process through which the 'increasingly manifest globalizing tendencies of previous periods and places gave way to a single, inexorable form' (Robertson, 1992: p. 59). These globalization processes are evident in several areas: the growth of agencies that straddle the globe; the establishment of global awards and prizes; the emergence of a global communications system; and the emergence of a standard-ized notion of human rights. As part of this general framework, Robertson is also keen to explore how standardized notions of 'civilization' emerged during this period. Robertson does not view ethnic reassertiveness as running counter to globalization processes. These processes are not mutually exclusive. Indeed, he suggests that 'the contemporary concern with civilizational and societal (as well as ethnic) uniqueness – as expressed via such motifs as identity, tradition and indigenization – largely rests on globally diffused ideas' (Robertson, 1992: p. 130). Roudometof and Robertson have recently further developed these ideas. Rejecting the idea that the process of globalization is a phase of capitalist development, and that economic integration necessarily leads to cultural convergence, they conclude:

> Cultural homogeneity and heterogeneity are consequences of the globalization process. Although cultural diffusion can transform a locale, the recurrent 'invention of tradition' makes it possible to pre-serve, create or recreate cultural heterogeneity at the local level.
> (Roudometof & Robertson, 1995: p. 284)

Significantly, it was in the third phase identified by Robertson that contemporary notions of national/ethnic identity and culture were formed. During the period of intense globalization (roughly 1880 to 1920), Featherstone (1991b) suggests that more nations were drawn together in a tighter global interdependency and set of power balances. Representatives of national cultures sought both to reinvent traditions of the nation and to marginalize local ethnic and regional differences. For Featherstone, this entailed the invok-ing of a collective memory. This was done through the perfor-mance of ritual, bodily practices and commemorative ceremonies. Royal Jubilees, the Olympic Games, international competitions and national days all performed this function. These practices became 'echoes of the sacred' where the fundamental elements of national culture and identity were revealed. Leisure events came to express myths, invoke memories, emphasize heroes and embody traditions. These tied popular consciousness together (Featherstone, 1991b). Significant issues arise from these observations and they will be returned to in chapter 2.

In this earlier phase of globalization, leisure practices functioned to bind nations together around *specific* invented traditions. In contrast, the more recent phase of globalization, dating from the 1960s, is forcing nation-states to reconstitute their collective identities along more pluralistic and multicultural lines. Significantly, leisure practices also take on new meanings. Featherstone notes in this connection:

> ... festive moments [such as Woodstock] in which the everyday routine world becomes transformed into an extraordinary sacred world enabled people to temporarily live in unison, near to the ideal. Subsequent gatherings often incorporate rituals which reinvoke the aura of the sacred.... Televised rock festivals such as the Band Aid, Food Aid, the Nelson Mandela concert and other transnational link-ups may also invoke a more direct sense of emotional solidarity which may reawaken and reinforce moral concerns such as the sense of common humanity, the sacredness of the person, human rights, and more recently the sacredness of nature and non-human species.
>
> (Featherstone, 1991b: p. 122)

Although global consumer culture can be perceived to be destroying local culture, Featherstone argues that it can also be used for reconstituting a sense of locality. Given the moral concerns about humanity, human rights and environmentalism, identified by Featherstone as permeating some leisure events, it is not surprising that he believes that global consumer culture is leading to polyculturalism and a sense of otherness. Global leisure practices do not automatically involve a homogenization process. In contrast, for Featherstone, 'the tendency ... within consumer culture to reproduce an overload of information and signs would also work against any coherent integrated universal global belief on the level of content' (Featherstone, 1991b: p. 127). More recently, Featherstone and Lash developed this argument further, and noted that analyses must 'become attuned to the nuances of the process of globalization and seek to develop theories which are sensitive to the different power potentials of the different players participating in the various global struggles' (Featherstone & Lash, 1995: p. 3). The very prevalence of images of the 'other' contained in global sport and leisure practices may both decentre the West and put other cultures more centre stage. Sport practices, such as the Olympic movement, will also be part of this global cultural contest. An even more robust case for viewing globalization as involving hybridization of the kind noted comes from the work of Nederveen Pieterse (1995).

For Nederveen Pieterse, there are many modes and forms of globalization. Seeking to avoid the potential Eurocentric and modernization connotations that can be associated with the concept, he stresses the plural, multidimensional and open-ended nature of the process. His approach is primarily a critique of essentialism. Advocating a geographically 'wide' and historically 'deep' analysis, Nederveen Pieterse emphasizes the flows between the West and the non-West and how globalization processes precede the recent 'rise of the west' to relative predominance. For Nederveen Pieterse, the problem of globalization involves a diverse range of currents and counter-currents, entails an active and critical reception by 'locals', and is leading to creolization of cultural forms and a hybridization of people's identities. For Nederveen Pieterse, cultural experiences have not been moving in the direction of cultural uniformity and standardization, but rather towards a global *mélange*. As he concludes:

> How do we come to terms with phenomena such as Thai boxing by Moroccan girls in Amsterdam, Asian rap in London, Irish bagels, Chinese tacos and Mardi Gras Indians in the United States? ... Cultural experiences, past or present, have not been simply moving in the direction of cultural uniformity and standardization. This is not to say that the notion of global cultural synchronization is irrelevant – on the contrary – but it is fundamentally incomplete.
>
> (Nederveen Pieterse, 1995: p. 53)

In reaching this conclusion, Nederveen Pieterse argues that the global cultural synchronization thesis fails to note the influence that non-Western cultures exercise on each other, leaves no room to explore cross-over cultures, overstates the homogeneity of the West and overlooks the fact that many of the standards and cultural forms exported by the West and its cultural industries turn out to be of a culturally mixed character. Adopting a long-term perspective allows him to stress that 'Europe', until the late fourteenth century, was the recipient of cultural influences from the Orient. While such observations provide a powerful corrective to the excesses of the homogenization thesis, in either its modernization or cultural imperialist guise, there is a danger that the analysis veers too far in the opposite direction.

The observations outlined in the Introduction to this text are supportive of aspects of the position adopted by Nederveen Pieterse. It is important to push the globalization process time-frame back beyond the so-called 'modern' period and also to account for the influence of non-Western cultures on the West. Likewise, as chapter 8 indicates, it is important to probe the hybridization of cultural identities. Equally, the creolization of sport cultures does, to some degree, parallel similar processes at work in the areas of music, art and food. Nevertheless, the analysis must not lose sight of the need to account for interrelated processes; that the contrasts between cultures have also diminished over time and that powerful groups do operate to construct, produce and provide global sport processes. This much is clear from the dependency and world-systems theorists. An uncritical deployment of concepts like hybridization and creolization can lead to a position where the individual is assumed to be sovereign and where people freely choose from the global sport *mélange*. The insights of scholars of cultural imperialism, dependency or world-system theory would thus be overlooked. That is too high a price to pay. At this juncture, it is appropriate therefore to see how the themes, questions and issues raised above have found expression in the cross-cultural study of sport.

Studying Sport in the Global Order: the State of Play

Judging by the number of perspectives that currently provide a range of competing explanations for the structure, meaning and significance of contemporary global sport processes, perhaps it is surprising that there is greater consensus regarding the origins of sport. Though the use of globalization concepts is a relatively new feature of research studying sport processes, cross-cultural analyses have been attempted for some time.[4] Johan Huizinga's 1949 work, for example, developed a cross-cultural account of the origins of modern sport and remains compelling reading. This is what Huizinga concluded.

> The great ball-games in particular require the existence of perman-
> ent teams, and herein lies the starting-point of modern sport. The
> process arises quite spontaneously in the meeting of village against
> village, school against school, one part of a town against the rest,

[4] Examples of these cross-cultural studies include Bale, 1985; Clignet & Stark, 1974; Jokl & Simon, 1964; Krotee, 1979; Mandell, 1984; Wagner, 1989.

etc. That the process started in nineteenth-century England is under-standable up to a point, though how far the specifically Anglo-Saxon bent of mind can be deemed an efficient cause is less certain. But it cannot be doubted that the structure of English life had much to do with it. Local self-government encouraged the spirit of associ-ation and solidarity. The absence of obligatory military training favoured the occasion for, and the need of, physical exercise. The peculiar form of education tended to work in the same direction, and finally the geography of the country and the nature of the terrain, on the whole flat and, in the ubiquitous commons, offering the most perfect playing-fields that could be desired, were of the greatest importance. Thus England became the cradle and focus of modern sporting life.

(Huizinga, 1949/1970: p. 223)

There are several features of this argument that require qualifica-tion and these will be dealt with in chapter 2. At this stage, it is suf-ficient to note that scholars accept the basic premise that 'England became the cradle and focus of modern sporting life' (Dunning & Sheard, 1979; Gruneau, 1988; Guttmann, 1991). Here the consensus breaks down. Different interpretations exist with regard to the dynamics underpinning the emergence and subsequent diffusion of modern sport (Dunning & Sheard, 1979; Gorn & Goldstein, 1993; Hargreaves, 1986; Hargreaves, 1994; Mandell, 1984). Similar themes, issues and questions that characterize the broader debate regarding global cultural flows also surface in discussing modern sport. Not surprisingly, similar fault-lines regarding homogene-ity/heterogeneity, monocausal/multicausal, unidimensional/multi-dimensional, unity/fragmentation, universalism/particularism are also evident. In the following section, I identify key research, and outline where such work is positioned along these fault-lines.

The clearest exposition of the modernization thesis as it applies to sport can be found in the work of Eric Wagner. Reviewing a diverse set of trends that are said to characterize global sport, Wagner correctly observes that 'Americanization is part of these trends but it is only one part of much broader processes; it is not by itself the key process' (Wagner, 1990: p. 400). This much is not incompatible with the argument presented in this text. Yet, Wagner mistakenly then assigns central status to what he terms 'international modernization' (Wagner, 1990: p. 402). While he acknowledges important caveats, such as 'sport culture flowing in all directions', and a 'blending of many sport traditions', Wagner does appear to downplay the conflictual nature of these processes, to overemphasize the ability of people to pick and choose as they wish from global sport cultures, and to see such development as a sign of progress. His concluding comments echo many of the features, and weaknesses, of the modernization perspective outlined earlier in this chapter. This is what he had to say:

> I think we make too much of cultural dependency in sports when in fact it is people themselves who generally determine what they do and do not want, and it is the people who modify and adapt the cultural imports, the sports, to fit their own needs and values. Bringing sports into a new cultural context probably serves more as examples available for people to pick up or trade if they wish, rather than any imposed or forced cultural change.... The long-term trend has to be, I think, towards greater homogenization, and I don't think there is anything bad or imperialistic about this; rather, these sports trends ultimately must reflect the will of the people.
>
> (Wagner, 1990: p. 402)

Though modernization was one of the first approaches within the field, ideas of this kind still surface in the literature on sport. Consider Baker and Mangan's collection of papers on sport in Africa (1987), Cashman's exploration of the phenomenon of Indian cricket (1988), Arbena's evaluation of literature relating to Latin America (1988) and papers published in comparative sport studies edited by Wilcox (1995). In his early writing on this subject, Allen Guttmann supported this position, arguing that Wagner was 'correct to insist that we are witnessing a homogenization of world sports rather than an Americanization', and that 'the concept of modernization is preferable because it also implies something about the nature of the global transformation' (Guttmann, 1991: pp. 187–8). Though he acknowledges that terms like '*Gemeinschaft* and *Gesellschaft*, the traditional and the modern, the particularistic and the universalistic' employ an 'admittedly simplified dichotomy', Guttmann still works within a modernization time frame, and overlooks what Robertson describes as the 'universalization of particularism' and not just the 'particularization of universalism' (Robertson, 1992). This is odd. In other work by Guttmann, important lines of enquiry are opened up when he refers to the diffusion of game forms in the ancient world and to the influence of the Orient on the West (Guttmann, 1993). Guttmann's solution, as we shall see later, has been to adopt a cultural hegemony position and to concentrate on more recent events.

While advocates of a cultural imperialist and dependency theory approach would reject several, if not all of the premises outlined by Wagner and Guttmann, these perspectives do share a common assumption that we are witnessing the homogenization of world sports. Within sport history research, informed by a

cultural imperialist perspective, several insightful case studies of
the connection between the diffusion of sport and imperialism
have been provided (Mangan, 1986; Stoddart, 1989). As chapter 3
highlights, the diffusion of sport, out of its European heartland,
moved along the formal and the informal lines of Empire –
particularly, though not exclusively, the British. But it was not just
the diffusion of specific sports, such as cricket, that reflected this
broader process (James, 1963). From a cultural imperialist perspective, what was also at stake was the diffusion of a cultural/sport-
ing ideology and a form of Western cosmology. This argument can
be highlighted with reference to the work of Henning Eichberg,
John Bale and Johan Galtung.

Eichberg's study probes several of the issues identified. He suggests that Olympism is a 'social pattern' that reflects the 'everyday
culture of the western (and east European) industrial society'
(Eichberg, 1984: p. 97). He emphasizes several negative consequences of Olympism, including drugs, violence and the scien-
tification of sport. Eichberg maintains that these excesses are not
accidental or marginal, but logically related to the configuration of
Western Olympic sport, with its emphasis on 'faster, higher,
stronger'. Olympism is seen to reflect the colonial dominance of
the West, and its spread across the globe has been remarkably successful. While it is possible to agree with Eichberg on this, Wilson
overstates this case when he suggests that 'the major impetus for
the globalization of sport was the Olympic movement' (Wilson,
1994: p. 356). The dynamics underpinning the globalization of
sport are, as Part II demonstrates, more multifaceted than this.
Indeed, as Eichberg argues, Western domination is increasingly
subject to resistance. Alternatives to Olympism are emerging.
These alternatives include a resurgence of national cultural games,
open-air movements, expressive activities and meditative exercises. He concludes that 'the age of Western colonial dominance is
coming to an end – and with it the predominance of Olympic
sports', and that, 'new physical cultures will arise ... from the different cultural traditions of the world' (Eichberg, 1984: p. 102). Not
all, as we shall see, share Eichberg's optimism.

Tackling these issues within the subdiscipline of sports geography, John Bale paints a more conflict-ridden and destructive
picture of the impact of the diffusion of sport along the lines of
Empire. As Bale records, 'western sports did not simply take root
in virgin soil; they were firmly implanted – sometimes ruthlessly –
by imperialists' (Bale, 1994: p. 8). For Bale, such 'sports colonisation' marginalized, or destroyed, indigenous movement cultures
and, 'as cultural imperialism swept the globe, sports played their

part in westernising the landscapes of the colonies' (Bale, 1994: p. 8). There is much in this latter argument and Bale's pioneering study raises our understanding of sport landscapes to a new level. There are, however, grounds for suggesting that the homogeniza- tion process is not as complete as these observations appear to indicate. This reservation is not, however, shared by Galtung. In similar vein to Bale and Eichberg, Galtung sets up his analysis with the following question: 'What happens when there is massive export of sports, radiating from Western centers, following old colonial trade and control lines, into the last little corner of the world, leaving cricket bats, soccer fields, racing tracks, courts of all sorts and what not behind?' (Galtung, 1991: p. 150). For Galtung, the answer is clear. Sports carry the sociocultural code of the senders, and those from the West 'serve as fully fledged carriers of the combination typical for expansionist occidental cosmology' (Galtung, 1991: p. 150). Unlike Eichberg, however, Galtung detects no hopeful alternatives. Whatever the merits of his overall argu- ment, Galtung rightly points to the role of the body in these processes, and insightfully observes that, as people learn these body cultures at an early stage in their lives, they leave 'imprints that may well be indelible' (Galtung, 1991: p. 150). I will return to the issue of body cultures in chapter 2.

Although the research highlighted above emphasizes a cultural imperialist perspective, variants of dependency theory have been used in the study of sport. Several studies have also examined Latin and South America (Arbena, 1993; Mandle & Mandle, 1988). Alan Klein's study of Dominican and Mexican baseball are examples of dependency research at its very best (Klein, 1991; 1997). Grounded in a careful and sophisticated anthropological approach, he probes the contradictory status and role of baseball in relations between the Dominican Republic and the USA. Klein skilfully observes:

> Because baseball is the only area in which Dominicans come up against Americans and demonstrate superiority, it fosters national pride and keeps foreign influence at bay. But the resistance is incomplete. At an organizational level American baseball interests have gained power and are now unwittingly dismantling Domini- can baseball. Therefore, just when the Dominicans are in a position to resist the influence of foreigners, the core of their resistance is slipping away into the hands of the foreigners themselves.
>
> (Klein, 1991: p. 3)

Despite noting, in similar fashion to Eichberg's interpretation of the Olympic movement, that 'Caribbean baseball is rooted in colonialism', Klein does not convey the sense of uniformity, or of total domination, that Galtung does. On the contrary, while pointing to the unequal nature of power relations, Klein remarks, 'having struggled in obscurity to refine the game Dominicans have made it their own, a game marked by their cadence and color' (Klein, 1991: p. 156). Local responses to broader processes are acknowledged. Klein goes further, and argues that 'the Dominicans are a beleaguered people who may someday rebel; to predict when the flash point will occur, look first to the firefights being waged in a game that has inspired their confidence. Look first at Sugarball' (Klein, 1991: p. 156). In studying the US–Mexican border, baseball and forms of nationalism Klein makes the same incisive case. As he remarks, 'an examination of the sport and the subculture of baseball in this region illustrates these nationalisms as well or better than other kinds of studies' (Klein, 1997: p. 13).

Other scholars working within this broad cultural imperialist/ dependency theory and cultural hegemony tradition either straddle these perspectives or downplay the role of Americanization and, instead, stress the role of global capitalism. Sugden and Tomlinson, for example, appear to draw on aspects of these traditions. Take, for example, their following remarks, 'although on the one hand FIFA has served as a forum for Third World resistance, on the other hand it has undoubtedly aided and abetted neocolonialist forms of economic and cultural exploitation' (Sugden & Tomlinson, 1998b: p. 314). In studies that Donnelly (1996) refers to as being located within a cultural hegemony position, the contested nature of global capitalism is highlighted. Guttmann, for example, argues that 'cultural imperialism is not … the most accurate term to characterize what happens during the process of ludic diffusion. Cultural hegemony comes closer' (Guttmann, 1994: p. 178). For Donnelly, the advantage of this cultural hegemony perspective lies in avoiding an overdeterministic view of Americanization: the transfer of cultural products is not one way, the ideological messages are not fixed and those who are exposed to such products have a degree of freedom to interpret and reinterpret these messages and products. As Donnelly concludes, 'cultural hegemony may be seen as a two-way but imbalanced process of cultural exchange, interpenetration, and interpretation' (Donnelly, 1996: p. 243). There is much in this that figurational sociology would share. Yet, interestingly, while Guttmann (1994: p. 179) also sees merit in this perspective, he argues that cultural hegemonists overstate the intentionality involved in ludic diffusion processes. Perhaps this is so, but equally important is the fact that the unintentional dynamics involved in global processes are overlooked. In addition, non-occidental influences on the West and the linkages between non-occidental societies and their impact on each other are still not accounted for. Civilizational struggles of a quite complex kind are the key to unlocking aspects of global processes.

Bruce Kidd's study of sport in Canada, located within a broader analysis of the development of Canadian national culture, insightfully explores the role of global capitalism (Kidd, 1981). Noting the potential importance of sport in the strengthening and enunciation of national identity, Kidd observes that the commodification of Canadian sport has served to undermine this potential. Focusing on the National Hockey League (NHL) as a 'critical case' in this regard, he highlights how both the ideological marketing strategy of the NHL and the general process of commodification between the two world wars served to 'accelerate the disintegration of beliefs and practices that had once supported and nurtured autonomous Canadian institutions' (Kidd, 1981: p. 713). For him, an explanation of these processes lies not in Americanization *per se* but in a critique of capitalism. Kidd observes:

> Explanation lies neither in U.S. expansion nor national betrayal, but in the dynamics of capital. Once sport became a sphere of commodity production ... then it was almost inevitable that the best Canadian hockey would be controlled by the richest and most powerful aggregates of capital and sold in the richer and more populous markets of the U.S. The disappearance of community control over Canadian hockey strengthened a much larger process – the centralization of all popular forms of culture.
>
> (Kidd, 1981: p. 714)

Whereas Kidd deals with issues between 'core' economies, George Sage (1995) draws on the work of Wallerstein and adopts a more 'world-system model' to explain the global sporting goods industry. Surveying the social and environmental costs associated with the relocation strategies of multinational corporations such as Nike, Sage concludes that such companies have been 'following a model which places exports over domestic needs, profits over worker rights, growth over the environment', and that a 'neo-colonial system of unequal economic and political relationships among the First and Third World countries envisioned by Wallerstein's world-system model of global development becomes abundantly evident to even a casual observer' (Sage, 1995: p. 48). The important insights provided by Sage and Harvey on the global sports goods industry will be further examined in chapter 6.

While noting the obvious American influences on Australian

popular culture, McKay and Miller (1991) adopt a similar stance to Sage. They view the concept of Americanization to be of limited help in explaining the form and content of Australian sport. For them, the political economy of Australian sport can best be analysed by concepts such as post-Fordism, the globalization of consumerism and the cultural logic of late capitalism. Though McKay and Miller (1991) and McKay, Lawrence, Miller and Rowe (1993) prefer the term 'corporate sport', Donnelly has argued that the 'notion of corporate sport may easily be extended to indicate the Americanization of sport, given that most of the conditions for corporate sport are either American in origin, or have been more fully developed in the United States' (Donnelly, 1996: p. 246). It would seem, however, that neither Sage, nor McKay and his fellow researchers, would accept this interpretation. As McKay and Miller remark, 'in the discourse of the daily report from the stock exchange, the Americans are not the only players in the cultural game' (McKay & Miller, 1991: p. 93).

Yet, Donnelly (1996) would have much in common with these writers. In certain respects his position, as noted, represents a modified and more sophisticated form of the Americanization thesis. Eschewing the excesses of the Americanization as imperialism argument, Donnelly views Americanization as a form of cultural hegemony with resistance and accommodation evident and also with other imperialist influences at work. There is some common ground with this approach and the figurational perspective and the conclusion that the American corporate model of sport is the dominant form at present would be accepted by both. While differences with regard to the dynamics of socio-historical processes remain, in the area of globalization a more fruitful dialogue is opening up between hegemony theory and figurational sociology than has previously been the case. The dynamics of this 'cultural game', with its links with both a colonial past, but also and with regard to the study of McKay and Miller (1991), a recognition of Australia's geographical position in relation to its Southeast Asian neighbours, will be returned to in chapter 8 when further consideration is given to global sport, nationhood and local identities.

Although McKay and Miller de-emphasize the pervasiveness of American control, and concentrate on the dynamics of global capitalism *per se*, the work by David Andrews would, at first sight, appear to be more in keeping with the position adopted by Donnelly. Andrews, for example, examines the 'global structure and local influence of the National Basketball Association (NBA) as a transnational corporation, whose global ubiquity inevitably contributes to the hyperreal remaking of local identities' (Andrews, 1997: p. 72). Andrews goes on to argue that the NBA has been turned 'into one of the popular commodity-signs which had usurped the material economic commodity as the dynamic force and structuring principle of everyday American existence' (Andrews, 1997: p. 74). In language sometimes akin to that used by Adorno and his fellow contributors to the Frankfurt School, Andrews argues that during the 1980s, 'the NBA became a hyper-real circus whose simulated, and hence self-perpetuating, popularity seduced the American masses' (Andrews, 1997: p. 74). This 'success' is not confined to the USA. Though it may be unwise to overestimate the knowledge of the powerful and underestimate the ability of 'locals' to reshape, resist, or simply ignore, the marketing strategies of multinationals, Andrews is correct to observe that the NBA does 'have a vivid global presence' (Andrews, 1997: p. 77). The source of debate, however, as he himself acknowledges, is 'the extent to which the circulation of universal American commodity-signs has resulted in the convergence of global markets, lifestyles and identities' (Andrews, 1997: p. 77). This debate will also be considered further in chapter 8. Despite the manner in which he formulates the early part of his argument, Andrews stresses the 'built-in particularity (or heterogeneity) in terms of the ways that products and images are consumed', and that, products, images and services from other societies 'to some extent . . . inalienably become indigenized' (Andrews, 1997: p. 77). As with the broader globalization literature, sociology of sport research is divided over the precise form and blend of homogeneity and heterogeneity characteristic of the global sport process.

What kind of assessment can be made regarding the state of play of the sociological study of global sport? Several writers have attempted some overall review (Donnelly, 1996; Harvey & Houle, 1994; Houlihan, 1994). While there are clear fault-lines along which the literature lies, reflecting the more general globalization debate, there is also some overlap. Research from both a modernization and a cultural imperialism perspective concludes that a homogenization process is occurring. This common ground can be seen in Guttmann's work. While his early work endorsed a modernization perspective, his more recent contribution has swung in favour of a form of cultural imperialism (Guttmann, 1991, 1994). While issues of cultural struggle and contestation are much more to the fore in this latter work, and in the work stemming from a cultural hegemony perspective, the common denominator is still a continued emphasis on homogenization.

Within the broad 'Marxist' tradition (cultural imperialism,

dependency theory, world-system theory and hegemony theory), common emphasis is placed on power, exploitation and the role that multinationals play in local markets. While the relative role of Americanization and/or global capitalism is disputed, what is agreed upon is that modern sport is structured by a political economy in which multinationals play a decisive part. In some instances, as we have seen, a particularly unidirectional and mono-causal focus is used to explain these processes. More recently, work by Andrews and Klein illustrates, to a greater extent, issues of local resistance, reinterpretation and indigenization. In this, they are in keeping with a trend in the more general globalization literature that emphasizes heterogeneity (Nederveen Pieterse, 1995). Harvey and Houle summarize aspects of this debate that have surfaced in the sociology of sport when they conclude:

> Thus, linking sport to globalization leads to an analysis of sport as part of an emergent global culture, as contributing to the definition of new identities, and to the development of a world economy. Therefore, the debate between globalization and Americanization is more than a question of vocabulary. Indeed, it is a question of para-digmatic choice, which leads to completely different interpretations of a series of phenomena.
>
> (Harvey & Houle, 1994: p. 346)

While the observations made in this chapter would endorse these writers when they argue that different interpretations of globalization more broadly, and global sport processes in particular, are 'a question of paradigmatic choice', there is room to doubt whether such interpre-tations are as polarized as they suggest. This chapter reveals a degree of common ground and a basis on which to build future work. It is not necessary to discard research from other traditions simply because we do not have all assumptions and concepts in common. That is not a sound strategy from which to develop a reality-congru-ent social scientific knowledge base (Elias, 1987). In the following chapter, a figurational/process-sociological perspective on globaliza-tion and sportization processes will be outlined. In doing so, I am mindful both to outline the specific contribution it can make, and also to indicate the degree of common ground that this perspective has with the approaches identified. In this respect, the links between a fig-urational/process-sociological perspective and the work of Robertson and Featherstone will be highlighted. What is clear from the literature reviewed in this chapter is that the study of global sport processes is a vibrant area, and that narrow, natiocentric analyses do not capture the complexity of modern sport in the late twentieth century.

2

Globalization, Process Sociology and Cross-cultural–Civilizational Analysis

From Western society – as a kind of upper class – Western 'civilized' patterns of conduct are today spreading over wide areas outside the West, whether through the settlement of Occidentals or through the assimilation of the upper strata of other nations, as models of conduct earlier spread within the West itself from this or that upper stratum, from certain courtly or commercial centres.... This spread of the same patterns of conduct from the 'white mother-countries or fatherlands' follows the incorporation of the other areas into the network of political and economic interdependencies, into the sphere of elimination struggles between and within the nations of the West.

Norbert Elias, The Civilising Process, 1939/1994

This chapter seeks to connect the study of globalization processes with a cross-cultural–civilizational analysis. In doing so, the degree to which a process-sociological perspective shares certain assumptions in common with other research on globalization processes will be indicated. In addition, using the work of Elias, several distinctive elements of process-sociology will be outlined.[1] Though

---

[1] It is not appropriate, in this context, to consider the central features of figurational/process-sociology more generally. For further elaboration, see Mennell

Elias wrote the comments cited above in 1939, and his 1939 study is more usually associated with tracing the emergence of the European civilizing process, it is clear that a cross-cultural–civilizational analysis was part of his broad research agenda.

A set of concepts and themes can thus be drawn from Elias's writings that are relevant to the study of globalization processes. These include: the emphasis placed on probing networks of power balances and interdependencies; the highlighting of the occidentals' practice of using their 'civilized' behaviour as a marker of prestige; the attention given to the dynamics of established/outsider relations, and how non-occidentals experienced and contested these inter-civilizational processes. This chapter also traces how several of these insights have been taken up and used by writers such as Featherstone, Mennell, Robertson and Wouters. Structuring the chapter in this way more effectively establishes the framework within which sportization/globalization processes are situated.

Process-Sociology and Globalization Research

A range of globalization research was reviewed in chapter 1. Several different traditions were identified and the relative merits of specific research noted. Certain common ground with a process-sociological perspective can thus be identified. Though postmodern writers are the exception, dependency and world-systems approaches emphasize that, in examining globalization, we are dealing with long-term processes that have occurred unevenly across all areas of the planet. Though, it should be added, the period in which such processes are said to have 'begun' is disputed. Other themes are also shared with research by Robertson (1992), King (1991) and Featherstone and Lash (1995). These long-term processes, involving, as noted in chapter 1, an increasing intensification of global interconnectedness, are seen to be gathering momentum, and despite the 'unevenness' of these processes, it is more difficult to understand local or national experiences without reference to global flows. For process-sociologists, every aspect of social reality – people's living conditions, beliefs, knowledge and actions – is intertwined with unfolding globalization

---

& Goudsblom (1998), Goudsblom & Mennell (1998) and Van Krieken (1998). A broad summary has also been provided by Mennell (1992) and Goudsblom (1977). For its application to sport and leisure, see Elias & Dunning (1986) and the review in Jarvie & Maguire (1994).

processes. These processes include the emergence of a global economy, a transnational cosmopolitan culture and a range of international social movements. The global development of sports organizations, such as the IOC, can be viewed in a similar light.

For process-sociology, the explanatory frame of reference must be global in perspective. As such, this approach is in keeping with the observations that Robertson (1995) and Featherstone and Lash (1995) have made regarding globalization. That is, as noted, we must 'move away from social change conceived as the internal development of societies to focusing on change as the outcome of struggles between the members of a figuration of interdependent and competing nation-states', and then, 'add to this an understanding of the intensification of trans-societal flows which are pushing towards a borderless global economy' (Featherstone & Lash, 1995: p. 2). Tracing the common ground that process-sociology shares with other approaches is not solely a question of how the dynamics of global processes are understood. Process-sociology overlaps with work by Arnason (1990) and Robertson (1992, 1995), for example, in the emphasis placed on the need to conduct comparative civilizational analysis.

Attention is rightly directed to the need to adopt a multidimensional interrogation of inter-civilizational encounters. Globalization refers 'in its most general sense, to the process whereby the world becomes a single place' and involves the development of a global culture (Robertson, 1992: p. 135). This culture, he argues, is not a homogeneous, binding whole, but refers to a 'general mode of discourse about the world as a whole and its variety' (Robertson, 1992: p. 133). In mapping how the world is ordered, Robertson traces a 'global field' that results from an interweaving of societies, individuals, international relations and humankind as a whole. In doing so reference to a single causal factor must be avoided.

There is not much that process-sociologists would disagree with here. Globalization is not the direct outcome of inter-state actions, but needs to be understood as operating relatively independently of conventionally designated societal and socio-cultural processes (Mennell, 1990). Stress is placed on the relative autonomy and long-term nature of the processes involved. While he refers to the development of a global culture, Robertson also stresses, as noted, that globalization processes do not lead to homogeneity. For Robertson, global processes involve both the particularization of universalism and the universalization of particularism (Robertson, 1992: p. 130). That is, as noted earlier, these processes are marked by heterogeneous tendencies and characteristics. In sum, 'globalization is . . . best understood as indicating the problem of the form in terms of which the world becomes "united" but by no means integrated' (Robertson, 1992: p. 51). In mapping out the global condition, Robertson identifies, as noted in chapter 1, five main phases in this long-term process.

Certain aspects of Robertson's pioneering work clearly dovetail well with the process-sociological approach being used here. This is no surprise, given that Robertson refers extensively to the work of Elias. Given this linkage, it is also appropriate to further map out the assumptions that these approaches have in common. In an earlier period, when social units were organized as tribes and states, sociological models of society corresponded, to a greater degree, to that reality. For, as Elias noted:

> The distances between many states and groups of states before the social development which generated the automobile and air transport and for a good time afterwards, were very great. Telecommunications, radio and television were still in their infancy. Global tourism and goods traffic were relatively limited, and the same was true of the whole network of interdependence between the states of the world. *The network has become visibly more dense in the course of the twentieth century.* People themselves, however, only perceived this in a very limited, inexact way. They were not used to thinking in terms of social processes. Hardly anyone spoke clearly about the rapidly increasing integration of humanity. It was seldom seen as a long-term, unplanned social process. Thus the shortening of distances, the increasing integration, happened, as it were, in secret. It did not obtrude itself on human experience as a global process of integration.
> (Elias, 1987/1991: p. 163; italics added)

For process-sociology, such very long-term globalization trends involve broad, multifaceted processes where, as Robertson also notes, no single causal factor predominates. Though Elias uses the term 'integrated' and Robertson prefers the term 'united', both mean the same thing. Integration refers to the interdependency chains that connect people together. It should be pointed out, however, that process-sociologists lay greater emphasis on the notion that these processes are the result of a complex interweaving of intended and unintended sets of actions. Past unintended consequences of intended acts are the seedbed of present and future intended acts (Bogner, 1986). A set of shifting power-balances of class, gender and ethnic allies and foes contour such global interchanges. Roudometof and Robertson (1995) commend, as will be detailed later in this chapter, the use of a figurational analysis of power networks in understanding these global processes. Ideological practices by individuals, key state officials and the representatives of transnational corporations, organizations and capitalist classes figure strongly in this.

For process-sociologists, there are, however, dangers in overstating the knowledge and power of 'established' groups and underestimating the knowledge and power of 'outsider' groups (Elias & Scotson, 1965/1994). At worst, this leads to crude ideas of global conspiracy, notions of cultural dupes and a simple homogenization thesis. While globalization processes do not necessarily lead to the destruction of 'local' culture, such cultures survive in a context more defined by powerful established nations and/or transnational groups. Inuit folk games, for example, have survived through to the late twentieth century, yet they too have undergone a sportization process in the form of the 'Inuit Olympics'.

The interweaving of the global field that Robertson identifies does not, however, *contra* those critics who confuse notions of 'development' with evolution in a process-sociological approach, follow any single inexorable path (Mennell, 1990). Many different variants to the existing global pattern were possible in the past, and the making of future global patterns is also open-ended and subject to different permutations. Nor should the use of cross-cultural–civilizational analysis in process-sociological accounts be confused with an ethnocentric approach to the study of global relations. Such a charge overlooks the degree to which Elias sought to 'debunk' the present stage of social development by adopting a comparative and developmental approach (Mennell, 1992: pp. 228–34).

Several key themes to a process-sociology perspective on globalization can thus be discerned. Globalization processes involve multidirectional movements of people, practices, customs and ideas. Yet, although the globe can be understood as an interdependent whole, in different figurational fields, established (core) and outsider (peripheral) groups and nation-states are constantly vying with each other for dominant positions. Global processes are multidirectional, involve a series of power-balances, yet have *neither* the hidden hand of progress *nor* some all-pervasive, overarching conspiracy guiding them. For process-sociologists, globalization processes have a blind, unplanned dimension to them and a relative autonomy from the intentions of specific groups of people. These processes, then, are also bound up in a multiple set of 'disjunctures' (Appadurai, 1990), which, given our present state of knowledge, have a high degree of unpredictability about them and which process-sociologists would view as an integral feature of human interdependencies.

Given this perceived growth in the multiplicity of linkages and networks that transcend nation-states, it is not surprising that we may be, as Robertson has argued, at the earliest stages of the development of a 'transnational culture' or 'global culture'. This process entails a shift from ethnic or national cultures to 'supranational' forms based upon either the culture of a 'superpower' or of 'cosmopolitan' communication and migrant networks, for example, Americanization. Sportization processes may, in certain respects, be more symptomatic of the emergence of a transnational culture than other aspects of social life. Despite this, for process-sociology, homogenization, at least in any simple sense, is not, as noted, a sufficient explanation of observed events. Processes of Europeanization, Orientalization, Africanization and Hispanicization have been and continue to be at work on a global stage.

This is clearly the case, as the following chapters will show, with regard to sport. This argument parts company with those researchers reviewed in chapter 1 who argued that Americanization has been *the* dominant theme of global sport development. If, as noted, Roudometof and Robertson are correct to argue that globalization research should be concerned with the 'multidimensional interrogation of these intercivilizational encounters' (1995: p. 287), then a process-sociological perspective is well placed to assist in the task of exploring this *range* of cultural flows. In order to justify further this claim, and to tie the analysis of sportization, globalization and comparative civilizational processes together, the more central features of how a process-sociological perspective views cross-cultural relations need to be outlined.

Globalization and Cross-Cultural–Civilizational Processes: Diminishing Contrasts and Increasing Varieties

The main dynamics involved in cross-cultural–civilizing processes can be illustrated with reference to Elias's study of the European civilizing process. In addition, concepts and ideas drawn from his other work, including that on established/outsider relations, shed further light on cross-cultural relations. Concepts such as diminishing contrasts and increasing varieties arguably steer the analysis between the excesses of homogenization and heterogenization. Likewise, a 'personal pronoun' approach ensures that a multi-causal, multidirectional approach to the study of globalization processes is used.[2] In the following section I want to consider these issues in greater detail.

[2] See Elias (1987/1991).

If, as is usually the case, a short time-frame is used to examine the differences between the social personality and customs of people *within* Western societies, then those differences identified will appear great. Over a longer-term perspective, however, what can be observed is that the sharp contrasts between different strata are diminishing. According to Elias, an important peculiarity of the Western civilizing process is that there is a reduction in the contrasts within society, as well as within individuals. Despite the urge of more powerful groups to use social customs and conduct to distinguish themselves from their social inferiors, a commingling of patterns of conduct derived from initially very different social strata gradually occurs.

What precisely, however, are the dynamics at work in the relations *between* Western societies? Elias shows how the upper classes were and are involved in a process of 'reciprocal supervision' of their and others' behaviour. Examining civilizing processes over the course of several centuries, he noted that the internalization of restraints by the upper classes lead to the habitual reproduction of distinctive conduct. The upper classes sought to keep this distinctive forms of conduct to themselves, yet also use it as a means to stigmatize others. Those who breached the dominant rules and codes were viewed as 'uncivilized'. The function of these codes then was to serve as marks of distinction and thereby preserve their threatened position, which was being challenged from lower down the social hierarchy. Throughout the course of these processes there was, however, a double-bind tendency at work. Elias noted that as functional differentiation increased and interdependencies widened, the upper classes were 'forced' to refine their behaviour and seek to retain exclusivity over the codes that maintain their distinction. Yet, growing interdependence and what Elias termed 'functional democratization' was inexorably leading to a diminution of their exclusivity, and thereby, a loss of social power. Let us examine these interlocking tendencies more closely.

In what Elias termed a 'phase of colonisation', the established upper class, intentionally or otherwise, interact with and colonize the culture of others. They permeate the lower or outsider class with their own pattern of conduct. They do so not simply for the land that these people occupy. They also seek their labour and to incorporate them into the network of social relations where hegemonic control lies with the established groups. These established groups seek to 'imprint' specific values, behaviour and habitus codes onto the outsider groups. As this process of colonization gains momentum, seemingly somewhat paradoxically 'phases of repulsion' also occur. That is, the upper classes build social barriers between themselves and the groups they colonize and whom they consider their inferiors. They do this in order to distinguish themselves from the outsiders and thus maintain their more established positions. This strict regulation of their established conduct, and that of the outsider class, is especially intense when the former feel threatened as the latter gain in power. Despite building social barriers and being constantly vigilant regarding the 'policing' of such cultural and social boundaries, the upper classes cannot prevent a gradual seepage of their distinguishing models of conduct into other strata. Indeed, the act of colonization requires that a degree of seepage occurs. Sooner or later, this process leads to a reduction in differences of social power and conduct – a process of functional democratization unfolds.

Markedly similar processes are at work in relations *between Western societies and non-Western societies*. In world terms, Western societies were (and still are in most, if not all fields of human endeavour) the equivalent of the established upper class within particular European nations. The spread of their 'civilized' patterns of conduct occurred through the colonial settlement of occidentals, or through the assimilation of the upper strata of other nations. Crucially, the same double-bind tendencies that marked the upper classes' colonization of 'outsiders' within the West was, and remains evident, in the West's dealings with outsider nations and peoples. With this spread came a particular contested view of civilization – of humanity as a whole. Elias described this process in the following way:

> The expansion of Western civilisation shows this double tendency clearly enough. This civilisation is the characteristic conferring distinction and superiority on occidentals. But at the same time the Western people, under the pressure of their own competitive struggle, bring about in large areas of the world a change in human relations and functions in line with their own standards. They make large parts of the world dependent on them and at the same time . . . become themselves dependent on them.
>
> (Elias, 1939/1994: p. 463)

Several points need stressing in this connection. Western societies were acting, as noted, as a form of established group on a world level. Their tastes and conduct, including their sports, were part of this, and these practices acted in similar ways to elite cultural activities and manners within Western societies. They were signs of distinction, prestige and power. Yet, just as established groups within Western societies found that their initially distinguishing forms of conduct seeped down to lower social strata, so the occidentals of the colonies discovered that a similar process occurred in their dealings with their colonial social inferiors. A double-bind tendency was at work. Indeed, as a result of this cultural interchange, outsider, non-Western codes and customs began to permeate back into Western societies. It was never a one-way traffic. Polo, for example, practised so avidly by established groups in southern England, is a game form derived, at the height of Empire, from the Indian subcontinent.

The manner and form of these processes of commingling – the two-way traffic between cultures – were dependent on several factors. These included: the form of colonization; the position of the area in the large network of political, economic and military interdependencies; and the particular region's own history and structure. In assessing the pattern of commingling, several other factors need consideration. Such processes were (and are) characterized by unequal power-relations and are also marked by a combination of intentional and unintentional features. That is, one means by which the established Western elites maintained their status and distinction was through the *embodied exercise* of specific forms of conduct. One example of this, as will be shown in chapter 3, was their recourse to specific status-enhancing sporting practices. Nevertheless, the social barriers that they built between themselves and the native outsiders proved semi-permeable. This was the case whether we consider the history of Raffles Hotel or the cricket club in Singapore. All-White outposts of Empire began to wither away. The contrasts between Western and non-Western people, and their societies, did indeed begin to diminish.

The form in and extent to which Western values spread through specific regions reflected the history and structure of the areas in question. This also applies, as noted, in the diffusion of non-Western conduct back to specific Western nations. The reception of Japanese art into Europe in the late nineteenth century is a case in point: in this instance, Japanese art permeated the French art salons and influenced the emergence and style of Impressionist painters (Nederveen Pieterse, 1995). It is also important to note that established and outsider groups were (and are) active in the interpretation of Western and non-Western conduct and cultural forms. This recognition points to the possibility that existing and new varieties of 'civilized' conduct could survive and emerge. Writing about these processes in 1939, Elias observed:

> In colonial regions too, according to the position and social strength of the various groups, Western standards are spreading downwards and occasionally even upwards from below, if we may adhere to

this spatial image, and fusing to form new unique entities, new varieties of civilised conduct. *The contrasts in conduct between the upper
and lower groups are reduced with the spread of civilisation; the varieties
or nuances of civilised conduct are increased.*

(Elias, 1939/1994: pp. 463–4; italics in original)

This, then, is not a simple process of homogenization. Nor does the
spread or diffusion of styles of behaviour solely depend on the
activities of established groups. A multiplicity of two-way
processes of cultural interaction crisscross the semi-permeable barriers that established groups, within Western societies, and
between Western and non-Western societies, deploy to maintain
their distinction, power and prestige. The more they become interconnected with outsider groups, the more they depend on them
for social tasks. In so doing, the contrasts between them diminish.
This is the key to understanding what Elias termed 'functional
democratization'. The power ratio between these groups moves in
an equalizing direction. Concomitantly, new styles of conduct
emerge. Elias commented on this issue in the following way:

> In accordance with the power-relationship, the product of interpen-
> etration is dominated first by models derived from the situation of
> the upper class, then by [the] pattern(s) of conduct of the lower,
> rising classes, until finally an amalgam emerges, a new style of
> unique character.

(Elias, 1939/1994: p. 464)

As 'civilized' forms of conduct spread across both the rising lower
classes of Western society and the different classes of the colonies,
an amalgamation of the Western and the indigenous pattern occurs.
Each time this happens, 'upper-class conduct and that of the rising
groups interpenetrate' (Elias, 1939/1994: p. 505). People placed in
this situation attempted to reconcile and fuse the pattern of 'occiden-
tally civilised societies with the habits and traditions of their own
society'. In this they achieve a 'higher or lesser degree of success'
(Elias, 1939/1994: pp. 509–10). The processes identified within the
West, and in the dealings between the West and non-Western countries, also occur *within* former colonized nations. As the rising class
of these nations shake off the shackles of the colonial overlords, they
too attempt to distinguish their behaviour. This attempt again
reflects the history and structure of a particular region, but also, the
specific dynamics of the new amalgam that emerged between themselves and the former masters. Just as their former masters became
bound to them, they too become bound to the rising class situated
below them in the hierarchy of social stratification.

In a shrewd conclusion, Elias notes that the watchword of the Western colonizing movement was 'civilization' and that what was at stake in this movement was not, as observed earlier, simply the land that people occupied but the people themselves. Their integration into wider political and economic interdependencies 'demands a civilisation of the colonised' (Elias, 1939/1994: p. 509). Whereas the formal possession of other nation-states is now much less common, the struggle for the thoughts and feelings of their populations remains ongoing. This is what Elias wrote as early as 1939:

> It is not a little characteristic of the structure of Western societies that the watchword of its colonising movement is 'civilisation'. For the people of a society with a high division of functions it is not enough simply to rule subject people and countries by force of arms like a warrior caste, although the old, simple goals of much of the earlier expansionist movements, the expulsion of other peoples from their land, the acquisition of new soil for cultivation and settlement, doubtless play no small part in Western expansion. *But it is not only the land that is needed but the people; these must be integrated, whether as workers or consumers, into the web of the hegemonial, the upper-class country*, with its highly developed differentiation of functions.
> (Elias, 1939/1994: p. 509; italics added)

Four key insights can be identified from the observations so far outlined. These are: the concepts of diminishing contrasts and increasing varieties; the idea of the commingling of Western and non-Western cultures; the subsequent emergence of a new amalgam; and the ongoing attempts by established groups to integrate outsider people(s) as workers and/or consumers. If these are some of the dynamics involved in cross-cultural–civilizational encounters, what other insights can be drawn from a process-sociological perspective?

The potential of this approach has been recognized by several writers, though the overall contribution of this approach has not been pulled together in one single analysis before. I am thinking here of Mennell's (1985) work on food, Featherstone's (1991a, 1995) analyses of global consumer culture, Robertson's general study of global processes (1992) and Wouters's study of stratification, informalization and globalization (1990). It is to the latter that I want to direct initial attention. In reviewing this research, aspects of a process-sociological approach can be extended and more fully elaborated.

Applications and Interpretations of a Process-Sociological Approach to the Study of Globalization

The significance of features of the comparative civilizing model outlined above was not overlooked by Wouters when he asked, 'Will the trend towards "diminishing contrasts and increasing varieties" between *classes* continue on a global scale between *states*? What are the chances that the structured changes in the West will spread to the global level?' (Wouters, 1990: p. 70; italics in original). Assessing a range of indices, Wouters argues that the use of an economic analysis alone is not sufficient. While the income differential between the 'rich' and the 'poor' may have increased, in other respects, the gap has diminished. In substantiating this argument, Wouters points to how the balance between power and prestige has moved in an equalizing direction. It is no longer possible to simply despatch a 'gun-boat' and enforce Western control over the 'natives'. Wouters continues, 'as far as standards of behaviour and demands on emotion management are concerned, the gap between rich and poor countries has diminished' (Wouters, 1990: p. 72). This process appears to stem less from some philanthropic policy of the West and more from what Elias terms the 'monopoly mechanism' (Elias, 1983: p. 106). That is, as the web of interconnections between the West and the non-West grows more dense, established groups become increasingly dependent upon their 'subordinates' in the international rank order of nations. As Wouters observes:

> In the longer run, the competitive drive inherent in this interdependency network tends towards diminishing power differences between colonists and colonized as well as towards diminishing contrasts in their standards of behaviour and feeling – a process similar to what had happened in the West.
>
> (Wouters, 1990: p. 75)

While Wouters in this instance is emphasizing the intended nature of this decrease in contrasts, non-Western people have also been active in resisting their incorporation. Such resistance is, in fact, an integral part of the model being outlined. For as Wouters observes:

> When these intertwining and intermingling processes come to a phase in which many begin to experience themselves as located somewhere at the bottom of a Western ladder of social stratification, counter-movements in which old, indigenous traditions are emphasised and practised in new ways, may expand and become dominant.
>
> (Wouters, 1990: pp. 86–7)

Though varying degrees of domination and colonization can be achieved by the West, the more powerful, over time, become dependent on the 'colonized'. Through processes of differentiation, integration and 'functional democratization' the seepage of high-status civilized conduct, and the resurgence of indigenous customs, leads to a decrease in the power of occidentals. Inequalities between established and outsider groups decrease and an informalization process, at a global level, gathers momentum. While such dynamics are discussed in the next chapter, at this stage I want to extend these arguments with reference to the development of food tastes.

Mennell's work on food also uses a process-sociological framework. An exploration of the long-term patterns of development, how contemporary tastes have emerged out of the past, and how changes have occurred within the West, and in the West's dealing with non-Western nations, is undertaken. Reviewing these processes, Mennell observes that 'underneath the many swirling cross-currents, the main trend has been towards diminishing contrasts and increasing varieties in food habits and culinary taste. One trend, not two: for in spite of the apparent contradiction between diminishing contrasts and increasing varieties, these are both facets of the same processes' (Mennell, 1985: p. 322). Over time, the contrasts between food consumption within the West and across a range of social groups have decreased.

What Mennell also stresses is the complex, interdependent nature of the changes in global food consumption and cuisine. Though, not unlike some scholars referred to in the previous chapter, he points to the impact of Americanization, especially in the fast-food sector of the market, Mennell also indicates that since World War II, four other 'major waves of foreign influence in British catering' can be identified (Mennell, 1985: p. 329). These include Italian, Chinese, Indian and Greek or Turkish. There are also significant subdivisions within these broad categories and such a listing excludes the long-standing influence and status of French cuisine within the West. From this, it is clear, Americanization processes alone do not explain the transformation of the purposes, patterns and pleasures associated with food consumption.

The reduction in contrasts in food consumption has meshed with the commingling of behaviour derived initially from very different social levels, ethnic groups and geographical locations. Mennell's overall assessment of the long-term processes he observes to be at work in the development of food also applies, as will be shown in chapter 3, with regard to the making of global sport. In a passage that could equally apply to the emergence of global sport as well as to food, he concludes:

> Likes and dislikes are never socially neutral, but always entangled with people's affiliations to class and other social groups. Higher social circles have repeatedly used food as one of the many means of distinguishing themselves from lower rising classes. This has been manifested in a succession of styles and attitudes towards food and eating. The tensions and competition have always been too strong in the end for establishment groups to maintain their culinary exclusiveness, and as each round led to ever-greater complexity and the rise of broader and broader classes, so a cultural and culinary blending has produced many varieties and nuances of cuisine. That same process also means that social contrasts can in long-term perspective be seen as well to have become more subtle and complex. They have diminished but by no means disappeared.
>
> (Mennell, 1985: pp. 331–2)[3]

If Mennell has provided an empirically grounded, topic-specific case study that fruitfully highlights the advantages of the figurational perspective, the more general work of Featherstone and Robertson also goes some way towards supporting the notion that process-sociology has something distinctive to offer the study of cross-cultural–civilizational processes. Featherstone has written extensively on global processes (1991b, 1995) and in these texts he regularly makes use of Elias's work. Clearly, process-sociology is viewed by Featherstone as one of the potential building blocks of a sociology of globalization – or should that be a global sociology? One of the first steps in this direction is to focus, as noted, 'on change as the outcome of struggles between the members of a figuration of interdependent and competing nation-states', and then, 'add to this an understanding of the intensification of trans-societal flows' (Featherstone & Lash, 1995: p. 2). Here, as in this book, these writers link the notion of a figuration of competing nation-states and blocs to the intensification of global flows. That is also the strategy that underpins the second part of this book. In other work, Featherstone develops this position and argues:

> Sociology needs to adopt not only a relational understanding of the shifting place of what have come to be known as 'societies' within their particular reference group, but also a long-term processual perspective which considers 'societies' as temporary phenomena.

---

[3] In addition to the study of sport outlined in this book, similar studies need to be conducted with regard to the development of music, dance and other movement forms.

> Societies then as processual entities should be considered as always
> in the process of formation and deformation: they do not always
> have to exist for social relations to take place, they come into being
> and fade away.
>
> (Featherstone, 1995: p. 135)

As Featherstone observes, the mode of analysis of Elias, and also of
Simmel and Weber, 'was always pointing towards the global'
(Featherstone, 1995: p. 135). Given that cultural contact and
exchange are increasingly bound up in power struggles and
lengthening interdependency chains, the work of Elias is seen by
Featherstone as of particular relevance.

> As Elias indicates in his synopsis to *The Civilizing Process* the cre-
> ation of larger nation-states and blocs and the nature of the power
> balances, interdependencies and linkages between and across them
> will influence the types of identity formation and personality struc-
> ture which develop in various parts of the world.
>
> (Featherstone, 1995: pp. 135–6)

Yet the growing web of interconnections, and the concomitant
influence that these have on processes of identity-testing and -for-
mation in different parts of the globe, brings with it a series of conceptual problems, and empirical questions. Conventional
sociological thinking does not well equip the researcher to deal
with these. Featherstone rightly observes that the cultural and
social, as well as the economic, dimensions of the flows that characterize these interdependency chains require equal attention. An
economically determined explanation does not capture the complexity of these global flows. Process-sociologists would concur
with this and argue, as noted, that a multicausal, multidimensional
explanation is needed. In this regard, Featherstone draws on
the insights provided by the latter section of Elias's work, *The
Civilizing Process* and concludes:

> The process of globalization, then, can be understood as the increas-
> ing extension of the reference group of societies which are estab-
> lished in a process of contact which necessarily form a world,
> however inchoate and limited that world might be when compared
> to the sense of the finite known world we inhabit. This larger trans-
> and supra-societal process forms the context within which societies
> are able to develop. The process of state formation in Europe, for
> example, produced a series of power struggles, rivalries, alliances
> and elimination contests. The competition for additional power
> resources to draw upon and use in these struggles increasingly
> became widened to take in the whole world.
>
> (Featherstone, 1995: p. 136)

The competition and elimination contests between established and outsider nations to which reference is made also contoured and shaped the sportization processes. The global diffusion of sport was also bound up in the quest for status and distinction by representatives of different nations. Process-sociology assists in the task of explaining these processes by its emphasis on multidimensional and poly-directional analysis, be it of migrant sport labour, the media–sport production complex or the sports goods/equipment/body culture nexus. The exploration of long-term structured processes holds the key to understanding what is involved. In addition, as Featherstone notes, power struggles, elimination contests and state-formation processes, were integral to the analysis of civilizing processes proposed by Elias. The relevance of process-sociology to the study of globalization processes does not end here. Featherstone correctly connects together the twin related concepts of diminishing contrasts/increasing varieties and established/outsider relations.

In discussing the broad development of consumer culture, Featherstone uses Elias's work on court society (1983) to stress the dynamics involved in the cut and thrust of status games that characterize this culture. The emergence of court society led to the nobility becoming specialists in the art of consumption and a process whereby individuals cultivated the habit of both presenting themselves in a fashionable demeanour and appropriate style, but also learning to read the appearance of others. Social action of this kind centred on a quest for status, distinction, style and power. This theme in Elias's work has been taken up, to good effect, by Bourdieu (1984).

Yet, as Featherstone notes, this was only one of several interrelated themes in Elias's work, and 'should not blind us to the existence of the counter tendency which mass consumption and democratization favoured, the tendency towards equalization and the diminishing of contrasts' (Featherstone, 1991b: p. 115). The development of consumer culture is seen as 'part of a process of functional democratization', and was 'accompanied by a greater levelling-out of balances of power', due to the fact that 'the less powerful were for the first time able to emulate, within the limitations of mass fashion, the consumption practices and styles of the more powerful' (ibid.). There is much here that is relevant to the study of globalization. This needs further explanation.

The dynamics of global interchange are characterized both by tendencies towards a diminishing of contrasts, emulation, equalization and imitation, but also by tendencies towards increasing varieties, differentiation, individuality and distinction. These

tendencies relate closely to Elias's other concept of established/
outsider relations. Elias used this concept both to explain aspects
of long-term civilizing processes, and contemporary community
relations (Elias & Scotson, 1965/1994). Process-sociology does not
only engage in the study of long-term 'macro' processes.
Local/global networks figure strongly as well. How is this
accomplished?

Though the nature of the power resources on which superior
social status is founded varies considerably, Elias argued that the
'established–outsider figuration itself shows in many different settings common characteristics and regularities' (Elias, 1994a: p. xix).
Key features of this established/outsider figuration include: the
relative degrees of cohesion of the groups involved; the strength of
collective identifications; the commonality of norms; the establishment of a powerful 'I/we/they/them images' that emphasizes
comparative superiority; the development and enforcement of
exclusion strategies; and the stigmatization of less powerful
groups. Commenting on aspects of this established/outsider
figuration, Elias observed:

> The centrepiece of that figuration is an uneven balance of power and
> the tensions inherent in it. It is also the decisive condition of any
> effective stigmatisation of an outsider group by an established
> group. One group can effectively stigmatise another only as long as
> it is well established in positions of power from which the stigma-
> tised group is excluded. As long as that is the case, the stigma of
> collective disgrace attached to the outsiders can be made to stick.
>
> (Elias, 1994a: p. xx)

Once a group's monopolization of the principal power resources and
its ability to exclude other interdependent groups diminishes, the
power to stigmatize – or for the stigmatization process to have real
'sting' – is reduced. Yet, though the balance of power may change
considerably over time, the once-established group finds it difficult
to shed itself of the group-charismatic we-image that conferred on its
members a sense of superiority and self-worth. The dreams and
group-charismatic we-ideals and images that Elias refers to apply not
just to nations or the people who compose them. Such fantasy-laden
images, and dreams of special charisma, are also part of how citizens
of the West encounter non-occidentals. Westerners' sense of superiority still surfaces even when they work for non-Western multinational firms such as Toyota, Sony and Samsung; this is evident
in British attitudes towards the establishment of car and electronic
factories in the UK. The dreams of nations, and the idealized

'we-identities' of once powerful groups, also live on, as chapter 8 explores, in the contemporary sports world. The nostalgic response of the English to defeats on and off the sports field is a case in point.

In discussing localism, globalism and cultural identities, Featherstone also makes this connection to established/outsider relations. In phases of colonization, the established groups are able to develop both a collective 'we-image' based on a sense of civilized superiority and group charisma, but also a 'they-image', in which outsiders are viewed with disdain and mistrust, and stigmatized as 'inferiors' – especially in phases of repulsion. Such processes, however, are subject to contestation and change. Highlighting the relevance of both these phases of colonization/repulsion and established/outsider relations for the study of global social relations, Featherstone comments:

> This colonization phase of the relationship between the established and the outsiders can give way with a shift in interdependencies and the relative power balance to a second phase, that of 'functional democratization'. In this second phase of differentiation and eman- cipation, people become enmeshed in longer and denser webs of interdependencies, which the established group finds difficulty in controlling. Outsider groups gain in social power and confidence and the contrasts and tensions in society increase.
>
> (Featherstone, 1991b: pp. 124–5)

In the British/English case, processes of established/outsider relations and diminishing contrasts/increasing varieties are ac- companied by a notion of a cultured person – specifically a *'gentle- man'*. For make no mistake, the struggles over style, status and distinction, on the one hand, and the trends towards emulation, equalization and imitation on the other, involved gender as well as class and ethnic relations. The cultivated English gentleman *embod- ied* qualities of honour, chivalry and fair play. During the nine- teenth century, these qualities would be developed on the playing fields of Eton and other public schools. These gentlemen would then display such attributes by their deeds of valour on the playing, or battle, fields of Empire.

A more critical, yet also sympathetic, use of the process- sociological approach to the study of globalization is provided by Robertson (1990b), and, more recently, by Robertson with his co- writer Roudometof (1995). They dispute the extent to which Elias paid attention to the link that the West had with other civilizations. *Contra* to this, it should be observed that Elias did refer to migra- tion processes across the Eurasian landmass and also examined the sociogenesis of the Crusades. While it is clear that Elias did not fully explore this interconnectedness with reference to the medieval phase in the European civilizing process, as the themes outlined above indicate he did discuss the links between occidental and non-occidental cultures in the more recent past.

Despite their reservation in this regard, Roudometof and Robertson find that the process-sociological approach is well suited to the study of globalization processes. This stems from both its mode of enquiry and the emphasis it places on conducting an inter-civilizational analysis. These points need some elaboration. Instead of adopting a monocausal explanation, and separating the economic from the political or the cultural, these writers propose that a more helpful way of conducting 'world-historical sociology' is to conceive of the processes involved as power networks. As they comment:

> The theorization of historical processes in terms of contact among different power networks allows for the examination of the key issue of the causal connections among power networks. In this regard, the legacy of the sociology of Norbert Elias can be used for the development of an approach that systematically attempts to discern the impact that changes in one or more power networks have on the others.
>
> (Roudometof & Robertson, 1995: p. 292)

Looking at the European civilizing process, Elias made connections between feudalism, inter-state conflict, the internal pacification of societies, changes in personality development and social customs. He did so in a manner that emphasized the multifaceted and interwoven nature of the processes that were contoured by the unintended consequences of intentional acts of individuals across many generations. It is not, as noted, solely a question of the mode of enquiry that prompts writers such as Roudometof and Robertson to emphasize the merits of process-sociology. Elias's use of the concept 'civilization' was neither ethnocentric nor essentialist. As Roudometof and Robertson remark:

> In contrast to other viewpoints, Elias's theory avoids the reification that Wallerstein finds so characteristic of the civilizational perspective. 'Civilization' refers to a number of features generated under particular sociohistorical processes in a specific territory within a given *longue durée*. The extension of Elias's figurational perspective outside Europe represents, of course, the major challenge faced by figurational sociologists. Although it is by no means certain that identical outcomes will be present everywhere, the logical connections established between external power relations and internal

emotional and affective control constitute a novel contribution to the topic.

(Roudometof & Robertson, 1995: p. 281)

Elias himself, as noted, was not unaware of the need to explore how the West was interconnected with non-Western nations. In addition, writing in 1939, Elias also emphasized that studies of non-occidental civilizations were required. But Elias did not assume that civilizing processes would be identical within the West or between occidental and non-occidental societies. This is what he wrote in this connection:

> A number of examples ... have shown how remarkably similar the forces of social interweaving that led to feudal relations and institutions in Japan are to the structures and forces which have been established here in relation to Western feudalism. A comparative structural analysis of this kind would prove a more useful way of explaining the peculiarities by which the feudal institutions of Japan and their historical change differ from those of the West.
>
> (Elias, 1939/1994: p. 527)

Elias viewed his work as one symptom of a beginning. Other process-sociologists have continued the task of inter-civilizational analysis to which Elias directed attention.[4]

Conclusion: Sport and Cross-civilizational Processes

In drawing this chapter to a close it is helpful to re-emphasize three key interwoven levels of civilizing processes. Two of these, as Mennell records, are more familiar. Each individual, from one generation to the next, experiences a 'civilizing process', though this is more usually termed socialization. In addition, a second level of civilizing processes is that of the development of social standards and codes of acting, thinking and feeling in particular societies. These two levels are interwoven. This much is clear, and those who have used Elias have tended to draw on these levels of analysis.[5] The third level and the one being dealt with in this chapter is, however, less familiar. It concerns the links between societies and the development of humanity as a whole. This is what Mennell demonstrates in the following passage:

---

[4] For research on the taming of the samurai and the development of Japan, see Ikegami (1995).

[5] For further discussion of this, see Burkitt (1991) and Mennell (1994).

No civilizing process in any particular society, it must be remembered, represents an absolute beginning. It never proceeds *in vacuo*, without reference to other – earlier or contemporary – civilizing processes undergone by other human groups. . . . Just as every individual lifetime civilizing process is a part of the longer-term development of a particular society, so also are civilizing processes in every society parts of a still longer-term civilizing process which encompasses humanity as a whole.

(Mennell, 1992: p. 201)

The European civilizing process itself is but one small example of an overall very long-term trend. Testing the connections between external power relations and internal emotional and affect control requires a fuller study that 'would have to deal with the great variety of competitive figurations in different continents at different stages of the development of society' (Mennell, 1992: p. 218). The study of global sport processes can contribute, in some small measure, to this task.

Several questions that arise in this regard centre on how the emergence and diffusion of modern sport is bound up in cross-cultural–civilizational processes. Have we seen a decrease in contrasts of the kind described? Is there a 'monopoly mechanism' at work within the global sport process? Are sportization processes marked by a kind of functional democratization? Are cross-cultural–civilizational exchanges a feature of the sport process? Can phases of colonization and repulsion be witnessed in the development of sport? Has sport been used as a sign of cultural status, exclusivity and power? What has been the role of Western and non-Western people in the established/outsider relations that arguably characterize the global sportization process? What is the nature of the power networks that characterize the global sport process and which social groups are the winners and losers in this cross-cultural contest? It is to a more detailed consideration of these questions that attention now turns.

3

Globalization, Civilizing Offensives and Sportization Processes

> As is well known, England was the cradle and the loving
> 'Mother' of sport ... It appears that English technical terms
> referring to this field might become the common possession of
> all nations in the same way as Italian technical terms in the
> field of music. It is probably rare that a piece of culture has
> migrated with so few changes from one country to another.
>   A. Stiven, *Englands Einfluss auf den Deutschen Wortschatz*; cited in
>   Elias, 1970

Written in 1936, by a German scholar, these observations reinforce
the conclusion reached in chapter 1: there is little dispute that
England is viewed as the 'cradle' of modern sport. Stiven is also
correct to point out that the *lingua franca* of modern sport is
English. This holds true in terms of the naming of specific sports
and also the technical terms associated with a range of sports that
have spread across the globe. People in different societies have
proved to be remarkably receptive to and emulating of 'English'
customs and pastimes. Sports such as association football, golf and
tennis are examples of these processes at work. There are,
however, two qualifications to be made to this argument. The
sports mentioned also highlight the 'European' influence on the
development of 'English' sports. That is, the development of golf,

for example, was strongly influenced by events in the Netherlands and Scotland. The role of the French in the development of tennis also cannot be underestimated. Indeed, some of the technical terms associated with tennis are derived from French. In addition, if consideration is also given to sports such as basketball and volleyball, which spread across the globe at a later stage in the sportization process, account has to be taken of the Americanization of sporting terms.

Stiven was therefore correct to a degree, but consideration of other cultural flows has to be undertaken. In addition, while it is correct to observe that the 'constitutive' rules of sport are commonly accepted across the globe, and form part of a global idiom, the rules and codes that regulate the 'playing' of a sport form vary considerably in different parts of the world. Here we see how both homogenization and heterogenization processes – or diminishing contrasts/increasing varieties – are at work. With the diffusion of Anglo/European, and Euro/American sports, the contrasts between cultures did diminish. However, comments of the kind expressed by Stiven tend to overlook how a process of indigenization was at work in the diffusion of these sport forms, and that global sport is characterized by an increasing variety of styles of play.

These comments are by way of introducing several themes that will be explored in this chapter. Two main goals underpin the structure of what follows. First, a processual frame of reference for understanding global sport will be emphasized. Several observations that act as key points of departure are identified. Second, links between sportization, civilizing processes and globalization will be made. Aspects of the sportization concept will be detailed and reference will be made to the work of Elias and Dunning (1986). This work will be extended by viewing sportization processes as involving a quest for 'exciting significance'. Elias commented on the importance of these sportization processes in the following way:

> It is as significant for our understanding of the development of European societies as it is for that of sport itself that the first types of English sports which were taken up by other countries were horse-racing, boxing, fox-hunting, and similar pastimes, and that the diffusion of ball games such as football, tennis and of 'sport' generally in the more contemporary sense began only in the second part of the nineteenth century.
>
> (Elias, 1970: p. 89)

In their research, Elias and Dunning identified two initial sportization phases, to which Elias alluded in the comments above. This

schema will be developed in chapter 4 by mapping out three additional phases in the sportization process. Clarification of the links
between the West and non-Western countries in the initial sportization phase will also be undertaken. Hence, what follows is of
significance not just to an understanding of European societies to
which Elias directed our attention, but also to globalization
processes more broadly. In this connection, it is relevant, at this
stage, to record that the five-phase sportization process model
corresponds, to a degree, to the main globalization phases outlined
in preliminary form by Robertson (1990).

Before attempting to tackle the goals identified, it is appropriate
to trace how the development of this approach has emerged. The
purpose of doing so is to emphasize that no final solution has been
achieved. Such comments also indicate that the model can be
subject to further modification and revision. The arguments contained in this chapter are preliminary in nature, and viewed as
but a contribution to the construction of a developmental, or
structured processes, model of global sport (Maguire, 1995b).

In the late 1980s and early 1990s, several case studies were conducted that examined the diffusion of basketball and American
football. A processual/figurational approach assisted in locating
the specific changes identified on a wider canvas (Maguire, 1988;
1990). This work acknowledged the fruitfulness of the concept of
Americanization but specific reservations were expressed regarding the adequacy of the cultural imperialism thesis, for example
with respect to properly analysing the interdependencies and
power-balances involved in what has come to be called globalization. Such work was closer, in certain respects, to some cultural
dependency research than the present text might be seen by others
to be. Questions concerning knowledgeability, local resistance and
competing cultural flows, such as Europeanization and Japanization, were also raised in this connection. The contested nature of
the processes involved was also highlighted. In summary,
though aspects of the Americanization thesis were used, several
modifications of and qualifications to this thesis were proposed.

Whatever their shortcomings, these studies also set out, as part
of a broader process/figurational sociology project, to examine
aspects of the political economy of specific sports developments.
Perhaps as a result of this focus, some commentators have located
these studies along with Marxist political economic work, and
suggested that they favour 'the American imperialism thesis'
(Harvey & Houle, 1994: p. 339). Guttmann goes so far as to refer to
this early work as involving an 'economic analysis of ludic
diffusion' (Guttmann, 1994: p. 175). Given that some observers are

predisposed to suggest that figurational sociology overlooks these dimensions (Horne & Jary, 1987), or that, as Rowe (1995: p. 104) maintains, 'the drive for capitalist accumulation [that] propelled the global diffusion and expansion of sport is given insufficient weight', there is a certain irony in these assessments.

Rowe also asserts that a 'second shortcoming of this figurational perspective concerns its handling of the power relations driving the global dissemination of sports' (ibid.). Chapter 1 illustrated some of the problems associated with an economic determinist view of globalization, and the exploration of power networks and interdependency chains that is a feature of a process-sociological perspective on globalization was dealt with at some length in chapter 2. Such critiques seem not only unfamiliar with specific features of this perspective, but also overlook that previous accounts have dealt with commodification processes in the sports world (Dunning, 1975; 1992c; Dunning & Sheard, 1979; Maguire, 1988; 1990). I think the problem with such evaluations is also a question of a reluctance to distinguish between different approaches and to tease out the distinctive perspective that process-figurational sociology has to offer. That is one of the central objectives of this text.

To be fair, in certain respects the position mapped out here has moved on since that early work. While issues of Americanization were then central to that work, the analysis conducted was relational in character and conceptualized this process as part of an interdependent network of competing global cultural flows (Maguire, 1993a). This chapter will, as noted, have a different emphasis. Above all, greater attention is paid here to how an understanding of sport and globalization is part of a broader inter-civilizational analysis. In order to avoid the usual conceptual squabble – and misunderstandings – that such comments generate in some quarters, let me be clear about this point. There is, undoubtedly, a political economy at work which plays a part in contouring aspects of global sport development. One has only to observe that on the London Stock Exchange there is a Global Sports Fund that invests in 250 of the top sport and leisure businesses, such as Nike, Adidas and BSkyB. It is accordingly crucial to probe the power dynamics at work in specific figurations. While people in different societies are not powerless dupes, equally they are not 'free' to choose as they please. Indeed, their taste for global goods is itself a reflection of wider societal power relations. By emphasizing issues of difference and diversity, the analysis contained in this chapter seeks to acknowledge that challenges to specific flows do occur. This allows for consideration of the role of counter-flows and the emergence of new styles. Yet I am also aware that the personnel of multinational companies market 'difference' to 'similar' segments of people on a global scale. It is not beyond our wit as social scientists to see how these processes are interrelated. We do not have to remain trapped in monocausal, unidirectional and reductionist thinking.

The process-sociological approach outlined in chapter 2, and particularly the concepts of diminishing contrasts and increasing varieties, will be used to assist in making sense of the global diffusion, patterning and differential popularization of cultural wares, including sports. Diminishing contrasts and increasing varieties have not, however, been given due prominence in previous figurational accounts of sport. This may explain, in part, some of the misunderstandings and misinterpretations that have arisen over the past three decades. Perhaps this is one of the reasons why Rick Gruneau, in an otherwise splendid account of the early stages in the making of modern sport, simply asserted that the process-figurational approach belonged to the 'industrial society' thesis that he identified. The argument contained in this chapter rejects such a classification. Similarly, the process-sociological interpretation of sport and globalization differs somewhat from the view offered by Peter Donnelly. In asking whether the globalization concept is a satisfactory description and explanation of world sport, Donnelly concludes:

> If it were, we would have to accept that various countries had contributed in relatively equal ways to the observed changes in sport; that such changes did not have a similar source, but were so blended that we have lost sight of any specific national origins; and that there was evidence of interdependency rather than evident and specific hegemonic interests involved in asserting *a* particular set of meanings and *a* particular way of playing and presenting sport as *the* only true meanings and *the* only way of playing and presenting sport.
>
> (Donnelly, 1996: p. 248)

This interpretation of globalization is rather at odds with the literature surveyed in chapter 1 and with the process-sociological view outlined in chapter 2. Neither process-sociologists nor writers such as Robertson (1992) and Featherstone and Lash (1995) use the concept in the way expressed by Donnelly. None of these writers views globalization in this manner. If such an appraisal has substance, it could possibly be seen to apply to the work of Nederveen Pieterse, with his emphasis on heterogenization, or to the work of Wagner on *Mundialization*. The observations that provide the key points of departure here certainly approach the study of global sport in a manner different from that which Donnelly assigns to the use of the globalization concept. This obviously needs consideration in more detail.

Sportization, Globalization and the Commingling of Global Sports Cultures

Referring to the initial phases in the sportization process and the organizational developments that characterized the second phase occurring in the mid-nineteenth century, Elias noted:

> Every variety of sport ... has a relative autonomy in relation not only to the individuals who play at a given time, but also to the society where it developed. That is the reason why some sports which first developed in England could be transferred to and adopted by other societies as their own. The recognition of this fact opens up a wide field for further investigation.
>
> (Elias, 1986: p. 39)

Investigations of this type lie at the heart of an analysis of the links between sportization and globalization. In opening up this field of study for further investigation, several observations will act as key points of departure. The first observation and crucial point of departure is that an understanding of the global sportization for- mation is bound up in inter-civilizational exchanges. While the argument presented here will reach different conclusions from those offered by Huizinga, in one telling passage of his work *Homo Ludens* he posed several important questions that relate to this kind of inter-civilizational analysis:

> The question to which we address ourselves is this: To what extent does the civilization we live in still develop in play-forms? How far does the play-spirit dominate the lives of those who share that civil- ization? The nineteenth century, we observed, had lost many of the play-elements so characteristic of former ages. Has this leeway been made up or has it increased? It might seem at first sight that certain phenomena in modern life have more than compensated for the loss of play-forms. Sport and athletics, as social functions, have steadily increased in scope and conquered ever fresh fields both nationally and internationally.... Now, with the increasing systematization and regimentation of sport, something of the pure play-quality is inevitably lost.
>
> (Huizinga, 1949/1970: pp. 221–3)

While it is perhaps appropriate, at this stage, to leave aside an assessment of the extent to which the play-element has disappeared in global sport, it is possible to conclude that sports which initially appeared in the West do appear to have some 'universal' significance and value, whatever that might be, but it is also clear that these sports have local and 'particular' meanings. Closely related to the observation that the global sportization formation is bound up in inter-civilizational exchanges is the second point of departure. The adoption of a very long-term perspective in exploring globalization processes can yield many benefits. Although, as Elias (1987) noted, sociologists may mistakenly 'retreat to the present' in exploring global processes, in examining the making of modern sports, long-term inter-civilizational analysis of European societies is much more fruitful. Here, as with regard to other observations that act as points of departure, questions concerning what constitutes modern sport need to be addressed.

In examining the initial sportization phase, it is important to stress a third key observation. The longer-term links of non-occidental ancient civilizations with the making of modern sport should not be overlooked. Though reference has already been made to England being the cradle of modern sport, it was acknowledged in that context that other European societies played a part in its formation, and indeed, in the sportization process more generally. This issue needs to be developed to refer to an assessment of how, if at all, Islam, and the Orient, influenced European folk games and royal pastimes. This is no easy task.

If this third point of departure applies to an understanding of the early phase of sportization processes, it is equally applicable to more recent developments. The interdependency chains that tie more recent developments within the West to non-occidental cultures require consideration. In stressing these points the analysis seeks to steer clear of an overly 'Western' interpretation of global sport processes. A Western ethnocentric approach is eschewed. Yet, this is not to overlook that representatives of some cultural traditions have proved more powerful in the development of global sport. The importance of this issue should not be underestimated. Writing about the different cultural traditions that influenced African women's sports, Ali Mazrui has observed:

> While the *jihad* legacy reinforces the warrior tradition of indigenous Africa, the continent's triple heritage of cultures works dialectically to improve the prospects of African sportswomen. Islam and African culture sometimes fuse and sometimes recoil from each other, only to turn around and confront the powerful

sporting forces of the Western world in which women athletes are increasingly encouraged and honored. The whistle has sounded. The match between cultures has begun.

(Mazrui, 1976: p. 228)

This issue of Western and non-Western cultural interchange can be further clarified with reference to the work of Max Weber, who also undertook an examination of inter-civilizational relations. Apart from rational forms of capitalism, Weber himself, like Huizinga, focused on the emergence of science, architecture and music. While he went to some length to demonstrate the specific role of the West, he also noted that 'the technical basis of our architecture came from the Orient' and that 'programme music, tone poetry, alteration of tones and chromatics, have existed in various musical traditions as means of expression' (Weber, 1920/1992: p. 15). Likewise, while the development of modern sport can be clearly associated with the West, it is important to probe, as noted, both the interconnections with already existing non-occidental body cultures and to assess the degree to which contemporary sport has been permeated by oriental forms and values. At this stage of our knowledge development it is only possible to point to the direction which the analysis must take. It will be for others to follow up these suggestions with detailed empirically based case studies. Yet, such issues lie at the heart of the debate concerning globalization, inter-civilizational analysis and the role, function and meaning sport plays within global processes. The approach being outlined here therefore shares with Arnason the assumption that 'among the identities that are thus reinforced and reoriented by the global context, civilizational complexes and traditions are not the least important' (Arnason, 1990: p. 224).

It is also necessary to grasp an additional observation that acts as a fourth point of departure. This relates to the local/global debate, and refers to the internal dynamics at work within any specific society. 'Local' cultures were and are never hermetically sealed from 'other' cultures. There is no past sporting *Gemeinschaft* waiting to be discovered. The local was always semi-permeable and contoured by centrifugal and centripetal forces (Elias, 1987/1991). What is needed is an understanding of the competing centrifugal and centripetal forces that characterize the new geographical arena (Robins, 1991).

A further observation that guides a process-sociological account of sport and globalization processes needs to be emphasized. The balance of forces at work in inter-cultural exchanges is marked by a series of power networks, 'elimination struggles' and a mutual contest of cultural sameness, difference and commingling between competing groups. In this regard, as Mazrui's observations highlighted, the gendered, ethnic, class- and age-based nature of these processes requires careful unravelling. The inter-civilizational analysis outlined in chapter 2 provided some important guidelines along which to conduct this task. While allowing for non-occidental linkages, and resistance and indigenization processes, an account has also to be given of the rise and relative dominance of the West. In chapter 2 it was emphasized that such an inter-civilizational analysis must avoid the pursuit of mono-causal explanations, the use of dichotomous thinking and the tendency to view global processes as governed by either the intended or the unintended actions of established or outsider groups of people. Analyses that emphasize the multifaceted, multidirectional and complex sets of power-balances are better placed to probe and trace the global sport process. In conducting this long-term, inter-civilizational analysis of global sport processes it is also important to be clear about what the term 'modern sport' refers to. Consideration is given to this issue in the next section. The meaning and significance of modern sport is also discussed.

Sportization, Subcultures and Body Cultures

Commenting on the diffusion of English pastimes to continental Europe and beyond, Elias addressed the connection between sportization and civilizing processes. Noting the reining-in of violence, the development of a tighter, standardized sets of rules, the development of governing bodies and the shift in body habitus, Elias observed that 'the sportization of pastimes, if I may use this expression as shorthand for their transformation in English society into sports and the export of some of them on an almost global scale, is another example of a civilizing spurt' (Elias, 1986: pp. 21–2). This export of English sports did not merely involve, as Part II explores, the multilayered flow of capital, personnel, technologies, landscapes. As Elias observed, more important than simply the global movement of cultural wares, this shift towards the competitive, regularized, rationalized and gendered bodily exertions of achievement sport involved changes at the level of personality, body deportment and social interaction. A more rationalized male body habitus was evident that was going to affect people and groups in different societies in fairly fundamental ways. Several issues are raised by these observations and require further consideration.

Though Elias and Dunning (1986) did not express the concept in these terms, as sportization processes unfolded, two broad interwoven dimensions emerged. The first dimension involves the emergence and diffusion of a specific body culture that centres on 'achievement sport', in either its elite or leisure-level forms. Several features of this achievement sport subculture, and thereby the motivation of the individual athlete, can be identified. These features vary, as noted, according to the level at which sport is being played, but are also influenced by the degree of seriousness that members of a particular society invest in sports involvement. One of the main features includes an emphasis on achievement striving which is closely connected to and reinforced by a quest for excellence embodied in the notion of the 'ultimate performance'. The quest for the ultimate performance appears to rest on what might be termed the myth of the super*man* – a performance so great that it eclipses the efforts of 'mere mortals'. Though varying in intensity across time and different societies, this subculture is also marked by rationalization and scientization processes. The most efficient and technically competent display has to be developed that would produce the 'optimal performance'. Laboratories across the world seek this holy grail!

As this sport science research emerged out of the shadow of physical education, in the guise of exercise physiology, biomechanics and sport psychology, it was increasingly funded and developed by the state and sport organizations. Being tied so closely to these agencies, sport science research has tended to reflect the demands of competitive sport: the achievement of records and 'winning' outcomes. Tracing sportization processes over time, it can be observed, from one society to the next, that in the development of sport science, research into human well-being, the quality of the sport experience and aesthetic values have been squeezed out. Other features of this subculture are closely connected to this achievement striving, rationalization and scientization. Over time, sportization processes have been marked by a high degree of specialization. Sports performers increasingly participated in only one sport and, within that sport, they specialized according to task or position requirements. The demands of elite-level achievement sport became so great that professionalization processes have also been a recurring feature, as one sport after another, in different societies, in different time periods, moves in the direction described. These sportization processes both reflect and reinforce trends at work in society more broadly. Various aspects of these trends are shown in figure 1. People's bodies are many layered. In sport, as in society, we do not simply have a 'physical' body. Several perspectives on people's bodies can be

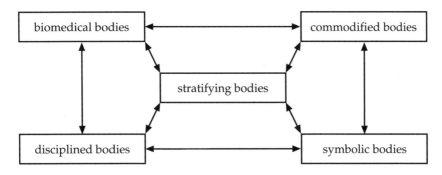

Figure 1 *Dimensions of sporting bodies*

identified: at its core however, we are dealing with bodies that are highly stratified – along, for example, 'ability', class, gender, ethnic and age lines.

These perspectives on people's bodies include biomedical, commodified, disciplined and symbolic bodies (Maguire, 1993b). For people participating at different levels in the sports world the *biomedical* aspect can appear to be more or less important but it is a significant issue for all people if viewed from a process-sociological perspective. That is, this scientization and technologization of human performance at the elite level also manifests itself through individualized, biomedical discourse governing health-related fitness programmes for the population as a whole. Aspects of diet, drugs and illness are also areas permeated by biomedical discourse.

Closely connected to this is the issue of the *disciplined* body. Physical education programmes, training regimes and elite competition all school or regulate people's bodies in specific ways. Sportization processes are also permeated, to a greater or lesser extent, by commodification processes and the notion of the *commodified* body highlights how such commodification processes structure and contour people's bodies and bodies of people. Elite sports performers are increasingly the bearers of sponsors' names and clothing. Sports competitions carry the sponsor's name and the timing and location of the event reflect the market profile of the companies involved in the economy of the sport. Questions concerning whether the needs which find expression in the commodified sportization process are 'real' or 'false' – rather than if such needs are primary, secondary or tertiary – emerge. All of these trends that mark sportization processes tend to depict a 'negative', 'deterministic' or 'pessimistic' picture of the sports world. But there is one trend that stands in opposition to these. A concern with how sportization processes are also a site of symbolic inter-action and subcultural resistance, of oppositional space and exis-tential experience, of body rituals and the pursuit of exciting significance, shows the *symbolic* body at play and at work. It is not a question of stressing the *symbolic* body to the neglect of the other features identified. If people are understood as interdependent human beings living out their lives in formations of numerous other human beings, then their involvement in sportization processes needs to be viewed in terms of a subtle blend or colour-ing of *biomedical, disciplining, commodified and symbolic* bodies that develop local meanings in a global context.

The second broad dimension of sportization processes involves the spread of a specific body culture into society more broadly. That is, though varying in intensity over time, and within and between societies, the sportization of culture has also been taking place as a widespread long-term process. To be seen and labelled as 'sporting' entails the expression of a specific body habitus. This habitus involves both the use of the body in specific 'physical' ways, but also the expression of a set of ethics that characterize a 'sporting' person. That is, as sportization processes gathered momentum, we have witnessed 'sport' breaking out of its tradi-tional school and subcultural boundaries. To be sportive, via exer-cise, athletic fitness or the consumption of sports products, increasingly becomes a moral imperative – especially in the West. To act according to notions of fair play, in politics and in everyday life, to demonstrate health consciousness and style, and to be viewed as an object of desire and respect by the wearing of appro-priate clothing, are also features of this sportization of culture. Ommo Grupe, developing ideas drawn from Elias and Dunning, thus concludes:

> Sport as a cultural phenomenon reaches far beyond the traditional boundaries of sport itself, it is an expression of a new understanding of culture. This process has been called the 'sportization' of culture and it means that sport-related values, norms and models of behavi-our have penetrated deeply into the cultural life courses. This situ-ation leads to an increase in the influence of those organizations and institutions which offer and disseminate sport-related sense-patterns. No longer are sport organizations the only entities con-cerned; media, business, and political institutions are also involved.
>
> (Grupe, 1991: p. 141)

Two points additional to these insightful comments need to be made. First, this cultural phenomenon is global in scope. That is, sportization processes spread out not simply beyond the

traditional boundaries within the West, but also outside conventional boundaries in non-Western societies. Second, it is not simply
a question of separate political, media or economic organizations
becoming involved. What we see in sportization processes is the
emergence of what Maguire and Mansfield (1998) have termed the
'exercise body-beautiful complex'.

This complex entails, as figure 2 shows, a range of interdependent groups whose actions are mutually reinforcing of the sportization of different cultures. Yet, the long-term impact was neither
planned nor intended by any one specific group. Though the exponents of different areas of this complex have their own short-term
goals, collectively their actions mesh to form the figurational
dynamics that characterize aspects of the sportization of cultures.
This complex is not confined to the West but straddles the globe
(Maguire & Mansfield, 1998). Tracing both the intended and the
unintended dimensions of sportization processes in this way
derives from an attempt to apply to this field the earlier work of
Elias and Dunning. Before tracing the main phases of these sportization processes in chapter 4, attention needs to be given to outlin-
ing some of the main features of this general approach as it applies
to the study of global sport.

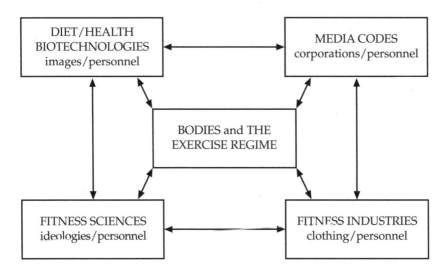

Figure 2 *The exercise gender–body complex*
Source: adapted from Maguire & Mansfield (1998)

Sportization, Human Emotions and the Quest for Exciting Significance

Based on this model of human relations – with what Elias (1986) terms the theory of civilizing processes at its core – the study of the sportization of English folk pastimes enables Elias and Dunning to formulate an answer to the question of why modern sports, that is, highly regulated contests requiring physical exertion and skill, made their appearance first of all during the eighteenth century among the English upper classes, the landed aristocracy and gentry. The importance of these observations lies in the fact that the early stages of this sportization process set the tone for future sporting developments. In examining the sports of boxing, cricket, fox-hunting, horse-racing and the early forms of modern football, Elias and Dunning (1986) conclude that all of these cultural forms mark attempts to prolong the point-like emotional pleasure of victory in the mock-battle of a sport and are symptomatic of a far-reaching change in the personality structure of human beings and that this in turn was closely connected with specific changes in the power structure of society at large. In particular, the changing balance of power between the landed aristocracy and gentry and the rising bourgeoisie was to prove crucial. It is here that the function of sport and leisure forms becomes more evident.

A principal feature of global sport is the 'arousal of pleasurable forms of excitement' (Elias & Dunning, 1986). One important feature of a civilizing process is a marked narrowing of what is acceptable in public life. As a direct corollary of this, the need for a social enclave in which socially approved moderate pleasurable excitement could be aroused and expressed increases. That is, the function of sport activities has to be assessed in relation to the ubiquity and steadiness of excitement control. What is the significance of this? The function which leisure serves in relatively 'civilized', 'modern' societies, according to Elias and Dunning, is based on a view of people according to which they have, in growing numbers, a socially conditioned psychological need to experience various kinds of spontaneous, elementary, unreflective yet pleasurable excitement.

The precise meaning and significance of sports activities is assessed in relation to a number of interrelated criteria. These include: the degree of controlled decontrolling of emotions that is evident; the degree to which emotions flow freely; the degree of eliciting or imitating of excitement akin to that which is generated in 'real' life situations; the nature of the tension-balances created;

and the degree to which the activity serves to counteract what Elias termed 'stress tensions'. Here we are dealing with tension-balances of varying blends. But the perpetual tension between routinization and deroutinization within leisure activities is the principal source of their dynamics: this is the 'shift to risk' which is integral to the activity being experienced. Indeed, as societies grow 'more serious', the cultural centrality of leisure sport increases.

In rejecting conventional work–leisure analyses, Elias and Dunning (1986) also map out what they term the spare-time spectrum. It is important to note that leisure activities are seen to fall into three forms. These are purely or mainly sociable activities; activities involving motility or movement; and 'mimetic' activities. 'Mimetic' activities vary considerably across the globe, both in terms of their intensity and style, but they have basic structural characteristics in common. That is, they provide a 'make-believe' setting which allows emotions to flow more easily, and which elicits excitement of some kind imitating that produced by 'real-life situations', yet without their dangers or risks. 'Mimetic' activities, locally constructed or globally generated, thus allow, within certain limits, for socially permitted self-centredness. Excitement is elicited by the creation of tensions: this can involve imaginary or controlled 'real' danger, mimetic fear and/or pleasure, sadness and/or joy. For Elias and Dunning (1986), writing initially in the late 1960s, this controlled decontrolling of excitement lies at 'the heart of leisure sport'. The different moods evoked in this 'make-believe' setting are the 'siblings' of those aroused in 'real-life' situations. This applies whether the setting is a Shakespearean tragedy enacted at Stratford-upon-Avon, a pleasure ride at EuroDisney or a closely contested play-off in the US Masters at Augusta. These moods involve the experience of pleasurable excitement which is, according to Elias and Dunning, at the core of most play needs. But whereas both leisure and sports events involve pleasurable excitement, in sport, but especially in 'achievement sport', struggles between human beings play a central part. Indeed, some global sports contests, like rugby union's world cup tournament, more closely resemble real battles between hostile groups.

Other key features of the process-sociological perspective on leisure, sport and the emotions deserve some consideration in this context. The mimetic sphere, though creating imaginary settings, forms a distinct and integral part of social reality. It is no less real than any other part of social life. The manner in which the quest for enjoyable excitement finds expression in social institutions and customs also varies greatly over time and space. Local traditions are maintained and local meanings attached to global sports. Nevertheless, the 'mimetic' sphere does contain three basic elements, namely sociability, motility and mimesis. There is no leisure activity where all of these elements are absent and more usually two or three elements combine with varying intensity. In studying the problems of sport, pleasure and the emotions therefore, Elias and Dunning focused on two interdependent questions: what are the characteristics of the personal leisure needs developed in the more complex societies of our time and what are the characteristics of the specific types of leisure events developed in societies of this type for the satisfaction of these needs? An additional question needs to be raised. How do global sport production and consumption processes reflect, create and/or fulfil these needs?

Elias and Dunning are to be commended for providing an analysis of sport-games and of tension-balances in leisure activities more generally, which avoids the dichotomy between the 'micro' and 'macro' dimensions of emotional experience. In teasing out the nature and extent of the emotional experiences involved in sport and leisure, reference to the interconnections between game dynamics, the mimetic sphere and the civilizing process was a crucial insight provided by these writers. However, this early work did not exhaust the debate about the gendered character of leisure practices nor the identity-formation qualities of achievement or leisure forms of sport. That is, as Dunning and Maguire (1996) argue, the quest for excitement is bound up in gender relations and the changing balance of power that contours and shapes aspects of the character of the global sport experience. Sport, both in its achievement-sport and leisure-sport forms, involves the quest not simply for unreflective excitement, but also for 'exciting significance'. The *symbolic* body cannot, as noted, be overlooked. Equally, however, to argue this should not blind the analysis to the existence of the 'masculine gaze' and commodified forms of pleasure provided by the global media–sport production complex. This issue will be examined more closely in chapter 7.

In tackling global sport processes, other qualifications to the perspective provided by Elias and Dunning are required. While these writers note that sport and art forms share the same mimetic function in producing an enjoyable and controlled decontrolling of emotions, they distinguish between them in terms of the fact that sport has the character of a battle which resembles real battles fought between rival groups. The quest is for battles enacted playfully in a contrived context which can produce enjoyable battle excitement with a minimum of injuries to the human participants. Compared with the arts, the scope involved for the exercise of the imagination appears to be of a rather restricted and heavily rule-bound kind. Yet, symbolic interactionist and phenomenological research rightly emphasizes the social construction and presentation of emotions. Emotions are seen to involve interwoven cognitive and affective dimensions. An understanding of how various emotional vocabularies are used and how some aspects of emotions are culturally relative and others culturally universal is required. Our ability to describe feelings varies between cultures and may be more sophisticated than the actual physiological processes involved. Although Elias and Dunning (1986) are correct to point to differences within and between mimetic events, in doing so they appear to have overlooked, or at least to have underplayed, the fact that identity-formation in leisure-sport also involves the quest for self-realization, the presentation of embodied emotions and emotion management (Hochschild, 1983; Rail, 1990). These issues were, however, explored by Dunning in his more recent work (Dunning, in press). They are at the heart of the *symbolic* body. Notwithstanding this, Elias and Dunning have provided crucial insights for our understanding of the pleasure and excitement associated with global sport. This issue, and a general assessment of global sport, will be returned to in the concluding chapter.

Conclusion: A Process-Sociological Perspective

This chapter has sought to demonstrate the value of a processual frame of reference for understanding global sport. In doing so, several observations that act as key points of departure were identified. In addition, links between sportization, civilizing processes and globalization were made. While reference was made to the contribution made by Elias and Dunning, their work was also subject to re-evaluation and extension. Two important revisions were offered. First, the notion that sport involves a quest for excitement was refined and developed and a greater emphasis given to the idea that sportization processes involve a quest for 'exciting significance'. In their research, Elias and Dunning correctly identified two initial sportization phases. This schema needs development and, as the next chapter details, three additional phases in the sportization process have been identified. This chapter has also sought to emphasize to a greater extent than Elias and Dunning did the link between these phases and globalization processes more broadly. In particular, clarification of the links between the West and non-Western countries in the initial sportization phases is also required. Chapter 4 seeks to flesh out in greater detail these additional phases and non-occidental linkages.

4

The Global Sports Formation: Meaning, Power and Control

The achievement sport culminating today in the Olympic Games provides telling examples. There the struggle for world records has given the development of sport a different direction. In the form of achievement sport the playful mimetic tensions of leisure sport become dominated and patterned by global tensions and rivalries between different states.

Norbert Elias, in *Quest for Excitement*, 1986

The analysis in chapter 2 concluded by raising several questions regarding the emergence and diffusion of modern sport. The common theme to these questions centred on issues of power and control, what constitutes 'achievement sport', and what is possible, pleasurable and permissible in global sport relations. Chapter 3 mapped out how a figurational/process-sociological perspective tackles aspects of these questions. Certain key points of departure were outlined and the framework for considering the risk and pleasure associated with modern sport was discussed. On the basis of these chapters and the review of existing research conducted in chapter 1, it is clear that while a great deal of attention has been given to the function and meaning of sport in specific societies, it is only since the late 1980s that the role it plays in global cultural exchange has been subject to investigation in the sociology of sport and, to a lesser extent, in the subdisciplines of sport geography and sport history.

In a thoughtful assessment of the role that sport plays in global processes, Houlihan (1994) at times downplays the general significance of sport in society. Sport, he argues, is not part of the 'core' of a person's and a nation's identity. Viewed in this light the impact of sport could be seen to be superficial and ephemeral. In contrast, Galtung has argued that sport was and is a 'carrier of deep culture and structure' and that this culture carries a 'message of western social cosmology' (1982: pp. 136–7). More recently, he concluded that sport is 'one of the most powerful transfer mechanisms for culture and structure ever known to humankind' (Galtung, 1991: p. 150).

In certain respects the perspective adopted here tries to steer a path between these two positions. Sport is a significant touchstone of prevailing global, national and local patterns of interchange. As chapter 3 highlighted, there are several indices that demonstrate that the social significance of sport is considerable. Notwithstanding this, Galtung may well overstate the impact of Westernization on world body cultures. There are dangers in claiming that 'Western' and/or American domination of global 'sport' cultures was and is complete. As Said noted, 'it was the case nearly everywhere in the non-European world that the coming of the white man brought forth some sort of resistance' (1993: p. xii). Galtung appears to overlook, as will be argued at various points in this chapter, issues of reinterpretation, resistance and recycling by indigenous peoples located in various positions within the power geometry of the global sport system. In that respect Houlihan is correct to point to the need for careful calibration of the effect that sport has on 'society' and on global processes more broadly.

In developing this point it is clear that non-Western people have, on occasions, not only resisted 'Western' masculine sport personnel and reinterpreted 'Western' forms, models and marketing of sport, but have also maintained, fostered and promoted, on a global scale, their indigenous recreational pursuits. It is correct to state that during the twentieth century sport was to become a 'global idiom'. Its laws were, as Mazrui (1976: p. 411) noted, the first to be voluntarily embraced across the globe. This does not mean, however, that Western achievement sport totally 'captured' all groups of people in different nations. Nor has it obliterated local body cultures in non-occidental or indeed occidental countries (Avedon & Sutton-Smith, 1971; Harris & Park, 1983). These are some of the themes and issues that will be dealt with in this chapter.

A developmental account of the globalizing of 'sport' shows how this Western form of body culture was itself subject to change, contestation and reinterpretation among and between a range of gender, ethnic, class and able/disabled-bodied groups. Yet, as a feature of the global cultural nexus, its significance, for better or worse, cannot be denied. In order to substantiate such an assessment, this chapter will trace the main sportization phases that have led to the present global sports formation. Each of these phases is, of course, worthy of extensive separate analysis. Here, I shall attempt only to outline, in preliminary form, some of the core features of these phases and, by necessity, some of my observations are speculative in nature. While I am certain that modification of the basic schema will be undertaken, the connections made between inter-civilizational processes and broader globalization phases have potential with which to embark on a developmental account of sport. Building on this base, the second part of this chapter seeks to outline the contemporary global sport system. A range of cultural flows that contour and shape global sport are examined. Attention is given to the power networks and control strategies that characterize the production and consumption of sport performances, equipment and merchandising operations, mediated accounts and international tournaments. These observations will provide the framework in which the detailed case studies presented in Part II are located.

Globalization Processes and Sportization Phases

The main phases of globalization identified by Robertson and described in earlier chapters are relevant to the understanding of the specific changes which occurred in the emergence and diffusion of modern forms of sport. While there is not a precise overlap, the general pattern outlined by Robertson has much in common with the main sportization phases already referred to. In what Robertson terms the 'germinal phase', lasting in Europe from the early fifteenth until the mid-eighteenth century, several important shifts occurred. In this phase, the incipient growth of national communities, the accentuation of the notion of the individual and of ideas about humanity and the development of a scientific worldview emerged. Though the first sportization phase occurred later in this period it, too, was bound up in the changes identified by Robertson as taking place within European societies more generally. Phase II lasted from the mid-eighteenth century until the 1870s. The notion of a homogeneous unitary state took shape; conceptions of standardized notions of individual rights, humanity and international relations also crystallized. Legal conventions regulating international trade and communication were also increasingly established. The timing of this phase matches up to the second sportization phase referred to by Dunning.

Phase III is called the 'take-off' phase by Robertson. In this phase, lasting from the 1870s until the mid-1920s, 'the increasingly manifest globalizing tendencies of previous periods and places gave way to a single, inexorable form' (Robertson, 1992: p. 59). Changes took place at the level of national societies, international relations, the generic individual and humanity as a whole. The growth of worldwide agencies, the establishment of global awards and prizes, the emergence of a global communications system and the emergence of a standardized notion of human rights are all indicative of this take-off phase. The parallels and linkages with sport development in the same period are quite marked. Between 1870 and 1920 the take-off in international sport unfolded. Robertson terms phase IV the 'struggle for hegemony phase'. In this phase the Cold War struggle between the West and the Soviet bloc also found expression in sport. Likewise, the gradual crystallization of the third world occurred in a sporting context. Phase V is named by Robertson the 'uncertainty phase' – here the number of global institutions and movements greatly increased, problems of multiculturality and polyethnicity developed and a concern with humankind as a whole emerged more fully. These uncertainties also surfaced in the sports world. Let me examine in greater detail how Robertson's model relates to the main global sportization phases.

While Elias did not develop the link between sport and globalization processes to any great extent, Dunning, in examining the growing seriousness and cultural significance of sport, observed that three interrelated processes appear particularly significant in explaining these sportization processes. These are state formation, functional democratization and the spread of sport through the widening network of international interdependencies (Dunning, 1986: p. 213). Dunning went on to conclude:

> it remains necessary to spell out precisely what the connections were between, on the one hand, the growing seriousness of sports participation and, on the other, state-formation, functional democratization and the civilizing process. It also remains to show how this trend was connected with the international spread of sport.
>
> (Dunning, 1986: p. 214)

The necessary development of this argument was not made.

Nevertheless, more recently, Dunning (1992b) has extended this perspective and argued that in the European case there are several principal requirements that can also be applied to a globalization analysis: (1) very long-term structured processes are involved; (2) there is a varying balance of centripetal and centrifugal forces involved in the developing chains of interdependence; (3) there is a need to examine the changing balance of power between those groups and institutions that benefit and those that lose out at various stages in this process; and (4) there is a need to avoid both natio-centrism and Euro-centrism and view the emergent European sport figurations in the context of wider, and increasingly global, networks of interdependencies. With these key principles and three interrelated processes in mind, attention can now be given to the five main sportization phases that have characterized the emergence and diffusion of global sport (see figure 3).

The Sociogenesis of the Initial Sportization Processes

The term *sportization* is used here to describe the transformation of English pastimes into sports and the export of some of them on a global scale. Though the English term *sport* has a long history, dating back as far as 1440, only in the eighteenth century did it begin to acquire its specific modern connotations. Did its emergence and subsequent spread correspond to some human social requirement by then more widespread? Why did the highly regulated contests requiring physical exertion and skill to which the term *sport* became increasingly applied first appear among the landed aristocracy and gentry? According to this perspective, answers to these questions require linking sportization processes to 'parliamentarization'. In turn, this requires a probing of the power structure and cultural relations in seventeenth- and eighteenth-century England.

Briefly, Elias and advocates of this approach argue that the emergence of sport as a form of physical combat of a relatively non-violent type was connected with a period when the cycle of violence between different political factions (Cavaliers and Roundheads during the English Civil War) 'calmed down'. Groups increasingly settled differences by non-violent means. Parliament became the symbolic battleground where conflicts of interest were resolved and defused. Military skills gave way to verbal skills of debate. Crucial in both the parliamentarization and sportization processes was the involvement of the landed aristocracy and gentry. But it is not argued that parliamentarization 'caused' sportization, still less that the sportization of pastimes 'caused' the parliamentarization of politics. Rather, the same people, the landed

The Global Sports Formation

aristocracy and gentry, were caught up in two aspects of a broad process of development in which there occurred a 'civilizing spurt'. According to Elias:

> The same class of people who participated in the pacification and greater regularization of factional contests in Parliament were instrumental in the greater pacification and regularization of their pastimes ... Sport and Parliament as they emerged in the 18th century were both characteristic of the same change in the power structure of England and in the social habitus of that class of people which emerged from the antecedent struggles as the ruling group.
>
> (Elias, 1986: p. 40)

In essence, then, the more 'civilized habitus' deployed by aristocrats and gentlemen to deal with the political aspects of their lives also led them to develop less violent, more civilized ways of enjoying themselves in their leisure time. One facet of this process was

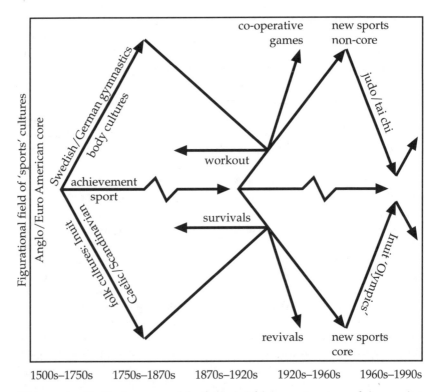

Figure 3 *Preliminary model of diminishing contrasts and increasing varieties in global sportization processes*

the formation of voluntary associations known as 'clubs'. Dunning neatly captures the processual nature of sportization when he observes:

> It is useful to think of this initial sportization of pastimes as occurring in two main waves: an 18th century wave in which the principal pastimes that began to emerge as modern sports were cricket, fox hunting, horse racing and boxing; and a second, 19th century wave in which soccer, rugby, tennis and athletics began to take on modern forms.
>
> (Dunning, 1992a: p. 13)

Several studies have been conducted that bear out this general picture and show how this 'calming down' of violence manifested itself in the development of sport (Dunning & Sheard, 1979; Sheard, 1997). Stressing the role of clubs and the impact of the enclosure movement in which the free English peasantry were 'broken', thus allowing the landed aristocracy and gentry to patronize, adopt and modify folk pastimes, this perspective has examined a range of sports. These include the development of cricket, boxing, folk football, fox-hunting, association football (soccer) and rugby (league and union). Modern achievement sport became the dominant body culture; over time folk games became less widely practised, though they did not die out completely. During the third sportization phase English achievement sport diffused to continental Europe. Here, competitor body cultures, both in the form of traditional folk games but also various forms of gymnastics, also existed. As in the case of Britain, folk games went into long-term decline, but, for a period, Czech, Danish, German and Swedish forms of gymnastics stemmed this tide of achievement sport. Although, as the later sportization phases reveal, these competitor body cultures re-emerge, it is achievement sport that becomes dominant within Europe and subsequently across the globe.

The Third Global Sportization Phase

Although Elias did not fully develop his analysis of the export of these sport forms, he did point to the significance of their relative autonomy for their adoption outside of England. Referring to organizational developments occurring in the nineteenth century, Elias asked the following questions which he initially formulated in the 1960s:

Why, for instance, were some initially English varieties of sport such as Association Football and tennis taken up by many different societies all over the world while the spread of cricket was mainly confined to an exclusive circle of Commonwealth countries? Why did the rugby variety of football not spread as widely as the Association variety? Why did the USA, without abandoning the English varieties completely, develop its own variety of football?

(Elias, 1986: pp. 39–40)

Questions of this type lie at the heart of an analysis of the links between sportization and globalization. Note that it is male achievement sport, emerging out of England, that is the dominant player. Though European rivals in the form of German and Swedish gymnastics existed, and some older folk pastimes survived, it was male achievement sport that was to affect people's body habitus on a global scale. Gradually, such achievement sports came 'to serve as symbolic representations of competition between states' (Elias, 1986: p. 23). What Elias did not fully appreciate and acknowledge, however, is that while male achievement sport culture developed in and diffused out of an English context, it was more fully developed in a later phase of sportization in the context of North America and, in particular, the USA. In England, achievement sport was regulated by the amateur ethos that emphasized 'fair play' and downplayed seriousness. Yet, during the third sportization phase, beginning around 1870 and lasting through to the early 1920s, along with the achievement sport body cultures, the notion of 'fair play' did diffuse to continental Europe and to both the formal and informal British Empire. The status competition between social groups within specific societies is one key element in accounting for this differential popularization of sports among and within European nations (Stokvis, 1989; Van Bottenburg, 1992). It is suggested here that the third phase in sportization processes connects to this 'take-off' phase. Several aspects of sports development illustrate these interconnections. The last quarter of the nineteenth century, for example, witnessed the international spread of sport, the establishment of international sports organizations, the growth of competition between national teams, the worldwide acceptance of rules governing specific sport forms and the establishment of global competitions such as the Olympic Games. The twentieth-century establishment of world championships in many sports is also indicative of the occurrence of globalization processes in the sports world. The exponents of rationalized achievement sport were spreading its tentacles across the globe.

The third sportization phase, then, entailed the differential diffusion of 'English' sport forms (Eisenberg, 1990; Van Bottenburg, 1992). The remarks made by one historian, Ensor, signify the British/English perception of this diffusion. In commenting on 'the development of organised games', Ensor observed that that '... on any reckoning may rank among England's leading contributions to world culture' (Ensor, 1936: p. 164). Whatever the merits of this evaluation, this diffusion was closely connected to two interrelated processes: the emergence of intense forms of nationalism, and a spurt in globalization processes. During this period we see the intensification of 'national' sentiment, the emergence of ethnic nation-states, and the invention of traditions. This was to be the seedbed of what Elias noted was a feature of twentieth-century sport, namely the 'self escalating pressure of inter-state competition in sport and its role as a status symbol of nations' (Elias, 1986: p. 23).

Reinforcing this position, Hobsbawm quite rightly observed that 'the last three decades of the nineteenth century marked a decisive transformation in the spread of the old, the invention of the new and the institutionalization of most sports on a national and even international stage' (Hobsbawm, 1983: p. 298). Sport synthesized people's habituses with the ongoing invention of political and social traditions, such as those surrounding the monarchy, to provide the medium for and a barometer of national identification and competitive community struggle. Although Hobsbawm is correct to point out that the 'rise of sport provided new expressions of nationalism through the choice or invention of nationally specific sports' (1983: p. 300), Welsh rugby, for example, it is also important to note that such nations were doing so in the context of the dominant standard setter, the English and by means of 'their' rationalized achievement sports. Equally, while Hobsbawm observes that 'international contests served to underline the unity of nations or empires much in the way that inter-regional contests did' (1983: p. 300), this formulation overlooks the interconnections between the sportization process, national habitus/identity formation and globalization.

Several important issues are raised by these interconnections. In this phase of sportization, 'Westerners', and in particular the English, were the dominant 'players'. During this period we also see the spread of sport to all parts of Europe, Africa, Asia and South America. As highlighted in chapter 1, scholars working within various traditions have now added to our knowledge of these differential diffusion processes (Appadurai, 1995; Arbena, 1988; Baker & Mangan, 1987; Eisenberg, 1990; Goksøyr, 1996;

Mangan, 1986, 1988; Mazrui, 1976; Meinander, 1992; Vamplew & Stoddart, 1994; Wagner, 1989, 1990). The diffusion of specific sports such as association football has also been well studied (Murray, 1994; Sugden & Tomlinson, 1998a). But the English were not alone: Danish and Swedish gymnastics, the German *Turnverein* movement and the spread of *skiidraet* from Norway to North America and beyond, are all examples of the Europeanization phase in global sports development. Though, at this stage, the diffusion of sports personnel, forms, ideologies and images was not part of some global marketing ploy, it did reflect the prevailing balance of power in global cultural interchange. Increasingly, however, North American sports personnel, forms, ideologies and images began to compete with and supersede their English equivalents.

The Fourth Global Sportization Phase

During the 1920s and 1930s, sports such as baseball, basketball, ice hockey and volleyball diffused to those parts of the world more centrally linked to the 'American' sphere of influence: Europe, South America and parts of the Asian Pacific Rim. While notions of fair play might have been viewed as a sign of distinction and a cultural marker of English gentle*men*, sports advocates in other societies chose to practise their sports differently and more seriously. By the fourth sportization phase (1920s–1960s), it was an American version of the achievement sport ethos that had gained ascendancy. As David Quanz has remarked:

> The American ideals thus replaced the Antique and English models. The Europeans copied the approaches which they judged were responsible for American successes in physical education, sport and the Olympic Games: the pedagogical and social system underlying the park and playground movement [and] the academic and scientific approach to sport as a broad concept of physical education . . .
> (Quanz, 1991: p. 130)

While there has been a struggle for world hegemony since the 1920s, in sport this occurred not only between the 'West' and the 'rest', but also within the 'West' itself. Workers Sports Movements were established in several European countries: these movements were designed to challenge the capitalist control of sport and organize sports along more democratic lines (Hoberman, 1984). In addition, women began to develop their own international sport movements and in the early 1920s organized their own track and field international competitions in Monte Carlo and elsewhere (Dyer, 1982). Despite these movements American male versions of sport practice won out. The management, administration and marketing of sport increasingly came to be organized along American lines. While there were intended and unintended aspects to this process, the main long-term effect was a reduction in the contrasts between global 'sport' cultures. In addition, some of the more recent aspects of global sports development had their equivalents in the third and fourth sportization phases. For example, during earlier phases, attempts were made to establish transnational teams to compete against what was rapidly becoming the most powerful sporting nation, the USA. This was evident in the attempts in the third sportization phase to form a British Empire team for the Stockholm Olympics in 1912 (Jobling, 1986: p. 102) and parallels the efforts to form transnational 'European' teams in the fifth sportization phase (since the 1960s) to play the USA in sports such as golf and tennis.

From the 1920s through to the late 1960s then, the 'West' regulated the field of play, sports organizations, the financial surpluses generated by sporting festivals and the ideological meanings associated with such events. 'Western' and non-Western people actively – as opposed to passively – embraced some aspects of the sports that diffused out of the Anglo/Euro-American core. While sport was and is a carrier of deep culture and structure, and in the fourth phase this culture was 'Western' in orientation, on occasions non-Western people not only resisted and reinterpreted 'Western' masculine sport personnel, forms, models and marketing, they also maintained, fostered and promoted, on a global scale, their indigenous recreational pursuits. People from non-occidental and indeed some occidental cultures did not accept sport uncritically between the 1920s and the late 1960s. Studies of Trobriand cricket (Cashman, 1988), baseball in Japan (Snyder & Spreitzer, 1984), the diffusion of sport to Papua New Guinea (Seward, 1986) and the early twentieth-century development of 'Finnish baseball' (Meinander, 1992) all highlight the dynamic interchange between the local, national and the global. Trobriand cricket, for example, is a modified form of the cricket that spread to those islands as part of a broader colonial process. Local people adapted this game form to suit their local culture. Indeed, indigenous cultures have proved adept at embracing a sport form, reinventing it and then recycling it back to the country of origin. Ironically, American football is a prime example of this (Maguire, 1990). In turn, the core country also embraces cultural flows from outsider states and the 'reinvented' sport form diffuses further around the core. Examples of this include Nordic sports, diffusing to North America and then subsequently spreading to other Western nations, and polo, which originated in the Indian subcontinent but which then, via England, diffused around the Empire. It should also be observed that this phase of sportization/globalization witnessed the slow relative decline of modern sport's founding nation. In the emerging global sport figuration, English*men* were being increasingly beaten – in the early stages of this fourth phase, by fellow occidentals – at games that they felt they had, by birthright, a 'God-given' right to be winners.

The Fifth Global Sportization Phase

Whereas the fourth phase of sportization clearly involved an elaborate political economy in which hegemonic control of sport lay with the 'West', control was never complete. Resistance took a variety of forms such as the Cold War rivalry between the Soviet bloc and the West that was also played out in the sports world. There also occurred the slow assertion of women's rights, such as through Title IX in the USA, and the challenge to hegemonic masculinity. More recently, this movement has become global in nature through the principles contained in what has become known as 'the Brighton Declaration'. Stemming from a meeting held in Brighton, England, in 1994 to discuss 'Women, Sport and the Challenge of Change', a series of global gender equity principles was enunciated. In addition, whereas the latter stages of the fourth phase were characterized by the rise of non-Western nations to sporting prominence, and, sometimes, pre-eminence, this process has intensified in the fifth phase of sportization beginning in the late 1960s. Non-Western nations began to beat their former colonial masters, especially the English, and this trend is apparent in a range of sports including badminton, cricket, soccer, table tennis and track and field. Here, African, Asian and South American nations were (and are) increasingly to the fore. In a sense, however, they still do so on 'Western' terms, for they do so through 'Western' sports.

Anglo/Euro and American control of global sport has also begun to wane off the playing field. The control of international sports organizations and the Olympic movement is beginning, although slowly and unevenly, to slip out of the exclusive hands of the 'West'. These trends are being reinforced by the accelerating commingling process occurring between sport cultures. Eastern martial arts as well as a range of revived 'folk games' have and continue to diffuse into and/or survive in residual form in the 'Western' core. Similar processes are at work in Scandinavia (Goodger, 1986; Hellspong, 1989; Korsgaard, 1989). Despite this, the media–sport complex markets 'sameness' – especially in the form of American sports – and the global political economy that regulates global flows ensures that the 'local' does not freely choose which cultural products are consumed (Maguire, 1990; 1993e).

Yet, this should not lead the analyst to overlook the point that global marketing strategies also celebrate difference (Hall, 1991). That is, the cultural industries constantly seek out new varieties of ethnic wares. These ethnic wares are targeted at specific 'niches' within a local culture. Difference may be targeted to similar sections of a global audience, but at least in this way alternatives 'survive'. The spread of Japanese Sumo to Britain is an example. There is also reason to suggest that the national cultures and identities most affected by these processes appear to be those at the 'centre', not the 'periphery' of the global system; these are the people who are, to the greatest extent, subject to the dislocating processes stemming from globalization. Globalization processes are also unevenly distributed within central regions.

Just as in music (Hall, 1992), food (Mennell, 1985) and cultural processes more generally (Nederveen Pieterse, 1995), so too in sport: this fifth phase of global sportization involves a degree of creolization of sport cultures – increasing varieties are evident. New sports such as wind-surfing, hang-gliding and snow-boarding have emerged and 'extreme sports' have become the cutting edge for some devotees of peak experiences. We need to develop criteria by which to judge the 'reach' and 'response' of global flows on local cultures. In this regard Houlihan is correct to observe that it is important to assess whether these processes affect what he terms the 'core' or the 'ephemeral' aspects of that culture (Houlihan, 1994). Similar observations have been made with regard to assessing the impact of Americanization processes (Maguire, 1990). Equally, while Houlihan is right to 'distinguish between the globalization of particular sports and the globalization of the organizational processes and values of modern sport' (Houlihan, 1994: p. 367), it is important not to lose sight of the interconnections between the achievement sport ethos and how it is played out in different kinds of sports. Not all modern sports are the same in this regard. Further, while I would concur with Houlihan that it is foolish to claim that victory on the playing field can, in itself, be seen as having a dramatic effect on relations between nations, the data contained in chapter 8 on national identity would reinforce the argument that 'profound differences will nonetheless still divide states and that these differences might be reflected in the sports they play' (Houlihan, 1994: p. 364).

Traditional sports, as chapter 8 stresses, bind people to those dominant invented traditions associated with 'nation'/sport formation in the third sportization phase. Just as a British Empire team was not formed because of assertive colonial nationhood, the European Union's questionnaire in the early 1990s regarding the entry of a common European team for future Olympic competitions was firmly rejected by community citizens. Indeed the national Olympic committees of the twelve nations that then made up the EU also rejected these overtures. Folk games survive and both regional and national identity politics are still a crucial part of European life (Nelson, Roberts & Veit, 1992).

In ultra-modern Switzerland, for example, *Ringen* and *Schwingen* – forms of wrestling done at the *Schwingfest* – and *Waffenlauf*, a type of gruelling cross-country run which originally involved carrying weapons, survive and have recently been used by sections of Swiss society to reaffirm a specific tradition, habitus and identity. As Hell-spong remarks with regard to the folk games on the Swedish island of Gotland, 'Traditional sports have experienced a renaissance on Gotland during recent decades and are today vital as an expression of the islanders' cultural identity' (Hellspong, 1989: p. 29). Attempts to form European sports teams are indicative of the early stages in the emergence of a we-identity at a European level that goes beyond localities like Gotland. Despite this, traditional sports continue to hold great attraction for large numbers of European people.

Yet, when national identities – and the sport forms of cultures as a whole – are undergoing a pluralization process, it is also increasingly difficult to sustain the notion that a *single* sport represents *the nation*. As chapter 5 shows, the global movement of sport labour reinforces the problems of multiculturality and polyethnicity (Maguire, 1994; Maguire & Stead, 1998). Yet, migration movements of this kind can also engender absentee patriotism, people born and living in a different society from where their parents were born and who hold an intense attachment to a place they may never have visited. With these trends in mind, perhaps it is less surprising that Western sports personnel and administrators may be experiencing aspects of the self-doubt and uncertainty that Robertson detects in 'Western' nations in general in the most recent globalization phase. These sport processes may parallel what Hall, discussing culture more generally, has termed the 'decentring of the west' (Hall, 1991).

This is not to overlook that the West is still very powerful. What I am seeking to highlight are trends that suggest that this hegemonic control is not complete, all-powerful and all-pervasive. Representatives of different civilizational traditions not only resist Westernization and Americanization but also seek to express and develop their own cultural heritage. And within the West itself there are processes at work which also undermine the dominant achievement sport ethic. Yet, there is a global sports figuration that is structured by a range of power-balances that enable and constrain people to different degrees across the planet. It is to the mapping-out of this global figuration that attention will now be turned.

The Global Sports Figuration

International sport success in the late twentieth century involves a contest between systems located within a global figuration. Sport success depends on several elements: the availability and identification of human resources; methods of coaching and training; the efficiency of the sports organization and the depth of knowledge of sports medicine and sports sciences (Heinilä, 1970). These national sport system mechanisms are, however, insufficient to explain international sport success. In addition to these elements the development of a sport within a particular society also depends on the status of that nation in the specific sports international rank order. Less developed nations tend to under-utilize their talent and performers and/or lose them to more powerful nations in the global sports figuration. Global sport figurations can thus lead to the under- or dependent development of a nation's talent. Kenyan athletics is a case in point (Bale & Sang, 1996). These global sport figurations, in addition to the elements already identified, are shaped and contoured by a range of global flows, particularly of people, technology, capital, mediated images and ideologies (see figure 4).

The movement of performers, coaches, administrators and sport scientists within and between nations and within and between continents and hemispheres is a pronounced feature of late twentieth-century sport. Chapter 5 maps out this global flow more fully but it is important to note that the migration of this elite talent has become a decisive feature that structures the experience of sport in different societies. The movement of technology and the manufacture of clothing, footwear and equipment is a worldwide industry that wealthier nations are able to access to a far greater degree than their poorer counterparts. Chapter 6 considers this

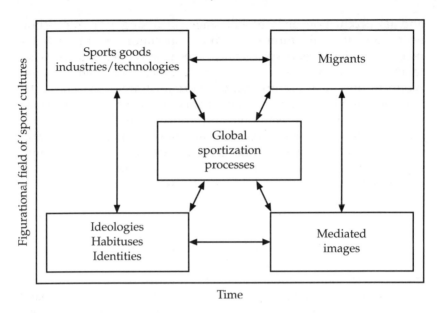

Figure 4   *Global sport flows*

global sports industry and examines the implications for sustainable sport systems. In addition to these global flows, the images of sports stars and tournaments flow round the globe via the media–sport complex. As chapter 7 demonstrates, this interconnected web of media and corporate interests structures, though it does not completely determine, the sports experience for performers and consumers alike.

Global sporting success, as noted, not only reflects national sport systems but also reinforces national esteem. Global sport involves, as chapter 8 will reveal, a form of patriot games in which images and stories are told and retold to ourselves, about ourselves and about others. This elite level achievement sport also tells us something about what it is to be 'human'. With its emphasis on rational and efficient performance, specialization, scientization, competition and professionalization, achievement sport reinforces the myth of the 'super*man*'. This myth is sustained by the ideology and findings of sports science which is concerned with identifying the conditions necessary to produce the ultimate performance.

The global sports figuration accordingly involves the following mechanisms of production, experience and consumption: achievement sport involves the identification and development of talent and its production on a global stage, in a single or multi-sport event, and its consumption by direct spectators or, through the media complex, a global mass audience. Traced over time there is a tendency towards the emergence of a global achievement sport monoculture – a culture where administrators, coaches and teachers promote and foster achievement sport values and ideologies and where competitions and tournaments are structured along highly commodified and rationalized lines. This global sport system is best exemplified with reference to the Olympic movement. Its importance as a global form of cultural communication has been captured by MacAloon when he remarked, 'The Olympic Games are one, indeed one of the most important sources of ... transnational forms for constituting differentiated identities' (MacAloon, 1991: p. 42).

Within the global sports figuration there is not only an international rank order of nations, but these nations can be grouped, more or less, along political, economic and cultural lines, into core, semi-peripheral and peripheral blocs. At the core of most team- and individual-based sports lie the countries of Western Europe, North America – excluding Mexico – and former 'White' Commonwealth countries such as Australia and New Zealand. Semi-peripheral countries tend to involve former socialist countries and some emerging nations such as South Korea. Peripheral countries include most Islamic nations, the majority of African countries and those from South Asia. Whereas the West may be challenged on the field of play by non-core countries, the control over the content, ideology and economic resources associated with sport still tends to lie within the West. Yet, through state policy, non-core countries can use major sports festivals to solidify internal national identification and enhance international recognition and prestige. Through sport, nations can have their *fifteen* minutes of fame!

Either in terms of hosting events or when the relevant decisions are taken, however, it is the West that dominates in international recognition, respectability, status and prestige. The more high tech and commodified the sport, the more reliant success is on the elements of the global sport figuration identified earlier. As a result, the West tends to win out. Indeed, with broader migration processes, the last decade has seen the recruitment by Western nations not only of sports scientists and coaches from the former Soviet bloc, but also the drain of athletic talent from Africa and South America in sports such as association football to the economically more powerful clubs of Europe. Non-core leagues remain in a dependent relationship with the dominant European core. In other sports such as track and field and baseball this drain of talent flows to the USA.

The West also remains dominant in terms of the design, production and marketing of sports equipment; new innovations emerge within the West; major sport federations are controlled by Western officials and global sports tournaments tend to be placed within the West. In the fifth sportization phase, there have, however, been challenges to the achievement sport ideology and to Western domination. Though no longer in existence, the Soviet bloc mounted a sustained challenge to the West for some forty years, though it too became incorporated into the ideology of achievement sport. Within the West itself feminism has developed and challenged the hegemonic masculinity associated with achievement sport. Some success has been achieved, though as some have observed, much more needs to be done (Hargreaves, 1994). The citizens of the West themselves have begun to be attracted by non-achievement sport activities such as the martial arts and extreme sports and, as noted, there has been a slow revival of traditional folk games (Pfister, Niewerth & Steins, 1993). Non-Western success on the field of play, in specific sports such as badminton and middle- and long-distance athletics, is gradually being matched by the involvement of non-Western personnel such as coaches, officials, administrators and producers of sports goods, media outlets and the hosting of major tournaments. Though England was, as Huizinga noted, the 'cradle of modern sport', its relative decline on the sports field is also matched by its fading influence in the corridors of power of global sport politics. This may be indicative of how things might develop in the next century for Europeans and perhaps Westerners more generally. One main source of potential dispute may well be the Olympic Games. As yet, however, the West still has hegemonic control in the global sport figuration.

Conclusion: Making Sense of Global Sport Processes

From what has been argued in this chapter it is possible to conclude that in world terms 'Western' societies became over time the equivalent of the established groups within particular European nations. The spread of 'civilized', that is, Western, patterns of conduct occurred through the settlement of occidentals or through their assimilation of Western standards by the upper strata of other nations. Crucially, the same 'double-bind' tendencies that marked the upper classes' colonization of outsiders within the 'West' were and remain evident in the West's dealings with 'outsider' (non-Western) nations and peoples. With this spread came a particular, contested view of civilization, of humanity as a whole. The members of 'Western' societies were acting as a form of established group on a world level. Their tastes and conduct, including their sports, formed part of this, and these practices had similar effects to those of elite cultural activities within 'Western' societies themselves. They acted as signs of distinction, prestige and power. The rise of the 'West', however, was contested and its 'triumph' was not inevitable. Furthermore, 'Western' culture had long been permeated by non-Western cultural forms, people, technologies and knowledge. In a word, these cultural interchanges stretch back to long before the 'West' momentarily achieved relative dominance in cultural interchange.

There are other key points that need stressing. Both the intended and unintended aspects of global sport development need probing. That is, while the intended acts of representatives of transnational agencies or the transnational capitalist class are potentially more significant in the *short term*, over the *longer term* unintended, relatively autonomous transnational practices predominate. These practices 'structure' the subsequent plans and actions of the personnel of transnational agencies and the transnational capitalist class. In addition, the consumption of non-indigenous cultural wares by different national groups can be both active and heterogeneous. Resistance to global sportization processes is possible. Yet, there is a political economy at work in the production and consumption of global sport/leisure products that can lead to the relative ascendancy of a narrow selection of capitalist and Western sport cultures. Globalization can therefore be understood in terms of the attempts by more established groups to control and regulate access to global flows and also in terms of how indigenous peoples both resist these processes and recycle their own cultural products. We are currently witnessing the globalization of sports and an increase in the diversity of sports cultures.

It is possible then to overstate the extent to which the West has triumphed in terms of global sport structures, organizations, ideologies and performances. Non-Western cultures resist and reinterpret Western sports and maintain, foster and promote, on a global scale, their own indigenous recreational pursuits. While the speed, scale and volume of sports development is interwoven with the broader global flows of people, technology, finance, images and ideologies that are controlled by the West, in the longer term it is possible to detect signs that this is also leading to the decentring of the West in a variety of contexts. Sport may be no exception. By adopting a multicausal, multidirectional analysis that examines the production of both homogeneity and heterogeneity, researchers will be better placed to probe the global cultural commingling that is taking place. Sociological research would indicate, as Part II maps out, that sport will increasingly become contested, with different civilizational blocs challenging both nineteenth- and twentieth-century notions regarding the content, meaning, control, organization and ideology of sport. In examining this contestation sociologists of sport will be probing some important aspects of international sport and the global human condition.

Part II

The Globalization of Sport and its Consequences

5

Global Trails: Migrant Labour and Elite Sport Cultures

It's still England against Scotland, no matter who's playing, but the rivalry is born into the British lads. The Canadians tell you they're British when they get a British passport. That might be so but it doesn't make them English or Scottish.

Peter Johnson, England ice hockey coach
Guardian, 29 January 1993

Whereas 'cultural workers' such as artists, musicians, poets and scholars have moved around royal courts, salons and universities for a considerable period of time, today, the migration of sports talent as athletic labour is a major feature of the 'new global cultural economy' (Appadurai, 1990). This interchange, as Part II of this book demonstrates, also involves the flow of sporting goods, clothing and equipment, media images, ideologies and capital. These interdependent flows are a feature of both the political economy and the cross-civilizational struggles that characterize the global sport system. These interdependencies are marked by a complex and shifting 'power-geometry' in which different groups seek to control, regulate, supervise and profit, resist or counter these flows (Massey, 1993). In this chapter, the main dimensions and issues of sport labour migration will be outlined and, based on existing research, the patterns that exist within and among sports will be explored. A 'critical case study' examining ice hockey will also be mapped out to indicate the broader processes at work in global sport. Some preliminary conclusions will be reached and connections made to other global sport flows.

Global Sports Labour Migration: Dimensions and Issues

Sports labour migration occurs at three levels: within nations, between nations located within the same continent and between nations located in different continents and hemispheres. Discernible national patterns in several countries have been identified in the recruitment and subsequent retention of people in sports such as American football, basketball, cricket, ice hockey, track and field and soccer (Bale & Maguire, 1994). Examples of intra-continental movement include the involvement of US citizens in 'Canadian' baseball teams and athletes from the Dominican Republic in 'American' baseball teams (Klein, 1991). In the countries that composed the former Soviet Union similar migration patterns are evident. That is, sports performers from different republics, such as Ukraine and Georgia, move within the former territory of the Soviet Union. This migration of eastern Europeans westward, in particular to the EU, is even more marked.

These processes are also evident on an inter-continental level. Movement of sports labour occurs between North America, Europe, South America and Asia. This is evident in sports such as American football, baseball, basketball and soccer. In specific sports, such as cricket and rugby, this migration has a seasonal pattern. The northern and southern hemispheres offer two seasons of continuous play; the 'natural' rhythm of the traditional sporting calendar has thus diminished in importance. Other sports stars experience an even more transitory form of migration: their 'workplace' is constantly shifting. Sometimes, seasonal and transitory migration patterns interweave, as with golf and tennis players (Bale & Maguire, 1994). British tennis star Tim Henman, for example, crisscrossed the globe in search of a world ranking in 1996. Beginning in Sydney in January 1996, Henman played in twenty-eight different ATP tournaments, visited fifteen countries and five continents. During 1996 he travelled over 65,000 miles, more than 2.5 times the circumference of the earth. These migratory forays tended to last no more than eight days at each tournament venue. In this respect, golf and tennis players are arguably the nomads of the sports labour migration process with constantly shifting workplaces and places of residence.

Though both men and women have their global circuits in these sports – as well as in skiing – the enabling and constraining figurational dynamics that characterize their experiences may well be markedly different. Sports migrants in general have to do their body work in various locations and, as a group, experience varying degrees of exploitation, dislocation and cultural adjustment. Whatever advantages there are, they appear to flow along gender lines since the global migration pattern so far described involving players, coaches and officials predominantly, though not exclusively, involves men. In some sports such as golf, skiing, tennis, track and field and, to a lesser extent, basketball, women are travelling more frequently and in greater numbers. Despite this, the dominant trend of men moving, more freely and in greater numbers, over time and across space, is based on a social structure that ensures that it is usually women who perform domestic and reproductive labour, whether in the company of their travelling partners or waiting 'at home' (Massey, 1994).

Gender relations then are one dimension that plays a crucial part in contouring a migrant's life. In figure 5, several other dimensions of sports labour migration that interconnect with gender relations are highlighted. From the evidence to hand, these dimensions and issues repeatedly surface and permeate the lives of elite labour migrants (Bale & Maguire, 1994; Maguire, 1996; Maguire & Stead, 1996).

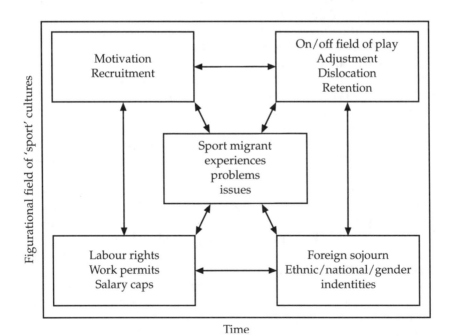

Figure 5   *Sport migrant experiences, problems and issues*

Questions of labour rights are central to migrant experiences. The rights enjoyed by sports migrants, and indeed indigenous sports workers, vary considerably between sports and across continents, and have changed considerably over time. The employment rights achieved by players in team sports such as European soccer are minimal compared to the 'freedoms' gained by sports people in individual sports, particularly in tennis and golf. Pete Sampras, Martina Hingis, Tiger Woods and Lotta Neumann all enjoy greater control over the production and exploitation of their sports talent than do EU soccer players of comparable ability such as Alessandro Del Piero or Alan Shearer. Not all participants in individual sports enjoy the advantages of tennis players or golfers, of course. Young female gymnasts also experience specific forms of exploitation regarding the control of their bodies, training, diet and performance (Maguire & Roberts, 1998; Ryan, 1995).

Track and field athletes have only recently begun to flex their collective muscle, and for the first time organized – without success – to press the IAAF to pay prize money at the 1993 World Championships. The IAAF president, Primo Nebiolo, threatened to withdraw recognition of boycotters, which would have prevented them from competing at the 1996 Atlanta Olympic Games. This threat was subsequently withdrawn. Though payments of some $50,000 were made for winners in the 1997 World Indoor Championships held in Paris, athletes still do not enjoy comparable control to that experienced by tennis players and golfers. As Bale and Sang make clear, the experience of Kenyan athletes, as either 'jet-setters', 'journeymen' or as 'wannabees/unknowns', shows the mixed fortunes of sports stars from emerging nations (Bale & Sang, 1996; Hoberman, 1997).

Within team sports, employment rights also vary across sports played in different continents. Although North American athletes in sports such as American/Canadian football, ice hockey, basketball and baseball have unionized, conducted negotiations with owners based on collective bargaining and have involved themselves in strike action, they have not been all that successful in gaining greater employment rights (Beamish, 1982, 1988; Kidd, 1988; Sage, 1990). The draft, in which college athletes are 'assigned' to specific teams, still operates in North American sport. In comparison, the free movement of labour is now part of EU law. Individuals are technically free to perform and work where they wish within the EU. Employment protection legislation also applies to migrant labour. Despite existing social protocols, the European soccer transfer system was described by Euro MPs as a 'slave system'. Its legality was challenged in the European Court in an action brought by Jean-Marc Bosman against the European Football Association (UEFA). The Bosman case effectively secured the rights of EU sports stars to work in any country of the Community without restriction (Maguire & Stead, 1997). This judgement, as will be demonstrated in the case study examining ice hockey, is having ramifications for all professional sports played in the EU.

Yet, the rights that the Bosman case established are not applicable to all players. Individuals from countries outside the EU are subject to a selection procedure. Sports migrants have to prove international status in their respective sports. Further, as with migrants more generally, exploitative labour practices also take place. No detailed research on the lived experiences of migrants from less developed countries, for example, African and East European soccer players, so far exists. Questions concerning whether they receive comparable wages and conditions to their EU counterparts need to form part of any enquiry. Sport labour migration is not, then, a uniform experience. It has its own highly differentiated political economy that reflects its position as part of the global sport system.

This movement of athletic talent amounts, in specific instances, to the deskilling of 'donor' countries and also structures migrants' lives. Latin and Central American countries, for example, regularly experience the loss of baseball stars and soccer players to the USA and Europe. It is a case of less developed countries having invested in the production of athletic talent; once this talent reaches maturity, more economically developed leagues, such as Major League Baseball, cream off the best available talent (Klein, 1991). Not only is the indigenous audience denied direct access to the talent nurtured and developed in their country, but, in some instances, such as with African national soccer teams, sports lose some of their quality performers when the demands of European clubs clash with international matches. The central questions surrounding this issue concern national identity, underdevelopment and dependent development (Bale & Sang, 1996). Yet, Europeans also feel under pressure. In commenting on the increasing Asian domination in his sport of badminton, the elite Danish player Peter Axellson argued that national teams had to be abandoned in the face of this competition. Advocating a transnational solution, Axellson observed, 'We must unite as Europeans. We must play together with each other as Europeans. The Asians are so good at this sport and there are so many of them' (*TransWorld Sport*, Channel 4, 25 November 1995).

The reaction of sport labour migrants to the 'host' culture also requires consideration. The constant moving back and forth between different cultures requires that particular types of migrants develop new types of flexible personal controls, dispositions and means of orientation (King, 1991). In developing this new kind of habitus, migrants such as tennis players and golfers face problems of inter-cultural communication. Major global sports festivals and tournaments involve a multilayered form of cultural communication involving interaction with fellow players, coaches, officials, the crowd and media personnel. In the world of European soccer, Swedes, Norwegians, Dutch and Germans appear more adept than English players at deploying flexible personal controls and often communicate with ease in several different languages.

While some sports migrants may find the move from one culture to another relatively free of culture shock, this may not always be the case. The burn-out of young women tennis players may, in part, be connected to the processes under discussion. Further, there may be specific features of these processes which reflect broader gender inequalities that differentially hamper and constrain women. We need more evidence regarding the gendered nature of these processes. Further, the initial movement of eastern European male ice hockey and basketball players to North America may also bring problems of adjustment to free-market economic processes. Some elite sports migrants such as basketball and tennis players also work in and inhabit a specific type of urban space (King, 1991). Their sport workplaces include the Globe in Stockholm and the Skydome in Toronto. They are removed from the 'natural' rhythm of the sporting seasons and express themselves in a highly regulated, supervised and commodified space.

Apart from leading to problems of adjustment, sports migration can also engender hostility in the host country. Sport labour unions, such as in European soccer, have sought to protect indigenous workers (players) by arguing for quotas and qualification thresholds to be applied to potential migrants. During 1993, the English Professional Footballers' Association (PFA) called for tighter controls and checks on the playing credentials of foreign players (*Mail on Sunday*, 24 January 1993, p. 9). Despite the Bosman ruling – which deregulated the movement of sports labour within the EU – Gordon Taylor, general secretary of the PFA, has continued to demand restrictions on non-EU migrants. The common themes that run through the case studies we have examined – of basketball, cricket, ice hockey and soccer (Maguire, 1988; Maguire, 1996; Maguire & Stead, 1996; Maguire & Stead, 1997) – concern questions regarding the perceived threat to national team performances and the under-development of indigenous talent. These questions are also surfacing in the contentious debate between different groups regarding the recent professionalization of rugby union and the decision by officials of major English clubs to recruit overseas players in large numbers.

Debates of this kind also involve questions concerning national identity and identity politics. Issues of attachment to place, notions of self-identity and allegiance to a specific country are significant in this connection. The de-monopolization of economic structures in the world economy involves the concomitant deregulation and globalization of markets, trade and labour. The globalization of capital has also entailed the globalization of the market in services to finance, commerce and industry (Dezalay, 1990). Crucially, this has led to a new category of professionals. These professionals include international lawyers, corporate tax accountants, financial advisers and management consultants. It is this group that emerged in the attempts by transnational corporations to chart and formalize the newly globalized economic arena. While the experience of these professionals is not exactly the same as for all sports migrants, in certain respects some elite sports migrants appear to embody the characteristics of this new breed of entrepreneurs.

A new generation of agents, entrepreneurs and organizations, such as Mark McCormack and his IMG, Rupert Murdoch and his News International, and media–sport production executives more generally, have created a global system of sport spectacles by directly employing or facilitating the employment of elite sports migrants to perform in Super Leagues, World Series and exhibition tournaments. These executives – and some of the migrants they employ – are arguably the sporting equivalent of Dezalay's 'hired guns' in North American law firms who are hired to win court cases 'at all costs' (Dezalay, 1990). As with the globalization of legal services, so, too, regarding sport, elements of an American-ization process are evident within broader processes of globaliza-tion. The pervasiveness of what is in the main a distinctively American style of business practice in a range of exported sports such as American football, basketball and baseball has forced people in other more 'indigenous' sports such as soccer, rugby and European ice hockey to align themselves to this model. Failure to do so would jeopardize their place within the hierarchy of the global media–sport marketplace.

The new generation of sports migrants, such as the Americans performing in the World League of American Football or the Africans recruited by American universities, may have little sense of attachment to a specific space or community. Highly rational and technical criteria determine their status and market value. Just as the new generation of lawyers stresses technical competency, aggressive tactics and a meritocratic ethos, sports migrants embrace the ethos of hard work, differential rewards and a win-at-all-costs approach. As the case study on ice hockey reveals, aggressive and violent tactics characterize the occupational subculture of some elite sports migrants. Lawyers who adopt such practices are said to be 'perfect auxiliaries to the new breed of corporate raiders' (Dezalay, 1990). The 'rebel' cricket and rugby tours to South Africa illustrate how sports migrants can likewise act as mercenaries for 'big business'. Sometimes, the link between corporate raiders and sports migrants is only too clear. Take, for example, the World Series Cricket organized by Kerry Packer and the Rugby Super League developed by Murdoch: in both instances player contracts were bought to ensure a product would be displayed by the media outlet broadcasting such sports.

Several observations regarding the patterns, dimensions and issues described so far can now be made. The sports labour process is bound up in a complex political economy that is itself embedded in a series of cross-cultural struggles that characterize the global sport system. This process is marked by a series of political, cultural, economic and geographical issues and pressures that structure the migrants' lives. These issues and pressures vary between sports played in different continents; they interweave in a fashion where no one 'factor' dominates. Nevertheless, there is an overall structure of sport labour migration and that is the broader global sport system identified in earlier chapters. Similarly, the motivation of elite migrants cannot be reduced to any one cause. A complex range of motives is involved. In order to develop this point and to frame more effectively the case study on ice hockey that follows, a preliminary typology of sport labour migration can be outlined.

While it is important to explore the lived migrant experience, in order to understand how the sports star interprets relocation and the sense of being an outsider in an established culture, it is necessary to use a conceptual framework that avoids separating this experience from global cultural processes. The ethnographic description must be placed on a wider conceptual canvas. In similar vein, in discussing how the life of Mozart must be understood as part of an analysis of court society, Elias outlined the approach that underpins the present chapter. He wrote:

> Mozart's individual fate, his destiny as a unique human being and thus also a unique artist, was heavily influenced by his social situation, the dependence of a musician of his time on the court aristocracy. We can see here how difficult it is to elucidate – as a

biographer, for example, tries to do – the problems individuals encounter in their lives, no matter how incomparable an individual's personality or achievements may be, unless one has mastered the craft of the sociologist. One needs to be able to draw a clear picture of the social pressures acting on the individual. Such a study is not a historical narrative but the elaboration of a verifiable model of the figuration which a person – in this case an eighteenth-century artist – formed through his interdependence with other social figures of his time.

(Elias, 1994b, p. 14)

In examining court society more broadly, Elias also observed that neither the development of Louis XIV as an individual nor his actions as a king can be adequately understood without reference to a sociological model of court society and without knowledge of the development of the social position of the king within this structure (Elias, 1983). In keeping with this approach, labour migration is viewed as part of wider global sport processes. The processes that structure the enabling and constraining features of sport labour migration have been highlighted. In turn, several key categories of migrants can be identified. In this way the main features of a sociological model within which to locate the case studies examining ice hockey can be outlined. In doing so, I am aware that the categories identified are not rigid and that in the lived experience of migrants, the different dimensions overlap and shade together in different combinations. In addition, these types of migration are interconnected with the dimensions of labour migration identified in figure 5. At this point let me examine some specific examples that illustrate what I have in mind.

Those migrants identified in figure 6 as sport 'pioneers' possess an almost evangelical zeal in extolling the virtues of 'their' sport (Bromberger, 1994). Their words and actions can be seen as a form of proselytizing by which they seek to convert the natives to their body habitus and sport culture. Similarly, some migrants can be identified as 'settlers' who not only bring their sports with them but are sports migrants who subsequently stay and settle in the society where they perform their labour. Other migrants can be viewed as 'mercenaries' who are motivated more by short-term gains and are employed as 'hired guns' (Maguire, 1993d). These migrants have little or no attachment to the local, no sense of place in relation to the space where they currently reside or do their body work. In contrast, some migrants are 'nomads' who are more motivated by a cosmopolitan engagement with migration. They use their sports career to journey: they embark on a quest in which they seek the experience of the 'other' and indeed of being the

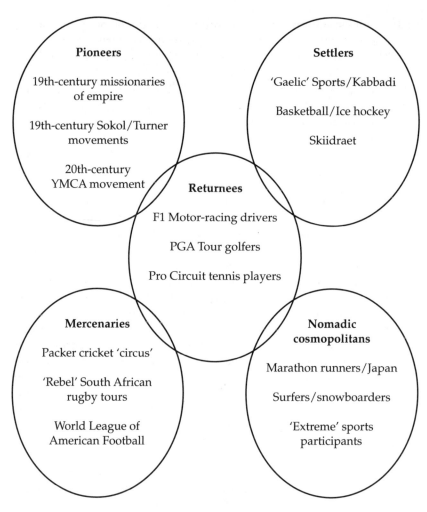

Figure 6 *Typology of sport labour migration*

'other'. That is, in Simmel's terms, of being, for example, a stranger in a foreign metropolitan culture (Maguire, 1996).

In English soccer during the 1990s overseas players such as Eric Cantona and Ruud Gullit typified the cosmopolitan stranger. But the stranger may also seek to journey away from the city. Surfers, snowboarders and participants in 'extreme' sports all share the desire to explore the experience of difference and diversity. Yet some cosmopolitans, along with pioneers, mercenaries and even long-term settlers, act as 'returnees' in the global process. The lure of 'home soil' can prove too strong. While this typology requires further investigation, in this context the aspects of sport labour migration identified are used to map out the patterns of migration as part of elite global competition (Maguire & Stead, 1996, 1997). In the light of the issues, questions and dimensions of sport labour migration raised, attention can now be turned to a case study on ice hockey. In this context, consideration is given to North American migration processes.

Canadians, Ice Hockey and Global Sport

Whereas the economic core of ice hockey can be located in North America and with the NHL in particular, the sport also flourishes in Europe and in parts of Asia (Gruneau & Whitson, 1993). With the exception of the NHL, global ice hockey is under the jurisdiction of the International Ice Hockey Federation (IIHF). Transfers between federations have to be recorded with the governing body at its Zurich headquarters. A quite discernible pattern to the import and export of players across the globe is evident. The main exporters of ice hockey players during the 1990s have been Canada and the former Soviet Union (Maguire, 1996). The migration of former Soviet citizens is, in part, accountable in terms of the collapse of that state and the consequent 'internal' migration between former Soviet republics. In addition, however, Russians and Ukrainians in particular have been flooding to the West. Besides the NHL, the key destination is the unified German republic. This movement parallels a similar process that has occurred in soccer (Maguire & Stead, 1997). Ice hockey clubs in Great Britain (GB) are also major recruiters – though primarily of Canadian talent.

Taking the 1994–95 season as an example, 34 per cent of hockey migrants came from Canada, while Germany and Great Britain imported some 40 per cent and 12 per cent respectively of the total number of migrants (Maguire, 1996). If the top ten destinations of the 433 Canadian 'blade runners' who migrated during the 1994–95 season are examined, it is clear that Germany (31 per cent) and GB (26 per cent) take the lion's share of these player transfers. There was also a general movement of Canadians across Europe and to Japan. During the 1990s, Canadians have, in fact, made up, on average, 33 per cent of the total number of migrants on the global ice hockey circuit (Maguire, 1996). On the basis of these figures it is impossible to determine why these migrants moved. It is feasible to speculate, however, that the main motivation of those who moved from the former Eastern bloc involved either a desire to relocate and settle in the West or to earn as much 'hard currency' as they could in as short a period of time, and then return 'home'. In terms of the migrant types identified in figure 6, former Eastern bloc citizens clearly act as 'settlers' or as 'mercenaries'.

The pattern of Canadian migration reflects a blend of economic, cultural, ethnic and political factors and involves a combination of all five types of migrants identified in figure 6. Yet again, mono-causal explanations do not capture the complexity of what is involved. A series of seemingly contradictory dynamics appears to be taking place. For example, the more economically powerful ice hockey leagues of mainland Europe (Germany, Switzerland and Italy) attract a higher-quality migrant player who may be motiv-ated more by short-term economic gains. Yet this pattern is also contoured by cultural factors. French Canadians tend to travel along talent flow lines whose destinations are French-speaking areas of Europe. Here a more cosmopolitan style may be at work. There is also a process of differential recruitment and perception by people in the potential host cultures. Italy actively recruits Canadians for both its domestic game and its national team. The Swedes, in contrast, appear to be more protective of their 'national game' and the degree of recruitment of Canadians is less than in other top Western European countries. Until recently, only one foreign migrant was allowed per team.

Largely on account of the demise of the Soviet Union and the eastern bloc, ice hockey clubs in Russia, the Czech Republic and Ukraine simply do not have, as yet, the economic or cultural capital available to recruit Western European or Canadian migrants. Indeed, the best East European talent is lured to the NHL. Valery Gushin, general manager of Moscow's Red Army team, is one of Eastern Europe's fiercest critics of this 'brawn drain'. Arguing that the NHL recruitment of players is another example of how Western entrepreneurs are taking Russian resources, he observed: 'The NHL comes here with tanks and takes away our best players' (*Macleans*, 22 January 1996: p. 54).

From the evidence available it is clear that the recruitment pat-terns relating to Canadian players are dominated by the strategies of Western European clubs (Maguire, 1996). Despite the SM-Liiga in Finland and the Elitserien in Sweden being regarded as Europe's premier leagues in terms of standards of play, it is to Germany and Great Britain that the vast majority of Canadians travel. In Great Britain in particular, where a lower standard of play is evident and where the sport has marginal status, the migrant can seek and play the role of 'pioneer', promoting the virtues of ice hockey. The flow of Canadian migrants across the

Atlantic is not, then, simply an economic affair. Migration is also contoured, in the case of France, GB, Italy and the Nordic countries, to cite just these examples, along lines of ethnic heritage. By claiming cultural affinity and nationality status, migrants are able to navigate a route through the thicket of eligibility regulations and quotas developed by sports organizations, national governments and the EU. In considering this overall movement, Jan-Ake Edvinsson, general secretary of IIHF, observed:

> It's a problem for the sport itself ... Then if a new player comes to a new country and plays for a team, he takes the place of one junior. And we like to develop ice hockey from as many countries as we can ... There should not be such a big movement.
>
> (personal interview, Zurich, March 1995)

This issue of dependent development is particularly evident in Great Britain. Recently, Canadian migrants have been joined in British ice hockey by a growing number of East Europeans. This has prompted a quite defensive ethnic response from Canadian migrants. In addition, very few West Europeans (e.g., Swedes, Finns, Germans or Swiss) have ever played in British ice hockey; it is basically a Canadian preserve. Given this, it is appropriate to note that, in a perhaps not unrelated development, the number of Canadians playing in the NHL declined from 97 per cent in 1967 to 75 per cent in 1988. By the 1993 season, some 17 per cent of the NHL players were European and the number of Canadians had fallen to some 66 per cent (MacGregor, 1993: p. 48). By 1995/96, 119 out of 605 NHL players were non-North American, with some forty-six Russians, twenty-seven Swedes and twenty-three Czechs/Slovaks on the club payrolls (*Calgary Herald*, 9 March 1996: p. E3). Once again, the scale of this migration flow prompted a quite negative response in some quarters. North American media viewed this migration as 'The European Invasion' (*Calgary Herald*, 9 March 1996: p. E3), whereas *The European* noted in its report 'NHL Invaders Upset Canadians' (*The European*, 4 October 1996: p. 12). A range of issues was identified by the North American media as underpinning the negative consequences of this over-recruitment. These include: the loss of 'Canadian' jobs; the lack of courage and fighting qualities evident in the 'European' style of play; and the fact that European players 'fake injury'. Despite these reservations, in addition to the Europeans playing in the NHL, over 200 European teenagers were reported to be employed in Canadian junior leagues (*Calgary Herald*, 9 March 1996: p. E3).

Despite this presence in North America, it is important to observe that during the 1994 NHL 'lock-out', many European players, acting as 'returnees', sought to 'return home' and play, on a temporary basis, for their former clubs. The IIHF, who signed in 1996 an agreement with the NHL whereby the latter agreed to support the development of ice hockey outside North America, sanctioned this 'return' migration. Given the Swedish desire to protect their home players, and their correlative reluctance to recruit Canadian migrants, it is perhaps unsurprising that the Swedish Ice Hockey Association refused to allow former Swedish-based players to return and play on a temporary basis. In order to bring the various tensions and issues that surround labour migration in general and ice hockey players in particular into sharper relief attention will now be given to one specific case study.

Canadian Players as Part of British Ice Hockey Subculture

Canadians have had a long involvement in British ice hockey. For example, British-born players who learnt their ice hockey in Canada had a significant impact in 1935–36 when Great Britain became the first team to win the Triple Crown of the Olympic, World and European Championships (Drackett, 1987). This success was to assist in the launch of a postwar British ice hockey boom that would last through to the late 1950s. In this phase, Canadian-born players made an increasingly important contribution. In contrast, from the late 1950s through to the early 1980s, British ice hockey experienced long-term decline. From this point on, however, and in a series of moves that have several parallels with developments then occurring in British basketball (Maguire, 1988), ice hockey exponents sought to establish the place of this sport among other marginal sports in the 'glocal' marketplace.

Here, the focus is on the post-1990 period of British ice hockey. During this period, the British team unexpectedly gained promotion from Pool C to Pool A of world ice hockey. Subsequently, they were relegated to Pool B. In addition, unusual success in qualification tournaments brought the national side to the final elimination stage for gaining a place at the 1994 (Lillehammer) Winter Olympics. More recently, the British team again narrowly failed to make the final elimination stage for the 1998 Winter Games in Nagano, Japan. Along with these changes, the domestic game underwent restructuring with the formation of a premier league. During the same period, the NHL arranged pre-season exhibition games involving major league teams (e.g., the Toronto Maple

Leafs) in Britain, and moves are under way for closer links between the NHL and the IIHF (e.g., negotiations led to the inclusion of NHL/professional players in Olympic ice hockey in Nagano, Japan, in 1998). In each of these areas, the role of media coverage, sponsorship revenue and the involvement of overseas migrants have figured prominently.

Using these events, the issues, problems and tensions associated with migrants more generally in global sport processes can be illustrated. In considering Canadian ice hockey migration, an examination of the occupational subculture that considers coaching strategies, playing styles and the centrality of instrumental forms of violence is also required. The problematic nationality status of Canadian migrants in British ice hockey is another powerful feature of the figuration in question. Simply put, the result of this long-term process is that GB players increasingly 'ride the pine' (sit on the bench as reserve players) while the 'Canucks' (Canadians) dominate the ice time.

The 'Canucks': Reliving 'Glory Days'?

The more recent recruitment of Canadians has been interwoven with the commodification and restructuring of the game that occurred in the 1980s and early 1990s. The reasons offered for the recruitment of Canadians into British ice hockey are similar to the sentiments expressed about the involvement of Americans in British basketball during the same period (Maguire, 1988). Their proponents argue that their presence will provide a better product to sell to live audiences, media networks and potential sponsors. In addition, Canadians are seen as providing a powerful role model and as acting as a spur to the development of indigenous talent. Given that the GB team was languishing in the bottom division of world hockey, the recruitment of foreign migrants came to be seen as desirable by key figures within the ice hockey federation and the club owners' association.

The motivation and mode of migration of the Canadians who play in British ice hockey reflect the ideal types of sport labour migration outlined previously. Those who settle and make Britain – at least for a limited period – 'their home' express an almost missionary zeal with regard to spreading a positive message about the attractions of the game. Canadians cast themselves in the role of 'pioneers' and 'proselytizers'. If only the 'Brits' would 'get the message' and 'see the light' their appreciation of and standard of playing the game would improve. For the majority of Britons, however, the significance of the 'blue line' (used for offside and to regulate the attack/defence balance of play) remains a mystery. By 1994 some 7500 players were registered with the British Ice Hockey Association (BIHA), of which 3000 were seniors playing in the men's leagues (Roberts, 1994).

For some Canadian players, British ice hockey is but another port of call. The turnover is rapid and this appears to stem from two main factors: the 'mercenary' desire of the migrant to 'make a fast buck' and skate swiftly to another rink in the same or a different society; or a wish to experience different cultures and 'to do the European tour'. Gary Yaremchuk, for example, played in five different European countries, including Britain, between 1987 and 1993. This temporary residence results sometimes from the inevitable downward spiral as a player ages and seeks more comfortable rinks to ply his craft. On the other hand, the pattern of migration may be the result of a miscalculated agent-inspired move. In the case of more talented players, the lure of the Swiss or French franc or the Deutschmark more usually ensures that their involvement in British ice hockey is a temporary affair. They are the 'hired mercenary guns' of European ice hockey. In some instances, departures by migrants can be rather conflict-ridden. Players simply walk out on clubs. Fife Flyers, a Scottish-based team, had one such experience in January 1995 when an American import, Tony Szabo, hastily departed Heathrow (London) airport bound for the USA. The Flyers' Canadian coach commented:

> When we got to his flat it was empty and even his car was gone ... By the time we contacted the Heathrow authorities we had missed him by 20 minutes. Thank God he's American – a fellow Canadian wouldn't do that to me.
>
> (*Daily Telegraph*, 10 January 1995: p. 32)

Yet for some Canadian migrants – including former NHL players such as Doug Smail – there are features of British ice hockey that outweigh the attractions of Zurich, Paris, Munich or indeed their 'home'. The close overlap between the Canadian and English versions of the English language avoids some of the problems associated with adjustment, relocation and foreign sojourn in a linguistically different country. Not for them the attractions of a nomadic lifestyle. Besides, as players come to the end of their playing careers, the desire to 'give back' something to the game dovetails well with the role of 'pioneer' in British ice hockey. In addition, being a local hero rekindles memories of 'glory days'.

The added advantage of British ice hockey is that it is

dominated by a Canadian ethos, coaching strategy and playing style. Europeans see British club and national teams as rough, violent clones of the Canadian game. Canadian migrants, by contrast, are welcomed into the fold, slide easily into the playing patterns and are assimilated into the Canadian network as smoothly as the British upper classes were into the Singapore cricket club in the days of Empire. Canadians can adopt the role of the pioneer, feel safe in the company of fellow 'Canucks', settle for a while, almost feel 'at home', yet are also secure in the knowledge that the option to 'return' to their roots is still available.

Migrants, National Identity and the Restructuring of Ice Hockey

Looking over the longer term, it is clear that the eligibility regulations and quotas regarding Canadian migrants have changed considerably. In the immediate post-World War II period, few restrictions were applied and, as a result, Canadians dominated the British game. More recently, the tensions between those who wish to use the migrants to gain a better position for Britain in the global ice hockey marketplace, and those who are more concerned to promote local talent and the long-term development of the British game, have become more evident. Until recently four 'foreign' players were allowed per team including three 'imports' and one dual national. This, however, underestimates the presence and influence of Canadians. Over time, several Canadians have stayed and made or remade Britain their 'home', however 'temporary'. As residents they qualify as GB players. Teams actively recruit this category of player and indeed they, along with the dual nationals who hold British passports, are eligible to play for the national team and thus do not count as part of the foreign quota.

The methods by which migrants enter Britain, however, can vary considerably. Though some clearly use official channels and their clubs apply for work permits, other methods are also employed. In the following comments by a reporter of *Ice Hockey News Review*, one of the methods used by Canadian migrants is outlined:

> I can vouch for the fact that many a Canuck was told that on entry to the mother country he was to tell the immigration officials that he was of course just visiting and on vacation. And that under no circumstances should he be seen to be carrying ice hockey sticks as hand luggage with his skates dangling round his neck. Needless to

say from time to time some Canucks from the backwoods managed
not to obey this simple instruction and found themselves being
turned straight around and shipped out on the next flight.
(*Ice Hockey News Review*, 25 December 1993: p. 9)

If the recent success of the GB team is considered, it is also clear
that their promotion from Pool C to Pool A and reaching the final
qualification stage for the Lillehammer Olympics were heavily
dependent on dual nationals. During the last three years, the
number of dual nationals has continued to grow. In the recent Pool
A World Championship tournament, fifteen out of twenty-three GB
players were Canadian dual nationals. Even this underestimates
their impact, for the team tends to operate a two-line game plan (of
two teams of five) that is made up almost exclusively of Canadians.
As with the domestic game, so with the national side. The 'Brits' are
left with goal-tending duties and with 'riding the pine' – acting as
substitutes for those Canadians who need a rest or who foul out of
the game. Defending this use of dual nationals, David Frame, the
chief executive of the BIHA, commented:

I think we're quietly confident of staying in Pool A and it's important for the sport's profile that we do so. People criticise dual nationals, but they're the only way we can compete at the top until we've
brought our youngsters on. Countries like Italy and Germany have
taken the same route as us and prospered.
(*Daily Telegraph*, 4 March 1994: p. 34)

Significantly, Frame referred to the fact that the use of dual nationals also occurs in Italy and Germany. However, their use is not
confined to these countries. In the World Championships to which
he was referring, some fifty-one 'Canadian'-born players and
players developed through Canadian local and provincial ice
hockey programmes were playing for non-Canadian national
sides. In the 1995 World Championships, the success of France was
heavily dependent on the role of French Canadians. 'Blade
runners', then, have a significant impact at both club and international levels. Such players are hired 'mercenaries' plying their
craft for other nations.

This pattern parallels the situation that prevails in international
cricket (Maguire & Stead, 1996). Yet, though economics play a part,
their representing another country appears to stem more from a
desire to test their skills against the very best. In this regard ice
hockey players are not unlike elite soccer and cricket migrants who
also perform for countries other than their place of birth (Maguire
& Stead, 1998). The equivalent of these ice hockey players in tennis

is the Canadian-born player Greg Rusedski who now represents Britain both in the Davis Cup competition and on the global tour in which he is highly ranked.

Local Heroes? Pioneers, Mercenary Labour and 'Brits with Canadian Accents'

How do the various groups who interact in the 'glocal' ice hockey subculture view these developments? In the British case, if groups from the host culture are considered, a variety of responses are evident. The owners of British ice hockey clubs welcome the involvement of the Canadians. Some of the elite clubs also welcome the imminent development of a European super league in which Canadians would play a prominent part. However, this view is not shared by all. Norman de Mesquita, writing in *Ice Hockey News Review*, remarked:

> Some overseas players do not give value for money, something we can identify with. We have all seen a few imports who fell into that category and who were just here to feather a financial nest and have a paid holiday. Then there is the feeling in cricket that too many native-bred players are being kept out of the first class game by foreigners. Isn't that familiar too? How many highly talented British-born players can you name who should, by now, be an integral part of the GB set-up if only we had included fewer mediocre veteran Canadians. It also applies to most clubs in our game and is the result of short-sighted management attitudes and the mistaken belief that short-term success is all that matters. [This is] exactly what killed off the game in the sixties.
>
> (*Ice Hockey News Review*, 20 August 1994: p. 5)

Criticisms of this kind centre on issues such as the 'over-reliance' on foreign stars, problems of financial instability, a lack of opportunity for British players, the lack of European players, regimented coaching, the adoption of a violent playing style and the presence in the GB team of 'Brits with Canadian accents' (*Ice Hockey News Review*, 20 August 1994). Discontent resulting from these features of the game manifests itself in several ways. British under-21 and B international players become disillusioned and refuse to make themselves available for selection. Although some Canadians see themselves as 'pioneers' whose aim is to promote the 'good of the game', British players see them as 'mercenaries' who settle and take over British ice hockey. Take the following remarks made by Tony Hand, a player for the Sheffield Steelers:

> I've nothing against imported players. I think they've been good for
> the game – to a certain extent. But obviously now there's too many
> and that's got to be to the detriment of the British player ... It's
> going to take an exceptional British player to come through, to actu-
> ally get the ice time they're going to need to develop. There's a lot of
> good British talent about and teams should realise that all they need
> is a little bit of development. But a lot of teams won't develop
> players.
>
> (*Guardian*, 4 December 1995: p. 16)

Such resentment about the underdevelopment of indigenous talent
is not confined to verbal criticism. Some British players target
Canadian players to ensure that they retaliate and then end up off
ice in the penalty box (*Ice Hockey News Review*, 11 December 1993).
Such criticism of Canadian players, and their presence as dual
nationals in the GB team, was held in check by advocates of their
use, but only for as long as the team was successful. Relegation
from Pool A and the failure to qualify for Lillehammer prompted
the critics of Canadian migrants to pose the question 'How British
is British?' (*Ice Hockey News Review*, 26 March 1994: p. 3). The editor
of the *Ice Hockey News Review* concluded:

> The BIHA should forget about artificially importing players eligible
> to play for GB because that has undoubtedly been a factor in the
> development of what I believe is currently a most unhealthy situ-
> ation for British youth. If we must have unlimited Canadians with
> British passports then so be it. But the genuine imports [designated
> as foreign players] must pay the price of that 'freedom'.
>
> (*Ice Hockey News Review*, 26 March 1994: p. 5)

In contrast to these sentiments, the Canadian-born coach of the GB
side not surprisingly defended the decision to rely on dual nationals. Arguing that Great Britain could not compete without their
involvement, Alex Dampier suggested that the presence of dual
nationals provides a powerful role model and that the long-term
strategy was to develop and play more British-born players. For
the players, representing another nation does not call into question
their sense of being Canadian. They aspire to be and to play
against the best. Representing another nation involves playing for
a 'flag of convenience'.

Though the advocates of the use of dual nationals appeared to
be in the ascendancy regarding the national team in the mid-1990s,
they did not hold total control over the domestic game. Significantly, those groups within the BIHA arguing for a more protec-
tionist strategy were able to ensure that even those dual nationals

who had played for the British team would be subject to the 'four foreigner' rule in the domestic game. That is, though they hold British passports and have played for Great Britain, they are classified as foreign and are therefore subject to the club quotas and eligibility regulations applied to other foreign players.

This issue, combined with wage-capping schemes designed to limit payments to players and developed by the BIHA and the club owners, prompted the players – Canadian and British – to form a Players' Association in late 1993 and early 1994, a move that pro-voked two responses. First, one of the instigators of the move, Kevin King, had to defend the launch protesting that the new Association would not be an organization run by and for imports (*Ice Hockey News Review*, 12 February 1994). The British players had to be won over. And second, the BIHA and the owners were fiercely critical and rejected the notion that the players could have any role to play in the governing of the game.

Significantly, one of the first actions of the Ice Hockey Players' Association (IHPA) was to begin conducting discussions with Department of Employment officials. Their meetings focused on the issuing of work permits for foreign, chiefly Canadian, but also other non-EU players. This prompted the BIHA secretary, David Pickles, to observe:

> We could not accept a situation where the IHPA has a right to veto work permit applications. We are asking the DOE to retract all of this and we have informed them, both verbally and in writing, that we will take it to the Home Office.
>
> (*Ice Hockey News Review*, 25 March 1994: p. 5)

Labour Rights: European Law and On-ice Enforcers

Questions of labour rights are not confined to ice hockey players (Bale & Maguire, 1994). Athletes in several sports face similar problems. In soccer, problems over freedom of contract, and the right to reside in and play for clubs within the EU, forced a Belgian player, Jean-Marc Bosman, to take the Belgian FA and the Euro-pean Union of Football Associations (UEFA) to the European Court (Maguire & Stead, 1997). In a landmark provisional judge-ment in September 1995, the advocate-general found in favour of the players' right to move, and concluded that quotas covering EU citizens were illegal and constituted a restraint of trade. This judgement was confirmed by the court in December 1995. Dis-cussing the issue of European legislation prior to this judgement, the general secretary of IIHF, Jan-Ake Edvinsson, observed, 'Even if we are not happy about it, we have to follow it. If it's the law, then also the sport must follow it' (personal interview conducted in Zurich, March 1995).

Significantly, though the case and the publicity that surrounded it centred on Bosman, the soccer player, Tim Cranston, a Canadian-born dual national, then playing for the Sheffield Steelers, was also named as part of the court action. Despite being a British passport-holder and also playing for Great Britain, he had been designated by the BIHA as an 'import'. As a result of this designation, his transfer to a top German club fell through: the 'foreign' quota was full. On hearing the advocate-general's provisional judgement, Cranston commented, 'When I heard about Bosman, I contacted his legal team and became part of the ruling. The only question now is who will be liable for the money I'm owed' (*Daily Telegraph*, 22 September 1995: p. 43). Senior soccer officials are having to face up to the deregulation of the transfer market that stemmed from this judgement, but ice hockey, with its dependence on foreign-born talent, has been particularly affected. Indeed, subsequent to the judgement, the BIHA held meetings with officials of the Canadian High Commission regarding the citizenship status of up to twenty players currently playing in Britain (*Guardian*, 7 October 1995: p. 20). In May 1995 the BIHA decided to abolish virtually every restriction on clubs signing foreign-born British passport-holders. Following the Bosman judgement, restrictions regarding EU citizens also had to be abandoned. While these changes strengthened the position of Canadian migrants, non-EU players from the former Soviet Union stood to gain little. Only internal sport migration by EU citizens had been seen to be subject to European legislation. The external controls remained in place. Work permits and international clearance issues still affected non-EU citizens. Hence the meetings of BIHA officials at the Canadian High Commission to establish the players' nationality status.

The British are not alone in being affected by the Bosman ruling. Coinciding with the launch of the inaugural European Ice Hockey League, (EHL), this judgement led, in effect, to 'free agency' for players. 'Out of contract' players quickly became the target for the general managers of the economically more powerful clubs, particularly those in Germany. As a consequence, Scandinavian clubs have been losing their top players to 'continental' Europe (*The European*, 2–8 May 1996: p. 14). This situation is not unlike that which exists in European soccer (Maguire & Stead, 1997).

Canadian migrants also appear to adopt less formal strategies to deal with issues of labour rights and the problems arising from, or threats to, their migrant position; on ice intimidation of non-Canadians is one of the tactics adopted. Though preceded by the defection of players from the Soviet bloc, since the people's revolutions of the late 1980s top-flight East Europeans have flowed across the Atlantic in greater numbers to be recruited to the ranks of the NHL. A similar process, albeit at a different standard, has occurred in mainland Western Europe and Great Britain. For club owners seeking to impose wage capping, the recruitment of East Europeans strengthened their negotiating position and allowed them to drive down wage costs because citizens from depressed Eastern economies are prepared to play for lower wages. Any Canadian who holds out for too long in salary negotiations risks being told to 'hit the highway'. Little wonder, then, that the Canadians viewed the flood from the East as a threat to their livelihoods. During the 1994–95 season, some 31 per cent of the total number of transfers recorded by the IIHF were from the countries that made up the former Soviet Union and Czechoslovakia (Maguire, 1996).

Whereas some migrants may feel that the newly formed Players' Association might be able to influence the decisions of the DOE regarding the regulation of the ice hockey inflow, the reaction of other Canadians in British ice hockey is more brutal and immediate. Following the recruitment of Ukrainian players to the Humberside Hawks club, the coach, Peter Johnson, observed that the East Europeans in general 'just get clobbered every game' (*Guardian*, 4 January 1994: p. 15). Referring to his own Ukrainian players, Johnson concluded:

> There is no question both he [Alexei Kuznetsov] and Alexander Kulikov have seen big threats and physical attention because Canadians see them as a threat to their jobs. I had a go at Durham's Chris Norton because he was hitting them so hard it was embarrassing. I told him that he should treat all players the same.
>
> (*Daily Telegraph*, 31 December 1993: p. 30)

The use of violent play is seemingly not confined to threats posed by East Europeans in the domestic game. The use of rough, violent play in international matches has gained the GB team the reputation of adhering to a 'Canadian style' (*Ice Hockey News Review*, 16 October 1994: p. 28). A report in the Swiss ice hockey magazine, discussing British ice hockey, highlighted these issues clearly:

> What the Panthers and Beavers exhibit is 'bush hockey' – good old Canadian style. First the man then the puck. The harder the check, the harder the thud against the board, the louder the jubilation from the crowd. Of European playing culture there is not a trace. Russian

technique; Slovakian cleverness; Swedish defensive teaching; these have not made their way over the channel between Calais and Dover ... [As] Peter Zahnen of the SIHF ... has written, 'Britain, a team without culture that technique and tactics are totally lost on'.

(cited in *Ice Hockey News Review*, 9 April 1994: p. 10)

There is, perhaps, a certain irony in this criticism. The Canadian commentator Don Cherry repeatedly denigrates European players for their alleged lack of a tough masculine style. Cherry also criticizes European involvement in the NHL *per se*, arguing that these foreigners are taking the jobs of 'good Canadian boys' (Gillett, White & Young, 1995: p. 15). This trend has not gone unnoticed by other commentators. As Roy MacGregor records:

> By 1992–93 ... there could be no dismissing the Europeans as a fad. In all, 88 Europeans had been drafted the previous June, with the most dramatic exodus coming from Russia. By the time the season ended, 49 Russians had skated with NHL teams and another 48 had played in the minor leagues or in Junior ice-hockey ... When NHL expansion began in 1967, Canadians held 96 percent of the available slots. By the time the 1993 playoffs opened, that figure had fallen to 66.2 percent – slightly below two-thirds. Don Cherry's response: 'There should be quotas'.

(MacGregor, 1993: pp. 47–8)

Despite Cherry's comments, the logic of the global expansion plans of the NHL and the unrestricted recruitment of labour by a dominant cartel ensure that top Europeans will continue to cross the Atlantic. Equally, the 'overproduction' of young Canadian men who dream of making the pros, or of older veterans who seek new rinks to relive glory days, also results in them following well-worn European migrant trails. The irony is that they then hold down team positions that EU and Eastern European citizens could occupy. Cherry overlooks the extent to which sports labour is part of a global marketplace. The Canadian migrants who already reside in Britain and play against mainland Europeans also appear aware of their violent reputation. The British national coach defended his players' tactics, yet was forced to conclude:

> It's inbred into you in Canada. Somebody hits you, you hit them right back. We have to play our normal week in, week out physical style but limited to body checking – and keep away from retaliation ... Our guys have had another 12 months of playing European competition. I'm confident they've toned it down and will realise that this year the most important thing in this tournament is winning. Your personal feelings can't come into it.

(*Guardian*, 18 March 1992: p. 19)

Yet the Canadian migrants do not just deal out pain (Messner, 1990; Young, White & McTeer, 1994). Given the frequency of hits and blows, one might have thought that the migrant experience is a trade in pain. As noted earlier, young Britons try to provoke the 'Canucks' and get them off the ice. On occasions, quite serious free fights occur. In October 1994, a Canadian migrant was subjected to a systematic attack while on the ice. Playing for Durham Wasps, Richard Little, a Canadian forward, sustained severe facial injuries. Subsequent to the game, the local police were called in to view the video evidence. The Durham Wasps' general manager, Paul Smith, commented on the case to the national press:

> He's been back [to hospital] this morning but they don't think it's fractured [cheekbone]. But it was terrible. You get the physical side to it but that was just callous. [The video] clearly shows it was a sucker punch from behind. After that the whole of Richard's body went limp, he just could not defend himself. As he went down he got another four or five very heavy blows to the face. We had to end the period around two minutes early just to get the blood off the ice.
>
> (*Guardian*, 25 October 1994: p. 23)

Despite the attention given to such cases, violence appears as a regular occurrence in the British game. Given Don Cherry's comments about how Europeans should be treated in Canada, it is somewhat ironic that a violent reception sometimes awaits Canadians in Europe. Indeed, in a game in 1995 between Durham Wasps and Sheffield Steelers, 231 minutes of penalties were clocked up, six dismissals occurred and play was held up for more than thirty minutes after a mass brawl. Nicky Chinn, one of the players dismissed after a Canadian-born forward, Ross Lambert, received injuries that needed seventeen stitches in a wound around his eye, was subsequently arrested by the police (*Guardian*, 18 December 1995: p. 22). During March 1996, a British Championship play-off match had to be abandoned after just fifty-eight seconds. This decision was based on instructions from the police following a mass brawl between players in the warm-up (*The Times*, 11 March 1996: p. 28). 'Doing migrant body labour' can be a painfully alienating experience. That is not the only consequence of such labour migration.

Blade Runners and 'Glocal' Ice Hockey

The involvement of Canadian migrants in British ice hockey raises a series of issues and questions that this chapter has sought to address. In figures 5 and 6, the main features of a sociological model of sport labour migration were outlined. To what extent does the case study of Canadian ice hockey migration substantiate this general model? It is clear that Canadian migrants to Great Britain are faced with a series of problems regarding labour rights, work permits and salary caps. The actions of the BIHA and, more recently, the judgement of the European Court help to shape the experience of these players. Yet the players are not passive victims of these processes. The formation of a players' union and the actions of individuals such as Tim Cranston demonstrate that migrants actively seek to improve their material conditions.

The case study also demonstrates the complex and, at times, seemingly contradictory nature of both the recruitment strategies of clubs and the desire of migrants to move. It is important to note that there is no single motivation driving Canadians around Europe or beyond. Elements of the pioneer spirit, the settler role, a mercenary style and cosmopolitan desire are all evident. To explore this further, more detailed fieldwork-based accounts of players doing their body work, but also of off-ice experiences high-lighting the nature of their lives between games, would be required. It is also clear from the evidence to hand that Canadians play for their adopted country out of a wish to play at the highest level possible rather than from a desire to represent the nation. They appear, like elite cricket migrants, less interested in 'patriot games' (Maguire & Stead, 1998). Canadian migrants accordingly illustrate several features of the general model of labour migration and share a number of experiences and problems faced by fellow migrants in other sports. What appears to be significantly different from the majority of sporting migrants, however, is that this experience involves the exercise of a violent masculine style. Located within a subculture where violent norms are tolerated and encouraged, Canadian migrant labour involves a trade in pain. Again, more fieldwork-based investigation of this feature is required.

It is also necessary to note that this pattern of migration and the sociological model of labour migration have to be seen as part of and in relation to the broader development of ice hockey and of global sportization processes. The IIHF is keen to establish a European super league, and the NHL is actively supporting this strat-egy, so far having funded IIHF developments to the tune of some £6 million. Though the IIHF had rejected these overtures for some time, they appear to have been forced into a compromise agree-ment. Plans by the USA-based International Hockey League (IHL) to expand into Europe by 1995–96 effectively forced the IIHF into the agreement during June 1994. These moves by the IHL prompted Rene Fasel, president of the IIHF, to observe: 'We are looking forward to working with the NHL instead of the IHL. If they [IHL] want to fight we are ready. They need our co-operation; if they think they can work without us that would be a mistake' (*Guardian*, 27 January 1995: p. 19).

In turn, such migration – and the strategies of the NHL and the IIHF – is part of a global sportization process that has both short-term features but also longer-term unplanned dimensions. Further analyses are needed which explore in greater detail and over a range of sports and countries the interdependencies that contour relations between, as in this case, insider/established countries, as well as those between such countries and the outsider nations that lie on the fringe of the global sport action. Both the strategies of multinational corporations and the unplanned features of global sportization processes need to be better traced and understood. Given that the NHL currently has a five-year, $210 million television contract with Fox TV, and that since 1992 its merchandising sales have nearly doubled to more than $1 billion annually, its global impact should not be underestimated (Deacon, 1995: p. 64). It is clear that the NHL is intent on emulating the NFL's global expansion strategy. This will be examined in chapter 7.

One of the keys to this was the working-out of an agreement between the IIHF, the IOC and the NHL players' association to enable NHL players to compete in the 1998 Winter Olympics. Despite the presence of such stars as Wayne Gretsky, however, the Canadians were eliminated at the semi-final stage. Given that Europe is the main target for licensing and merchandising expansion, it is no surprise that the NHL would like to establish a pan-European league. By the 1996–97 season, this was achieved. Some of those within the game observed that the collision between traditional ice hockey cultures and North American practices could wreak havoc on national leagues and indigenous player development. Mark Kelly, European scout for the Pittsburgh Penguins, observed:

> What we're seeing in all of Europe, Scandinavia and especially Russia and the rest of Eastern Europe, is a clash between an established culture of European sport and the business of North American sports. Europe has always had such strength at the grassroots level of the game and so has always produced a wealth of hockey talent. But the recent changes at the top levels of the game – dramatic changes – will eventually hurt the development of players. It might take a few years for the sport here and in Europe to feel it – sort of a four or five year trickle down – but I'm convinced that there will be some significant damage.
>
> (*The Globe and Mail*, 31 August 1996: p. A1)

As part of this general marketing process, the NHL held exhibition games in England to 'promote the game'. Yet this prompted contradictory reactions. When the BIHA president, Freddie Meredith, rejected NHL overtures and argued that the BIHA 'doesn't need or want the NHL to help promote the sport in Britain', he was described as 'uppity' in the Canadian media (*Toronto Sun*, 9 September 1993: p. 56). Given the subsequent compromise agreement reached between the NHL and the IIHF – designed to fend off the challenge of the IHL – Meredith was forced to change his position. In January 1995, he commented:

> We are within the framework of the IIHF, which has signed an exclusive agreement with the NHL to develop ice hockey internationally. The IIHF and the NHL are very serious about their relationship and clearly will take whatever steps are necessary to ensure that [they] can develop ice hockey in the way they wish.
>
> (*Guardian*, 27 January 1995: p. 19)

Yet, while the BIHA once proclaimed they did not need the NHL, along with officials of ice hockey federations across Europe they are now locked into a political economy structured by their agreement with the NHL. In addition, drawing on both the sociological model of labour migration outlined earlier and the data contained within the case study, it is clear that their mutually dependent development is based on a continuing reliance on Canadian 'blade runners'.

Conclusion: Globalization and Sport Migration

One dominant, but by no means exclusive, theme of global sports development in the late twentieth century has been Americanization. It is also legitimate, however, to talk of competing cultural flows including Japanization, Europeanization, Asiaticization, Africanization and Hispanicization which have, so far, been weaker. The present analysis is not, however, arguing a case for homogenization and integration. We have, as Golding & Harris (1996) remind us, to move beyond cruder forms of cultural imperialism and the Americanization thesis. The broad cultural processes identified in this book arguably interweave and commingle along the range of cultural flow lines outlined in Part II.

These cultural processes involve interdependencies out of which something emerges that was neither planned nor intended and which both reflects and contributes to broader globalization processes. Although sport migrants, officials and consumers are caught up in this unfolding globalization process, they do have the capacity to reinterpret cultural products and experiences into something distinct. Furthermore, the receptivity of national popular cultures to non-indigenous cultural wares can be both active and heterogeneous. These are areas in the study of global sport processes in which much more work needs to be done. Because of this interweaving and the possibly emergent 'decentring' of the West, sport migrants will be increasingly likely to come from non-Western as well as Western countries. The effect on their labour rights and sense of cultural identity is a question yet to be fully explored.

While it is important to probe the existence of relatively autonomous transnational practices, this should not lead research to be unaware that national and transnational agencies, including such sports organizations as the FA in Britain and the NFL, based in the USA, will attempt to manipulate and control such processes. Clearly, the actions of the NHL outlined in this chapter fit in as part of this general pattern. The similar strategy of the NFL will be focused on more closely in chapter 7. It is also appropriate to note, that although criticisms have been advanced here regarding aspects of the Americanization thesis, it is not being denied that the interlocked processes of commodification/Americanization have played a part in the unfolding developments under discussion. This can take several forms: the global migration of American sports personnel, the global spread of American sports forms and the global adoption of the marketing of sports along American lines. Usually, such developments mutually reinforce each other, though they have developed to varying degrees in different countries and continents. As chapter 7 will demonstrate, although the media–sport production complex markets diversity as well as sameness (Maguire 1993d), American football and basketball appear ready to become global sports. As such, American sports migrants would appear likely, for the time being, to be one of the dominant groups traversing the globe. With the marketing of soccer and rugby union as global sports, however, the significant presence within these global flows of Europeans, South Americans and Antipodeans should not be overlooked (Maguire & Stead, 1997). What consequences this will have for the donor and host cultures is, as yet, unexplored.

The conscious strategies adopted by personnel in particular sports organizations has sometimes led to the predominance of American sports migrants in specific sports. This can be shown if reference is again made to basketball. By the late 1980s over 400 Americans were playing at elite level in West European basketball leagues (Maguire, 1988). Those leagues that have undergone the most successful commercialization processes – many Italian and Spanish clubs are closely connected to transnational corporations, for example, 'Benetton Treviso' in northern Italy – tend to recruit higher-quality American migrants. The English case is thus not an isolated example. Further, just as English officials looked across the Atlantic for marketing models to follow, European basketball officials have been reported as considering 'their own version of the NBA ... creating a league of top clubs from across the continent. Plans also are under way for the creation of a world club championship tournament that would be an expanded version of the four-nation MacDonald's Open' (*USA Today*, 14 November 1990). Teams such as the Denver Nuggets, the Boston Celtics and the New York Knicks have competed in the MacDonald's Open tournament. As in the English case, some American migrants are beginning to 'settle' in specific European countries. During the last decade, Americanization processes have therefore involved not simply the quick raising of playing standards, but also the transformation of the structure and meaning of the game in Europe. In several respects these developments mirror the strategy adopted by the NFL in its marketing of American football both in specific countries and with regard to the formation of the World League of American Football (Maguire, 1990). Though located in Barcelona, Frankfurt and London, the vast majority of gridiron football players within this league are American. Little sign of resistance to such American migration is yet evident. But if sports have traditionally been closely tied to notions of community, what sense of attachment and identification can resident citizens and migrants have with each other?

These processes are not confined to England or to Europe, but are at work to greater or lesser degrees on a global basis. The 1990–91 NBA season's opening matches were held in Tokyo with the series being seen as 'a giant marketing test for the NBA'. Games were reported as having 'had an undeniable NBA stamp' (*Sports Illustrated*, 16 November 1990). This marketing image included official NBA clocks, baskets and floor, and the whole operation was supported by official NBA entertainment. The NBA Commissioner, David Stern, was reported as 'seeing the world as one big NBA supermarket' and Charles Grantham, the executive director of the NBA players' association, though conscious of the demands being increasingly made on American players, concluded, 'just think of this global picture as a big pie. The bigger the pie gets, the bigger the piece for the players' (*Sports Illustrated*, 16 November 1990). The squeezing out of indigenous players is overlooked by Grantham. Commenting on the marketing agreement reached between the NBA and a Japanese company, *Sports Illustrated* noted that 'last week's series was, in the words of Masanori Otsubo, a C. Itoh executive, "a kick off event" to promote the NBA in Japan. In other words, citizens of Japan, look for a blitz of those two big American T's – TV and T-shirts' (*Sports Illustrated*, 16 November 1990). The NBA subsequently realized that it was impracticable for them to administer franchise teams outside North America. By the mid-1990s they appeared content to accumulate revenue from the sale of clothing and other endorsed products while allowing local leagues to develop under the marketing arm of the NBA (Lyons, 1994). Ironically, the 1998/1999 lock-out of NBA players accelerated the involvement of North American players in European basketball (*Observer*, sport section, 16 November 1998: p. 13). Yet resistance to these processes, of a kind similar to that evident in the English case, may already be occurring. During the early 1990s some thirty leading American women basketball players lost their employment when the Japanese professional basketball league decided to ban foreigners (*Guardian*, 27 March 1993: p. 13). Similar processes of Americanization/commodification of Australian basketball have been highlighted by McKay et al. (1993).

In some ways, the operations of the NFL, the NBA and the NHL correspond to the marketing strategies of other large transnationals including the Disney Corporation and MacDonalds. Indeed, in ice hockey the Disney Corporation owns one major NHL franchise. While it is therefore correct to conclude that the globalization of sport is powered by the intended ideological and economic practices of specific groups of people from particular countries, its pattern and development cannot be explained solely with reference to these ideological practices. The interdependency chains that characterize globalization processes have intended and unintended dimensions. This issue will be returned to in subsequent chapters. As this chapter has shown there is evidence of contradictory cultural practices and patterns that cannot be explained with reference to some over-arching economic theory. In addition, reference to the resistance to and reinterpretation of the intended strategies of sport transnationals cannot be overlooked. Nevertheless, it is possible to conclude that it is along the lines of these cultural, economic, ideological and technological global flows that the speed, scale and volume of future sports labour migration will be contoured.

6

The Sports Industry, Global Commodity Chains and Sustainable Sport

> The globalization of Nike will certainly continue, in part because Global has become a Nike state of mind ... The completely global Nike will look much different than we look now, but we're closer all the time.
>
> Tom Clarke, Nike general manager; cited in Katz, 1994

The development of transnational sports industries is a significant feature of the global sport system. These industries involve a range of transnational corporations involved in the design, manufacture, production, distribution and marketing phases. Companies such as Nike, Reebok and Slazenger develop sports products including clothing, footwear and equipment which are consumed by large numbers of people across the globe. Changes to the urban, rural and wilderness landscapes occur as a result of the actions of the sports industry. The development of golf courses or new stadia, for example, changes the environment in significant ways – as a result of which a series of 'green' issues and environmental concerns surfaces in discussion of the global sports industries. How can we provide answers to these concerns and explain the development and patterns of this element of the global sport system?

In tracing broader globalization processes, emphasis in this book has been placed on the growing network of interdependencies that involve economic, political, cultural and technological dimensions. These chains of interdependency are marked by what Giddens (1986) would call features of 'time–space compression'. These features also characterize the commodity chains that tie the various strands of the sports industries together. Orders are placed 'just in time' for clothing or footwear niche markets created by beguiling mediated images. In addition, these interdependency chains are contoured and shaped by a series of unequal power-balances involving global transnational corporations, regional sub-contractors, sports organizations, media networks, workers and consumers. These chains crisscross the globe.

NHL ice hockey can illustrate some of the processes involved. As economist Robert Reich has observed, 'Precision ice hockey equipment is designed in Sweden, financed in Canada, and assembled in Cleveland and Denmark for distribution in North America and Europe, respectively, out of alloys whose molecular structure was researched and patented in Delaware and fabricated in Japan (Reich, 1991; cited in Sabo, 1993: pp. 2–3). Several transnational corporations are involved in the design, production and consumption phases of these globally endorsed NHL products. The appeal of slogans such as 'Planet Reebok', Nike's 'Just Do It' and Slazenger's 'Your Soul, Our System – The Spirit of Sport' hides the stark reality of the global sports industry. This chapter seeks to examine this reality.

Attention will be paid to the global sports industry market in general and to the operations of Nike in particular. While the actions of Nike illustrate the role of global subcontracting and flexibility in athletic footwear production (Donaghu & Barff, 1990), consideration will also be given to both the global ski industry and the British motor sports industry as further examples of the manufacture of sports equipment (Henry et al., 1996). This British industry and its development in what Henry et al. call a 'new industrial space' demonstrate how 'core' economies in specific sports can retain control over the design, production and distribution network within its own core, without sourcing to the Pacific Rim or elsewhere. The chapter concludes with an examination of the environmental concerns arising from the global sports industry and a mapping out of the notion of 'sustainable sport' (Chernushenko, 1994).

Interdependent Global Commodity Chains and the Sports Industry Complex

One of the key features of globalization in recent years has been the restructuring of the global economy. Increasingly, global networks of groups, organizations and regional blocs structure the production and distribution of goods and services (Dickens, 1992; Johnson et al., 1995). The term *global commodity chain* has been developed to capture production processes and the linkages that lie therein. While the production phase is clearly of importance, of equal concern is the role played by design, distribution and marketing 'nodes' within any global commodity chain (Korzeniewicz, 1994). For Korzeniewicz, a global commodity chain perspective 'helps us understand how marketing and consumption patterns in core areas of the world shape production patterns in peripheral and semi-peripheral countries' (Korzeniewicz, 1994: p. 247). While Korzeniewicz draws on a world-system model, the use of a global commodity chain perspective, with its emphasis on processes, linked networks and time–space dimensions, can be used here in conjunction with a process-sociological approach to understanding the sports industry complex.

These commodity chains – involving design, production and distribution – are clearly embedded in broader cultural patterns. Advertising, fashion and consumption shape the networks and crossover intersections of these global chains. Studying the global sports industry reveals important insights into broader concerns regarding these commodity chains. For example, companies such as Nike and Reebok have reshaped their production processes and focused company efforts on controlling the design, distribution, marketing and advertising phases. This links to their activities in other areas of the global sport system identified in this book, notably with regard to elite migrants and the media–sport complex. For Korzeniewicz the most fundamental innovation of sport companies over the past decade has been:

> the creation of a market, and this has entailed the construction of a convincing world of symbols, ideas, and values harnessing the desires of individuals to the consumption of athletic shoes. By focusing on the marketing and circulation nodes of a commodity chain, greater analytical precision can be gained in identifying the crucial features of these innovations.
>
> (Korzeniewicz, 1994: p. 251)

Clearly, these processes require further examination. While several studies focus on the athletic shoe segment of the industry, attention here will also be given to clothing and equipment. The social scientific study of the global sports industry is still in its early stages of development, and Jean Harvey and his Canadian colleagues have led the way in this regard (Harvey et al., 1996). In this context, attention will focus on the UK situation and what that market reveals about broader global patterns.

The UK sports industry complex involves both state and consumer expenditure. On the whole the expenditure by the state – at central and local government levels – centres on capital development and equipment. Increasingly, economic resources are funnelled into capital projects connected to major sports festivals and national/local facility development. Private clubs in a range of sports, most notably association football, are also involved in this capital investment. Such strategies bring with them a series of tensions and struggles regarding stadia redevelopment, relocation and design (Bale, 1994). Though worthy of sociological attention, issues surrounding sport, the stadia and the city will not be the focus of attention here (Maguire, 1995a). Rather, consideration will be given to the issue of consumer expenditure.

Consumers spend money on a range of services but of primary concern here is their expenditure on clothing, footwear and equipment. Of the total sports expenditure in the UK in 1995, amounting to some £2280 million, about 40 per cent was spent on clothing, 20 per cent on footwear and 40 per cent on equipment (*Mintel Special Report, Sport,* 1996). Expenditure on clothing increased during the 1990s: the development of high-tech fibres like Gore Tex and Lycra, and the increased market for replica association football kit, appears to account for at least part of this increase. During 1995, the UK market for sports clothing amounted to some £1400 million, equivalent to 6.5 per cent of the total expenditure on clothing in the country. As with footwear, sports clothing has increasingly become part of the leisure-wear market and consumer culture – particularly with regard to fleece tops, multilayered anoraks and waterproof clothing (*Mintel Special Report, Sport,* 1996). Using a global commodity chain perspective it can be observed that the UK mass market for sports clothing is satisfied by imported goods. Despite an increase in the importing of clothing from the Far East, EU countries still provide some 45 per cent of UK sportswear. The main brands, as with athletic shoes, tend to be Reebok, Nike and Adidas. The largest domestic producer is Umbro with UK sales in 1994 of some £57.9 million, increasing to £75.4 million in 1995 (*Mintel Special Report, Sport,* 1996). It should be noted, however, that Umbro is owned by US firm Stones Inc.

One of the major players in the UK market is the Pentland

Group, headed by Stephen Rubin, who became president of the World Federation of the Sporting Goods Industry in the late 1990s. This group owns companies such as Speedo, Mitre, Ellesse, Pony and Reusch. Perhaps due to the role of UK-based companies and the fact that EU countries provide a high share of imports, the sports clothing market has not prompted the degree of public or media criticism that the footwear area of the overall sports goods market has. With the exception of the criticism levelled at association football clubs for the excessive profits said to be being made on replica kit, none of the debates about the actions of the footwear subcontractors have surfaced in the clothing sector. It is to these debates that attention will now be turned.

As with the growing intersection between sport and consumer culture more broadly, the trend between the 1980s and the 1990s has been for athletic shoes, associated with a specific sport, to become part of all-purpose leisure wear. During the 1990s 'white trainers' became less fashionable in the UK market, and walking, hiking and climbing boots became the 'most dynamic segment' (*Mintel Special Report, Sport*, 1996: p. 21). Between the late 1980s and the mid-1990s this market segment grew from £100 million to £150 million. One of the other growth areas has been in shoes designed and marketed for the aerobics sector that women tend to dominate. Here, the American firm LA Gear is the major player.

Unlike the sports clothing industry, where British and European companies compete for market share, imports dominate and account for some 90 per cent of sales in the shoe sector (*Mintel Special Report, Sport*, 1996: p. 22). Even where 'British' brands exist, such as Hi-Tec, CICA and Mitre, the manufacturing of these athletic shoes takes place abroad. Overwhelmingly, these 'British' products, as well as US and European brands such as Adidas, Nike and Reebok, are produced in the Far East – in particular in Indonesia, South Korea, the Philippines, Taiwan, China and Thailand. A similar import profile is evident in the American market (Korzeniewicz, 1994; Sage, 1996). In the UK, Reebok is the top brand for women's sports wear. Nike, with a range of high-cost shoes, is also targeting association football as one of its growth areas in the late 1990s. In securing exclusive rights to the Brazilian national team, Nike, in order to enhance its own market share and profile, was able to dictate the playing schedule of the team in their build-up to the 1998 World Cup. The negative publicity that Nike received following revelations about the health of the Brazilian player Ronaldo on the day of the World Cup final in France shows how, even for the more powerful companies, events can overtake the best-laid marketing plans. In addition, the Nike brand is itself reported to have experienced a downturn in its fashionability. Susie Steiner, a writer for the *Daily Telegraph*, described this downturn in the following way:

> Re-structuring costs, including redundancies, have cost Nike £49 million and taken it to an overall loss of £41.7 million. There are those who blame the fashion backlash on Nike's own fervent advertising campaigns. The logo is everywhere and if it is every-where, it is no longer cool.
>
> (*Daily Telegraph*, 3 July 1998: p. 14)

It is these patterns of trade, marketing and degree of control over sport that have aroused most media attention. What are the issues involved? During the 1990s Western media attention began to focus on the activities of the athletic shoe companies. The operations of the subcontractors used by these leading firms were described as 'global sweatshops' (*Guardian*, 11 April 1994: p. 23). During the mid-1990s, Christian Aid, a British-based relief and development agency, commissioned and published research that offered a sustained critique of the actions of Reebok, Nike, Adidas and other major sports shoe companies. The main findings were:

1 Despite the intense rivalry between sports brands, rival products roll off parallel conveyor belts in factories in Southeast Asia.
2 While employment opportunities are created by these factories, the wages and conditions for the workers, especially child labour, often leave much to be desired.
3 Employment costs make up a fraction of the price of a pair of sports shoes. Reebok, Nike and others spend considerable amounts on the marketing, advertising and product endorse-ment phases of the global commodity chains.
4 Despite media and non-governmental organization pressure, corporate conduct suggests that, despite media public relations exercises, these companies do not take their share of respons-ibility for the people, mainly young women, who produce sports shoes. (Brookes & Madden, 1995)

Looking more closely at the details provided by the Christian Aid report, it is clear that the inequalities that exist along the global commodity chain involving athletic shoes are marked. In 1995 a typical pair of sports shoes would sell for £50 in Britain. The pro-duction process would involve forty or more factory workers who would share just over £1 between them. In the USA a Nike Air Pegasus shoe in the same year would retail at $70.00. Its ex-factory price was $14.95, of which $1.66 was labour costs (Brookes & Madden, 1995). In fact, two-thirds of the exports (by value) produced in the Far East go to the US market (Korzeniewicz, 1994). Initially, the major companies subcontracted to Taiwan and South Korea. Increasingly, however, such operations have been moved to lower labour cost countries such as China and Indonesia, notwithstanding the social and economic upheavals experienced by the latter during 1998. Three areas of concern were identified by the Christian Aid report. These were: discrimination against trade unions; forced overtime; and the hiring/firing policy of the companies concerned. Clearly these are issues that require detailed examination. Work by researchers such as Sage has begun this task. As Sage rightly concludes:

> The export manufacturing operations of companies that produce licensed merchandise under contracts with professional team sports have been built on a model that places profits over workers' needs, features violations of the human rights of workers, and often results in pervasive and cruel suppression of those workers. Corporations that make licensed merchandise and the pro sport industry that profits from the sales of this merchandise need to be evaluated by the slogan used by organized labor throughout the world: 'An injury to one is an injury to all'.
>
> (Sage, 1996: p. 8)

To what extent are these observations applicable to the sports shoe industry? As has been observed, Nike plays a crucial role in this industry. Along with several other companies, it is sensitive to charges of exploitation but evidence in this regard is being accumulated (Sage, 1995). Studying Nike also reveals important elements regarding global commodity chains more broadly. Identifying several phases in global commodity chains (design, obtaining and processing raw materials, manufacturing, import/export distribution, marketing and advertising), Korzeniewicz notes how Nike have ceded control over the raw material and manufacturing phases to local manufacturers, but through the other phases they promote 'the symbolic nature of the shoe and appropriate the greater share of the value resulting from its sales' (Korzeniewicz, 1994: p. 261). The global sports shoe commodity chain highlights complex transnational linkages at different stages of production and distribution. More importantly, as Korzeniewicz observes, it is the marketing and advertising that have driven the other phases in the commodity chain:

Marketing, advertising, and consumption trends dictate what will be manufactured, how it will be manufactured, and where it will be manufactured. In explaining Nike Corporation's success, manufacturing processes are secondary to the control over the symbolic nature and status of athletic shoes. A more refined breakdown of the service activities involved in the commodity chain improves the understanding of the different economic rewards accrued by core, semiperiphery and periphery organizations and groups.

(Korzeniewicz, 1994: p. 263)

Clearly the sales of athletic shoes are not due simply to the technical qualities of the shoe *per se*. In referring to the 'symbolic nature and status of athletic shoes' Korzeniewicz is demonstrating how the advertising associated with the marketing of Nike shoes carries a series of cultural messages. These messages relate to how products are marketing and consumed in consumer culture more generally (Featherstone, 1991b). The slogan 'Just Do It' dovetails well with the hedonism associated with consumer culture. These observations seem to be borne out by Nike's own declared position. Focusing on the issue of marketing, Phil Knight, founder and chairman of Nike, provided an important glimpse into the corporate logic of the company:

The way I relate to marketing is as sociology. What Nike does well is interpret what people are doing, what they are interested in, and we've been lucky enough to align ourselves completely with what we perceive ... For us, marketing is building awareness around the products and reminding people what we do.

(Knight, cited in Katz, 1994: pp. 150–1)

What they don't do is the manufacturing and, according to Christian Aid, that leads to a situation where subcontractors to Nike exploit Far Eastern workers. In studying this global commodity chain then, important clues can be gained regarding the relative distribution of rewards that flow between established and outsider groups. As the Christian Aid report emphasizes, the main winners appear to be transnational corporations.

The third segment of the global sports goods industry involves the manufacturing and marketing of sports equipment. This includes the more usual forms of equipment such as golf clubs, tennis and badminton rackets and outdoor climbing and ski equipment. In 1995, the sale of equipment represented 18 per cent of the UK sports goods market, golf equipment, with £180 million sales, being the most lucrative. In contrast to the athletic shoe market, in equipment the UK has retained a domestic manufacturing base – notably in cricket, snooker, darts, golf and outdoor athletics equipment. Fifty per cent of this production goes for export, with Dunlop Slazenger being a major exporter. In keeping with the more general global commodity chain of the sports industry, the manufacture of equipment also occurs to a significant degree in the Far East. Imports from this region account for 60 per cent of the overall UK imports. Unlike in other segments of the sports industry market, however, Far Eastern companies do not simply act as subcontractors for Western corporations. In some instances, this goes against the general idea of dependent development: Far Eastern companies, such as Mizumo and Daiwa in Japan and Pro-Kennex in Taiwan, are involved at all phases in the global commodity chain. While this may represent but the first, and a small, challenge to Western domination, it is clear that similar issues about worker exploitation also surface in this segment of the sports industry. This is most vividly highlighted with regard to the manufacture of soccer balls.

During the mid-1990s increased media attention was given to the use of child labour in the manufacture of soccer balls in Pakistan (*Sunday Times*, 14 May 1995: p. 6; *Guardian*, 12 May 1997: p. 3; *Guardian*, 11 December 1997: p. 15). Such negative publicity forced the issue of child labour onto the agenda of several non-governmental organizations including Save the Children Fund and Christian Aid. Faced with such criticism, both FIFA and the World Federation of the Sporting Goods Industry (WFSGI) were forced onto the defensive and felt that they had to be seen to be acting to resolve the exploitative practices on the Asian subcontinent. In a series of meetings, notably the Verbier conference in November 1995, the London conference in November 1996 and the Atlanta meeting in February 1997, the WFSGI, along with organizations such as the International Labour Organization, UNICEF and Save the Children Fund (UK), agreed to seek to eliminate child labour in Pakistan's soccer ball industry. Given that Pakistan is the production base of 75 per cent of the annual sales of hand-stitched soccer balls, this step, if implemented, would be significant. The WFSGI themselves claim:

> The agreement signed on February 14th 1997 marks the first time that multinational corporations and their local suppliers of any global industry have joined force with international organizations such as the International Labour Organization (ILO), UNICEF and non-government organizations such as Save the Children (UK) to address the problem of child labor ... More than 50 sporting goods brands connected with soccer – including virtually all the major

global brands – have pledged to purchase soccer balls produced in Pakistan only from local manufacturers who participate in the monitoring program.
(Official International Handbook for the Sporting Goods Industry, 1998: p. 6)

It is too early to tell if these claims are more than a publicity relations exercise. In order to monitor the effectiveness of this agreement and the proposed programme, it is clear that the role of non-government organizations such as Christian Aid will remain important. Whatever the merits of this specific agreement, the main funding for which stems from the US and UK governments and UNESCO, the evidence accumulated by Christian Aid regarding the conduct of the transnational companies involved in the sporting goods industry does suggest that a degree of scepticism is possible regarding some of the more general claims made by the WFSGI:

> Perhaps more than any other industry, the world sporting goods community has taken the lead in identifying and addressing the ethical and related challenges that arise in the globalized economy in which our industry competes. This leadership has involved a remarkable series of new relationships and partnerships that will place the sporting goods industry at the forefront of socially responsible sourcing and ethical trading practices.
> *(Official International Handbook for the Sporting Goods Industry, 1998: p. 4)*

With such claims in mind, future research will have a powerful benchmark by which to judge the actual practices of transnational companies involved in the global sporting goods commodity chain. Although this chapter has pointed to the role of Far East subcontractors in the raw material and manufacturing phases, with the attendant control of other phases by Western multinationals, this situation is not the same in all sports. The examples of ski-racing equipment and of the Formula One motor-racing industry suggest important qualifications to the general picture so far provided. High-tech equipment design, manufacturing and marketing in these sports still resides within the West.

Throughout the 1960s and into the 1970s Austrian firms such as Fischer, Blizzard, Nordica, Atomic and Kästle dominated the production of ski equipment. By the 1990s this ownership and control pattern had changed; French companies such as Rossignol and Salomon currently dominate. Former Austrian companies such as Atomic are now owned by the Finnish Amer group, headed by the Swede Johan Eliason, and Kästle is controlled by the Italian clothing firm Benetton. Only in a small number of cases has European control been challenged. Fischer, for example, has retained its independent Austrian status, though 30 per cent is now owned by Japanese concerns. Similarly, while Rossignol and Salomon dominate in integrated ski, boot and binding systems, they are being challenged in the ski and snowboard segment of the market by the American firm K2 (*Panorama*, 1997: pp. 17–22).

The annual ski and snowboard turnover for the Rossignol group in 1997 was reported to be $433 million; it leads in sales but Salomon targets higher-value ski products and its sales amounted to some $587 million in the same period. Though there have been internal changes in ownership and control, in this high-tech segment of the sports industry the Europeans remain the significant players at all phases of the global commodity chain. A similar situation exists in the British motor-sport industry.

Drawing on work by Henry et al. (1996), it is clear that the British motor-sport industry is an example of a dynamic, localized core economy that dominates the design and manufacturing phases of Formula One racing. Its study provides further insights into the global pattern of the sports industry. This requires elaboration. Though Italian and French companies such as Ferrari and Renault play a significant part in the industry, it is British firms that dominate and have done so throughout the 1990s. The Formula One constructors championship has been won by British firms in thirty-one out of the last forty years. Over the past decade the championship has been won repeatedly by either Williams or McLaren and in 1998 no fewer than nine out of the eleven teams in Formula One were British based.

This domination is reflected at several stages in the development of a Formula One car – including its design, assembly, engine and components sections. Despite competition from firms such as Renault and Honda, the major engine suppliers are British based, and include Cosworth and Ilmor, the latter also supplying 'Mercedes' engines for Indycar Racing. Indeed, in 1994, in this US-based form of racing, all of the teams used a car designed and built in Britain (Henry et al., 1996). Even in non-UK teams such as Ferrari, British designers and engineers such as Patrick Head play a prominent part. As well as the better-known teams such as McLaren, Williams, Jordan and, more recently, Stewart Racing, there exists a network of small and medium-sized firms that provide parts for the chassis, gearboxes, drive-by-wire throttles and active suspension systems used in Formula One.

This network involves what Henry et al. (1996) describe as a 'set of geographically concentrated, technologically advanced SMEs (small to medium enterprises) undergoing rapid growth on the back of success in international markets' (Henry et al., 1996: p. 28). Despite the more general decline of the UK's industrial base during the 1980s and 1990s, this sector of the British motor-sport industry has developed into an example of an 'untraded interdependency' that comprises 'conventions, rules, practices and institutions which combine to produce both possible and real "worlds of production" which present the action trajectories for firms within a world of uncertainty' (Henry et al., 1996: p. 31).

The key to these 'untraded interdependencies', especially the highly localized British motor-sport industry centred on southern England, is 'knowledge-intensiveness', a 'local world of product knowledge' that allows rival firms to remain competitive. Knowledge seeps through to other firms through the movement of drivers, designers, engineers and administrators. This knowledge is not bought or sold but, nevertheless, those involved are caught up in a network that binds them to each other. These processes not only assist specific firms but also allow the British motor-sport industry as a whole to maintain its global competitive advantage (Henry et al., 1996). Insights of this kind not only reveal the complex and diverse nature of the interdependencies that characterize the global sports industry but also highlight how social and cultural factors have to be considered in seeking to understand economic success or failure. Such insights are also relevant to understanding broader globalization processes. This knowledge-intensive, high-technology industry not only holds a monopolistic position relative to other European competitors, but also ensures that non-Western nations, including Japan, find it very difficult, though not impossible, to challenge such control.

Given the vested interests at stake this should not be surprising. The ownership and control of Formula One motor-racing is a complex affair. Up until 1987 Formula One had been governed by the Fédération Internationale de l'Automobile (FIA). Led by Jean-Marie Balestre, the 1987 Concorde Agreement resulted in the FIA receiving for the first time 30 per cent of Formula One's television revenue in return for leasing the sports commercial rights to the British entrepreneur, Bernie Ecclestone. During the late 1980s television revenue was relatively small and the FIA's income was less than $1m a year. Balestre, nervous about what he felt was the precarious nature of this income renegotiated the deal and the FIA were then to receive a royalty as opposed to a fixed percentage. This 30 per cent share was sold to Allsop, Parker and Marsh (APM), an Irish company owned by Patrick McNally – a figure who had connections with the sports marketing world more generally.

Income for the FIA did increase. In 1992 the figure was $5.6m rising to just over $9m in 1996 (*Financial Times*, 16 November 1988: p. 21). During the 1990s, however, instead of television revenues decreasing, such income into the sport soared. Between 1992 and 1996, TV revenues raised by Ecclestone totalled some $341m, with 30 per cent going to APM and McNally. By 1997 the FIA President Max Moseley renegotiated the agreement, this time with Ecclestone back as the key player. Under the new agreement the FIA still receive a royalty payment – in 1997 amounting to $9m. Yet gross television revenues amounted to $225m, the 30 per cent option giving FIA a $67m share. Moseley's decision to stay with the royalty option is bound up in the strategy of the motor-racing teams – with Ecclestone as the controlling figure – to float the Formula One business on the Stock Exchange. In return for this agreement, the FIA have secured $100m from the $2bn Eurobond flotation that Ecclestone has proposed. The FIA insiders were heavily aware of both the huge potential income and the work associated with Formula One. As with other sports, Formula One has become global, with two jumbo jets carrying the 22 teams of technicians, their racing cars and equipment around the globe. In any case, all rights to Formula One, from TV coverage to merchandising, revert to the FIA in 2002 when the governing body's commercial agreement with Ecclestone ends. Given this, and the role of Western multinational automobile firms, it is little surprise that non-Western companies have difficulty breaking this stranglehold. Yet, this globalized deregulated sport has attracted the attention of the European Commission. Not only are more stringent regulations regarding tobacco advertising threatening television revenues and direct sponsorship of teams, but the European Commission is also examining potential breaches of EU competition rules. The outcome of this struggle will provide a telling case regarding how national and supranational authorities try to regulate global capitalist concerns.

Sports Industry Development, Green Issues and the Global Environment

The need to adopt a 'global perspective' on human affairs is no better emphasized than with reference to environmental concerns. Across the world there is a growing awareness of environmental problems that affect humanity as a whole. These include the depletion of the globe's ozone layer, global warming, the dumping of various materials (nuclear, toxic and non-toxic) on land and in the seas, air and water pollution, urban sprawl and ecological damage to natural habitats, such as rainforests, alpine regions and tundra (Yearley, 1996). A related environmental issue is resource depletion of energy, minerals, soil and water. With such pressures on the global environment it is little surprise that commentators and scientists have become alarmed at the loss of biodiversity. Given this, as Yearley concludes, there are:

> Good grounds for regarding environmental problems as increasingly globalized. Modern pollution is very literally, in Robertson's terms, 'compressing' the world as, for instance, nations are obliged to worry about what their neighbours are doing about air pollution and emission control. The diminution of resources and the loss of species are making people aware that there are global limits to the things and the creatures which they count on. To some extent at least, these considerations are giving citizens, government and corporations a sense that there are real global ties and, perhaps, in principle at least a global identity for the occupants of spaceship Earth.
> (Yearley, 1996: p. 59)

How are sports players implicated in these processes? That is, how do these problems manifest themselves in and/or are exacerbated by sport cultures and to what extent are sports performers, administrators and consumers aware of this interrelationship? Despite the acknowledged impact that sport has on the environment, little attention has been paid to this issue in the sociology of sport (Bale, 1994: pp. 40–6). Clearly, the environment is affected by the way that sport is practised – whether this be as a result of ski development in alpine regions, golf-course development in the Far East or the by-products of the sports industry that produce the goods consumed by participants and spectators who then create waste products that go into landfills.

In a pioneering text on sport and environmental issues, David Chernushenko has captured several key issues in a thought-provoking manner. He argues:

> The sports 'industry', despite its enormous global economic impact and its inordinate influence on so many economic and societal decisions, is rarely recognized for what it is: a multi-billion dollar provider of goods and services to much of the world's population. While the nature of those goods and services can be relatively benign, their collective impact is both significant and wide-ranging. From ski resort development to stadium construction to running shoe manufacturing, the sports industry leaves a sizeable footprint on the planet. Just how big that footprint is, and how permanent depends on the way in which the industry conducts its activities.
> (Chernushenko, 1994: pp. 5–6)

How the sports industry conducts its activities and the impact they have on the environment vary according to the sport. However, certain common issues can be identified. Deteriorating environmental conditions make the playing of particular sports more difficult; sometimes the necessary land or water conditions simply no longer exist. In addition, air and water pollution put the health of athletes in jeopardy. For example, the British national water-sports centre in Nottingham has been closed on several occasions due to poor water quality. Yet, sport also impacts on the local and the global environment. One person's run through a forest creates little impact, but when that develops into a running, cycle and triathlon trail then the impact grows accordingly. Communities also resist the development of some sports facilities in 'protected' areas and action groups resist the granting of the Olympic Games to their city or region; examples include the activities of environmental groups surrounding the Toronto and Stockholm bids for the Summer Olympics. Even where facilities already exist, major sporting events consume vast amounts of energy and produce considerable amounts of waste. As Chernushenko (1994: p. 23) observes, a typical American football/baseball game adds between 30,000 and 50,000 disposable cups to the local landfill. Sport-resort development, whether it be skiing, golf or water-based, leads to destruction of natural vegetation, soil erosion, chemical pollution, loss of natural habitat, waste generation, increased energy demands and, at the very least, the disruption of wildlife, flora and fauna.

Both golf and skiing have attracted the attention of environmental protesters. The environmental impact of the 1992 Winter Olympic Games in Albertville has been heavily criticized (Chernushenko, 1994: p. 28). European alpine ski developments are increasingly coming under closer scrutiny but the development of golf courses in the Far East, though resisted by the 'Global Anti-Golf Movement', continues apace – despite the recent downturn in the 'tiger economies' of the Pacific Rim. In Japan alone, golf-course development led in the 1980s to 5000 hectares of forest being destroyed annually. By 1990 Japan had 1706 golf courses, with 325 more under construction; that trend continues to grow during the 1990s (Chernushenko, 1994: p. 25).

Despite the impact environmental changes have had on sport and the effect that the sports industry has on the environment, few senior officials in sports governing bodies appear to take the issues identified seriously – or certainly do not make them a priority in their future planning. There are exceptions. Article Ten of the European Sports Charter, entitled Sport and Sustainable Development, argues that:

Ensuring and improving people's physical, social and mental well-being from one generation to the next requires that sporting activities including those in urban, open country and water areas be adjusted to the planet's limited resources and be carried out in accordance with the principles of sustainable development and balanced management of the environment.

(European Sports Charter, Council of Europe, 1992)

In this light, the organizers of the 1994 Winter Olympic Games in Lillehammer, Norway, set out to structure and organize the range of activities involved – stadia construction, land use, energy consumption and waste management – to minimize the environmental footprint that Chernushenko refers to. Arguing that the way in which sport is presently practised is 'not sustainable', Chernushenko (1994: pp. 76–91) cogently outlines several principles for 'sustainable sport'. Sport practices become sustainable when materials and energy sources are used in continuous cycles without cumulative degradation of the environment. To achieve this the sport community as a whole must grasp that the principles of conservation, stewardship, eco-efficiency and partnership must be combined with responsibility, accountability and a decision-making process that is democratic and which emphasizes active living, ecosystem diversity and investment in the future. Hedonistic slogans such as 'Just Do It' simply won't create the conditions in which sustainable sport can develop. As Chernushenko concludes, 'Any harm done by the sport industry to the planet is thus a strike against the future of sport itself' (1994: p. 77).

This chapter has sought to critically examine the impact that the sports industry has in economic, cultural and environmental terms. Bound up in broader global concerns there are questions concerning human rights, exploitation of workers in a range of dependent countries and environmental impacts that members of the sport community rarely consider, let alone address. Yet, the sport community in the West, and elsewhere, must begin to tackle not only those issues that impinge on their experience of the global sport process but how that process impinges on the lives of their fellow human beings. Otherwise, to use a Victorian cliché, 'it's just not sport'. Clearly, much more research needs to be done and, in doing so, social scientists of sport have a responsibility to raise an awareness of these issues as and when they can. Using the reality-congruent knowledge generated by their research, social scientists can challenge both the beguiling appeal of market research and advertising and the siren voices of neo-liberal politicians who seemingly see the planet as humankind's playground. This chapter is but a small contribution to this task.

7

The Global Media–Sport Complex

We hope to revive some of the ancient traditions, bringing in a
cultural aspect which is very important, but also bringing in
the 'Olympic Truce'. In a new century, where we live in the
global village, the Olympic Games is the one event which
brings people together in the world. Not just governments, but
citizens of the world, and the man in the street (*sic*) through
television and the media in this one local festival. So it is very
important what message comes out of this . . .

Greek European Affairs Minister George Papandreou,
commenting on the Greek hosting of the 2004 Olympic Games,
Guardian, World Report 27 June 1998

Where sporting events were once localized affairs, news of which
barely filtered through to neighbouring villages, as we approach
the end of the twentieth century modern elite sports competitions
are global media spectacles. Examples include the Olympic Games,
the World Championships in track and field and soccer's World
Cup. By the early 1990s nearly 200 countries were receiving broadcasts of these events (*European TV Sports Databook*: p. 4). Specific
cases demonstrate the scale of what is involved. Television coverage of the Winter Olympics at Lillehammer, Norway, was received
in over 120 countries with a cumulative audience estimated at 10.7
billion people. The actual amount of sport coverage, on both terrestrial and satellite channels, also continues to grow. Between 1989
and 1995 European sport coverage increased from 24,000 hours to
some 58,000 hours annually (*European TV Sports Databook*: p. 9).
People are consuming more and more global media–sport

products. Media sport is also big business in terms of television advertising, merchandising and the sale of exclusive rights to specific events, leagues or tournaments. Given this, two points are clear: the development of the global sport 'system' is closely connected to the emergence of global media communications and the contemporary experience of sport is intertwined with global media concerns. How are we to make sense of global media sport?

As with studies of the mass media in general, the global media–sport complex can be explained by reference to the homogenization/Westernization/Americanization strand of the globalization debate. The merits of this line of argument were addressed in chapter 1. How much purchase does this approach have in connection to media sport matters? At first sight, examination of the patterns of the ownership and control of global media companies, consideration of the meanings attached to global media–sport content, and analysis of the images associated with media sport would lend itself to such an interpretation. Evidence to support such a position could be drawn from how American media concerns such as ABC and NBC influence the IOC's decision-making; American sports such as American football, basketball and baseball are packaged, marketed and franchised to and for a global audience, and American sporting heroes such as Michael Jordan become, through media marketing, global figures, promoting specific brands such as Nike. Jordan's image is consumed across the globe (Andrews et al., 1996). Yet, as noted earlier, a degree of sociological caution needs to be exercised over claims regarding the Americanization thesis and 'postmodern' discourse about it.

What is not in doubt is that sport has spread across the globe, that its administration and organization are global in scale and that the scope of the sport system's interconnectedness is global in nature. As such it meets the three conditions of globalization identified by Thompson (1995). Media networks and communications systems have played a significant part in this process and some writers have gone so far as to argue that 'the media are American'. This case can, however, be overstated.

The homogenization or Americanization thesis arguably overstates the degree of uniformity achieved and underestimates how global media content is understood and (re)interpreted by people in different societies. Indeed, other qualifiers to the general argument need to be stated. Global media–sport products may be resisted, misunderstood and/or 'recycled', and thus be subject to a process of hybridization. As with sport development more generally, the concepts of 'diminishing contrasts and increasing varieties' can provide a way of sensitizing us to these seemingly paradoxical tendencies.

Given these observations, several questions regarding media sport and the homogenization/Americanization thesis need to be addressed. What constitutes Westernization and/or Americanization? Is it simply a question of the presence of a cultural product from a 'foreign' culture or does it involve a shift in the habitus and conscious make-up of people? How 'intended' is the process described? How complete does the process have to be for domination to be said to have occurred? What abilities do people have to understand, embrace and/or resist these processes? What constitutes the 'indigenous/authentic' culture that the foreign culture threatens? In order to address these questions, and to map out how media sport has become part of the global sport process, this chapter will examine the available evidence with regard to three key areas: the production of media–sport cultural goods; the form and content of sport-mediated products and text; and the meaning and significance of the consumer consumption of sport. For this purpose, an examination of a specific sport will be undertaken that can act as a 'critical case study'. That is, in order to assess the relative merits of the different approaches to global media–sport issues, the spread and diffusion of American football will be considered. In this way, an overall assessment of global media sport as part of the more general sportization process will be developed.

Sport, the Media and Global Cultural Flows

In exploring global media sport several key points of departure need to be stressed. First, the nature and extent of the interdependencies involved must be traced and located within wider global developments. The media flow is a part of the interdependent global sport system that Part II of this book seeks to explore. Other global flows that structure this system include technology, capital, migrant labour and national symbols and ideologies. This system involves what Sklair (1991) terms transnational practices. Transnational practices, which take a variety of cultural forms, gain a degree of *relative autonomy* on a global level. These transnational processes sustain the exchange and flow of goods, people, information, knowledge and images. By utilizing terms such as *transnational*, a second main point can be made. The analysis being presented is moving beyond the nation-state as the sole reference point for understanding the growing 'integration' of the world. The media–sport production complex is an integral part of this general process. Think of the technological advances involved in the media coverage of the modern Olympics and how satellites now relay powerful images across the globe in an instant. For Real (1989a), these images reflect and help sustain the emergence of a global culture, however briefly and superficially.

The relative autonomy of these transnational practices needs to be linked to what Appadurai (1990) has termed the 'disjunctures' that occur as global flows crisscross each other. In recognizing this, a third point can be made. These 'disjunctures' are part of the figurational dynamics that lead to a whole series of *unintended* features of the global sport system. This global sport system possesses a relatively autonomous dynamic that is not dominated by any one group. Notwithstanding this, it is important not to overlook a related point concerning global media sport. Transnational practices are prone to attempts to control and regulate them. This can involve the actions of transnational agencies or individuals from the 'transnational capitalist class' (Sklair, 1991). Transnational organizations such as the IOC, FIFA and the IAAF, agencies such as the IMG and ISL, media corporations such as NBC, Eurosport and News International, and transnational companies such as Reebok and Nike, seek to regulate the cultural flows involved. Individuals who belong to the 'transnational capitalist class' (Samaranch, Nebiolo, McCormack, Murdoch) are also centrally involved as some of the key players whose plans and actions interweave in attempting to develop a global media–sport complex. Such interventions cause cultural struggles of various kinds and at different levels.

If these last two points are taken as interrelated, it can be observed that an analysis of global media sport has to examine *both* the intended and the unintended aspects of its development. The intended acts of representatives of transnational agencies or the transnational capitalist class are potentially more significant in the *short term*. Over the *long term*, however, the unintended, relatively autonomous transnational practices stressed in point three may predominate. These practices 'structure' the subsequent plans and actions of transnational agencies and the transnational capitalist class. As has been argued throughout this text, globalization processes involve a blend between intended and unintended practices.

The impact that global media–sport practices have on the global sport system should not be underestimated. Though such transnational practices cannot be explained solely by reference to nation-states, a fifth point regarding global media sport needs to be stated. The global media complex is influenced by American practice in sports such as American football, basketball and base-ball. Such practices have forced a range of sports, such as soccer and rugby, to align themselves to this model. Failure to do so would place in question their ability to survive in the global media marketplace. Questions concerning the political economy of global media sport cannot be avoided and need addressing. Despite pointing to the influence of American media models, it would be foolish to suggest that such practices are all-pervasive or not resisted and that the consumption of the products that flow from this media–sport complex is accomplished in an uncritical manner that does not reflect 'local' culture and circumstances. Exponents of cultural studies rightfully remind us of how meaning is pro-duced in and through particular expressive forms and how it is continually negotiated and deconstructed through the practices of everyday life (Fiske, 1989; Golding & Murdock, 1991; Turner, 1990).

On this basis, research concerning global media sport has to focus on both an analysis of cultural texts and the way that people in different societies interpret media artefacts and incorporate them into their worldview and lifestyles. A sixth point concerning global media sport can thus be made. While there is a political economy of media sport, global audiences are composed of know-ledgeable, creative active agents. Consumption involves an active process of interpretation and, at times, of resistance and rejection. Global media products relate to how local circumstances allow people to make sense of and give meaning to their particular situ-ation. At issue, therefore, is the role of popular culture both in the reproduction of global capitalist social relations and in resistance to those relations. These themes surface repeatedly in studies of sport, leisure and popular culture (Gruneau, 1988; Cantelon & Hollands, 1988; Rowe, 1996).

In highlighting how people across the globe are engaged in the practice of winning meaning and creating space from and within global media–sport consumption, a seventh point regarding these processes can be made. There is a danger in over-emphasizing the sovereignty of the consumer. At times the romantic celebration of resistance appears at odds with examining the way the mass media operate 'ideologically' to sustain and support the prevailing relations of domination. Attention also needs to be paid to how the global media–sport complex operates as an industry. By focusing only on the meaning of consumption, the transnational practices that impinge on the production and circulation of meaning and the ways in which people's consumption choices are structured by their position in the wider global formation can be neglected.

These links are important in studying globalization and the media–sport complex (Gruneau, 1989b; Jhally, 1989; Tomlinson, 1996; Wenner, 1989).

These seven, seemingly paradoxical, points of departure are meant to emphasize how the exploration of global media sport must avoid becoming trapped in false dichotomies and using uni-dimensional and monocausal analyses. A sensitivity to local responses to global flows has to be stressed. But so does the balance of power between the groups involved. Given these points of departure, three 'core tasks' can be identified that can serve to assess local/global processes involved in global media sport. These are an examination of the production of media–sport cultural goods, study of the political economy of sport mediated texts and a focus on the politico-economic aspect of consumer consumption.

The Production of Media–Sport Cultural Goods

Research in this area probes how changes in the array of groups that exercise control over cultural production and distribution limit or liberate what Golding and Murdock term the 'public sphere'. Two key issues arise in this connection. The pattern of ownership of and the consequences of this pattern for the control of cultural production must be traced. Consideration must also be given to the nature of the relationship between state regulation and the communications industry. There is not enough space here to review how these issues are dealt with in the study of the media, culture and leisure (Golding & Murdock, 1991; Critcher, 1992). Here attention will focus on the global sport arena. The global media–sport complex is arguably made up of three key groups. These groups are the sports organizations, media/market-ing organizations and personnel, and trans- or multinational cor-porations. The nature of the interdependency between them has varied over time and within and between continents (Whannel, 1989). There are, for example, important differences in this regard between North America and Europe. Indeed, in the USA there is greater cross-ownership of sport and media organizations than currently exists in Europe (Jhally, 1989). The involvement in the late 1980s and early 1990s of the late Robert Maxwell, Bernard Tapie and Silvio Berlusconi with a range of media and sports industry interests and with European soccer clubs, including Derby County, Olympique de Marseille and Associazione Calcio Milan, were clearly exceptions to this. Further, the nature of this interrelationship also varies from one sport to the next.

Some sports organizations, notably in well-established male sports, are more successful than others. All sports organizations, including the IOC, tend to negotiate separately with the media (Jackson & McPhail, 1989; Rowe et al., 1994; Tomlinson & Whannel, 1984; Whannel, 1992b). The ownership and control of global media sport rests with a few transnational corporations (Jhally, 1989). Sports have a largely dependent role in this media–sport complex. That is, sports organizations have little or no control over the nature and form in which 'their' sport is televised, reported or covered (Goldlust, 1987). This dependency on the media has grown over time and is arguably connected to sports organizations' increasing reliance on revenues from sponsorship and marketing (Jhally, 1984; Wenner, 1989). This is not always the case. As will be shown in the case study that follows, the relative power of the NFL in its negotiations with the media ensures that it has greater influence over the mediated sport product it helps to produce.

Traditional sources of revenue, for example spectator receipts and patronage, have declined in importance (Dunning, 1992c). Sports organizations have to ensure that they gain sufficient exposure and are visible in the sponsorship and endorsement marketplace. Media coverage secures this. The hegemonic position enjoyed by specific sports within this global media–sport complex requires less powerful sports to conform to the style and form in which the dominant sports are displayed. The glitz and spectacle of the NFL and the NBA become *the* benchmark by which other sports are judged (Andrews, 1997; Barnett, 1990; Goldlust, 1987; Larson & Park, 1993). The size of recent franchise sales indicates just what is at stake. In the NFL, for example, the Tampa Bay Buccaneers were sold in 1995 for $192 million; in the NBA, the Dallas Mavericks were sold for $125 million, while in the NHL, the Los Angeles Kings were sold for $119 million, again during 1995 (*Kagan World Media*, 1995). Since other sports have to 'survive' in such a marketplace, they adopt marketing strategies and business ethics the same as or similar to those associated with American sports production (Goldlust, 1987; Jhally, 1984; Lawrence & Rowe, 1986).

Media–sport production is also strongly influenced by commercial strategies built around 'synergies' that exploit the overlaps between a company's different media interests. These cannot be completely mapped here (Klatell & Marcus, 1988; Whannel, 1992b), but specific examples can serve to illustrate what is involved. Murdoch's sport and media empire is a case in point. Already the owner of extensive sport and media concerns in

Europe and Australasia, he is currently attempting to broaden his interests in the USA through the acquisition of a share in the Los Angeles Lakers basketball club. This would complement his ownership of several other US sports teams, including the Los Angeles Dodgers (baseball), the New York Knicks (basketball) and the New York Rangers (ice hockey). He also owns the Fox TV network. Presumably the building of this elaborate media–sport network will not stop here as Fox Group officials freely talk of taking over as many prime sports franchises as will be allowed by the various leagues (*Guardian*, 4 April 1998: p. 24). Indeed, during 1998 Murdoch and his company BSkyB have agreed to pay £623.4m for the English soccer club Manchester United. This move has not gone unopposed. Fan groups have protested against this takeover and the British government has referred the matter to the Office of Fair Trading, thereby raising questions concerning monopoly control. If this office concludes there is a case to answer, then the takeover will be examined by the Monopolies and Mergers Commission.

Similar processes were at work in the spread of American football to England. Interweaving of the actions of satellite broadcasters and newspaper and magazine proprietors is also evident in the spread of American football to continental Europe (Maguire, 1991). Likewise, in the NHL, the Los Angeles Kings, who as noted were sold for $119 million, are owned by the Disney Corporation who use their marketing to promote the club and the consumption of products related to the team. This interweaving of media, marketing, sponsor and sport organization commercial interests is vividly evident with regard to the Olympic movement (Klatell & Marcus, 1988; Jackson & McPhail, 1989; Larson & Park, 1993; Tomlinson & Whannel, 1984; Tomlinson, 1996). Connections can be traced with ISL, the marketing agent for the IOC, the companies recruited to the TOP sponsorship programme, the involvement of Coca Cola, the awarding of the games to Atlanta and the presence in that city of Ted Turner and news network CNN (Barnett, 1990; Whannel, 1992a). It should be observed that Turner then owned Atlanta's baseball and basketball teams, the Braves and the Hawks. Whannel (1992b) has shown how *Time/Sports Illustrated*, who were then a TOP programme sponsor, planned a special edition on the Olympics and devoted coverage to it in its regular sports service.

In the light of this research evidence, four main features of global media sport can be identified. Sport has become more compliant with media demands (Goldlust, 1987). Related to this it is clear that media–sport coverage has undergone a process of spectacularization (Sewart, 1987). Sport has also become a commodity whose media value is determined by the size and composition of the audience it can deliver to potential advertisers and sponsors of media broadcasts (Gruneau, 1989a; Klatell & Marcus, 1988; McKay & Rowe, 1997). There is also a trend towards establishing global media sports, such as American football, basketball, baseball and ice hockey (Maguire, 1991, 1996).

These processes have been accelerated by both the deregulation of media broadcasting and the growth in media forms (cable, satellite, video and pay per view). Network organizations able to deliver sports coverage to all homes with a television now compete in this new market with aggressive competitors. One consequence has been a narrowing of the public sphere of media sport broadcasting. Put simply, satellite broadcasters such as BSkyB (Sky Sport) and Eurosport have managed to secure sole rights for important sports events. These sports are then shown to a narrow sector of the viewing public. The consequences of this are evident in the scramble for rights to cover English soccer in the late 1990s. These processes may well accelerate in the first decade of the new century. Sky Sport has won out in the struggle to control access to English Premier League soccer.

The success of this Murdoch-owned company should not be underestimated. Sky Sport has not only exclusive rights to Premier League soccer but also to English rugby union and the European club competitions in that sport. Sky Sport also controls coverage of British and NBA basketball, the World League of American football, rugby league and one-day cricket matches (McKay & Rowe, 1997; Maguire & Possamai, in press). This company also secured exclusive rights to cover the 1997 Ryder Cup competition between Europe and the USA held in Valdarrama, Spain. Yet, despite this relative dominance, its control is not complete. Public service terrestrial broadcasters have fought to ensure access to European soccer club competitions and the clubs themselves have plans to develop their own channels.

Governments are also beginning to turn attention to this area of media consumption. During the 1990s, several calls have been made for the UK government, and indeed the EU Commission, to adopt a series of 'listed' sports events which would ensure that no one broadcaster could have exclusive rights to specific sports events and thus deny the general public access to these events. In 1998 a report to the British government recommended a new system whereby some sports events would remain 'protected' and broadcast by terrestrial channels. A 'free market' would exist for the majority of sports however, thus allowing satellite, cable and pay-as-you-view companies to bid for exclusive broadcasting rights. In 1998 attempts by Sky Sport to agree with the English Premier League a pay-as-you-view system prompted criticism from the game's 'traditionalists' and was, for the moment at any rate rejected by the chairmen of the clubs concerned. Likewise, while attempts to form a European Super League are under active discussion between UEFA, major clubs, sponsors and media firms, no final plans have been made, though it is anticipated that a new structure will be in place for the start of the 2000/2001 season.

The Meanings of Mediated Sport Texts

Research inspired by cultural studies has been concerned to analyse the structure of media texts and trace their role in sustaining systems of domination. In studying media sport it is recognized that there exist contending discourses, offering different ways of looking and speaking. The groups who propound these discourses are involved in an ongoing struggle for visibility and legitimacy. Global media–sport discourses are permeated by similar struggles. They are viewed as being multifaceted and containing a number of different meanings which can be 'read' by the 'skilled consumer'. Work of this kind signals a move away from the dominant ideology thesis associated with the Frankfurt School (Turner, 1990). The idea that global media–sport texts are dominated by a single monolithic ideology can be rejected. Cultural forms act as mechanisms for regulating public discourse. Sport is no exception. There are two dimensions to this process. In the first, the range of discourses that particular cultural forms allow into play is subject to regulation. This connects with the other dimension that explores the way the available discourses are handled in the text. The main concern is to examine the ways these mechanisms work within a particular media text or across a range of texts. Media–sport personnel play a crucial role in this process. That is, in producing a marketable commodity, both visual and verbal media codes are at work. For Whannel, four main elements are involved. These are: hierarchization, the process of signalling that some things are more important than others; personalization, the presentation of events from an individualized perspective; narrative, the telling of events in the form of stories; and the placing of events in the context of frames of reference (Whannel, 1992a: pp. 112–13).

This aspect of the media–sport production complex enhances the excitement/spectacle value of the sport. It does so in the following ways: cutting and editing of the 'live' match; use of camera positions, angles and focus; use of slow motion; use of graphics, music, interviews and 'expert' analysis. In so doing, the sport form 'gains pace', its spectacle value is heightened and thereby its marketable value increased (Cantelon & Gruneau, 1988; Gruneau, Whitson & Cantelon, 1988). These global media–sport discourses do not simply serve to enhance the commodity value of the product however. They also help to sustain systems of domination (Andrews, 1997). Research has examined how media–sport discourses reinforce racial and gender systems of inequality (Gruneau, 1989b). Work on gender and media sport demonstrates how women are marginalized, trivialized and objectified in media coverage (Duquin, 1989; MacNeil, 1988; Daddario, 1994; Duncan & Hasbrook, 1988; Williams, Lawrence & Rowe, 1986). In an excellent paper Duncan & Brummett (1989) highlight the types of gendered 'pleasures' associated with television sports. Wilson (1997) has provided an insightful study into media constructions of African-American athletes in Canadian basketball, while McKay captures the use of globalized corporate slogans and how this is a form of 'enlightened racism' (1995). The media–sport discourse on masculinity has also been subject to investigation. Trujillo (1991) analyses print and television representations of baseball pitcher Nolan Ryan and shows how hegemonic masculinity is reproduced in mediated sport. Studies on violence also show how mediated sport exploits violence for audience rating, marketing purposes and the reinforcement of specific forms of masculine identity (Hutchins & Phillips, 1997).

This work has contributed significantly to our understanding of global mediated sport. Cultural studies work, however, may be less suited to explaining how the economic dynamics of production structure public discourse by promoting specific cultural forms over others (Golding & Murdock, 1991). Exploring this issue further reveals that media interest in sport tends to stem from two factors: the low production costs and the potentially high audience ratings that can be achieved. The motivation that lies behind these factors again varies between Europe and North America and indeed within Europe itself. That is, the desire of media organizations such as the British Broadcasting Corporation and Swedish Television, to hold down costs and gain 'high' audience ratings is closely connected to the need to retain independence and perform what they see as their public broadcasting role. Commercial organizations such as CBS, NBC and ABC are also keen to hold down costs and produce appropriate audience profiles and ratings to secure advertising revenue. In addition, satellite and cable companies, such as Eurosport and Sky Sport, seek 'quality' sport broadcasts to bolster their entire programme schedule (Barnett, 1990; Whannel, 1992a).

The strategy of the media organizations in the global media–sport complex appears to be informed by at least three factors: the existing station style and ethos, scheduling constraints and the market for potential advertisers (Goldlust, 1987). With regard to the last, the social composition of both the media audience and the participants and spectators of the sport covered is important. Which of these elements is of greater importance varies with both the sport form covered and the potential sponsor and/or advertiser. Sometimes, the potential sponsor or advertiser may wish to use the media coverage to target one or more of these groups. The economic dynamics of production are one element that structures – without, of course, completely determining – public discourse by promoting specific cultural forms over others. If researchers accept this they are better placed to grasp why certain sport forms have appeared as global media sports. As noted, this issue has been subject to intense and ongoing debate within the sociology of sport (see Guttmann, 1991; Kidd, 1991; Klein, 1991; Maguire, 1990; McKay & Miller, 1991; Wagner, 1990), the debate centring around the issues of Americanization, modernization and globalization and interweaving with the general issues of globalization and the development of global sport (Tomlinson, 1996). Studies examining the content of sports coverage in specific societies are also beginning to appear (Valentine, 1997).

There is, without doubt, an unintended element in the diffusion of some sports to specific societies at particular historical moments. To acknowledge this does not mean that the establishment of a global media–sport complex and the emergence of global sport products are unconnected! Whatever the genesis of these processes, their impact has been to promote certain cultural forms over others, 'indigenous' or otherwise. Sensitivity to this issue allows researchers to trace the detailed connections between the financing and organization of cultural products and changes in the field of public discourse. Similar issues arise with regard to the form and content of broadcasts on Eurosport and other satellite broadcasters. Indeed, the sensitivity of the issue in Europe has prompted the launch of a 'European cultural channel' (Emanuel, 1992) and the formation of a European media policy (Van der Poel, 1991). The same degree of concern is not that evident regarding sport. Mediated texts appear to vary considerably in their degree of discursive openness – that is, how accessible and understood they are for people in different societies. If that is so, then that may in part explain the differential diffusion of some cultural products: specific forms of music, theatre and literature do not 'travel well'.

Sport, however, may be more 'open' and more easily interpreted by people across the globe. Whether this assumption is correct or in need of modification, it will also be necessary to explore the structural variation in people's response to different products. This issue relates to the political economy of consumerism and consumption.

Global Media Sport and Consumer Consumption

In research on the production, transmission and consumption of mediated sports it is conventionally asked whether people are skilled consumers or cultural dupes? This key question surfaces in several debates concerning the consumption of mediated sport within a nation, between nations and across continents. Think of 'British' consumption of 'English'-dominated media–sport products, of 'Canadian' consumption of 'American' media–sport products, the 'Asian' consumption of the 'European'-based Barcelona Olympics and visions of the Sydney 2000 Olympics (Tomlinson, 1996; Valentine, 1997; Wilson, 1994). Cultural studies research on media sport has reflected the more general tendency to see people as 'skilled consumers' (Hargreaves, 1986), that is, as people who could make informed choices regarding the consumption of media products. This is symptomatic of the more general attempt to recognize the knowledgeability of social actors and to move away from a view of the consumer as a 'cultural dupe'. The emphasis on informed choice can go too far, however. In the celebration of the viewer as 'resistance fighter', some cultural studies research comes close to occupying the pluralist position that celebrates the 'sovereignty of the individual' who enjoys unfettered choice.

This is not the case with all such work (Andrews, 1997; Rowe, 1995). Studies by Gantz (1981) and Wenner & Gantz (1989) point to the need to explore the audience experience ethnographically. Bryant's (1989) study of televised sports violence complements textual analysis of media–sport reporting more generally. More studies of this kind will be required in making sense of global media sport consumption. In doing so, a useful corrective to the excesses of postmodern discourse analysis will be provided (Gantz & Wenner, 1995; Gan et al., 1997). Yet, there are dangers in overstating the knowledgeability of individuals in consuming indigenous media–sport products. There are also hazards in placing too much emphasis on the 'agency' of the individual or on a culture's ability to resist cultural penetration by 'foreign' multinationals. To do so neglects the need for a detailed analysis of the political economy of the media–sport production complex and of the inter-relations between the elements that make it up. Though we are dealing with 'skilled' pleasurable consumption, people are relatively unaware of how such choices are structured by both global cultural struggles and by the media–sport production complex. To acknowledge this does not require the adoption of a cultural dupe thesis. This is where audience experience research is vital.

Some researchers have also sought to explore the ritual aspects of media representations of the Olympics (MacAloon, 1988). Real (1989a), for example, contentiously argues that 'the Olympics create McLuhan's global village' although briefly and superficially. He is correct to observe that the 'text of the super media Olympics is a rich one, the interpretations many, and the ideology complex'. He concludes that 'even as we point out its imperfections, we must be profoundly grateful for its international global potential for the human family' (Real, 1989a: p. 248). Globalization processes do not, however, necessarily lead to the promotion of the 'ideals' expounded by Pierre de Coubertin and those who now control the IOC. Moreover, ritual can be highly destructive. During the next decade global sport development may be a site for reconciliation and/or struggle between the representatives of different cultural traditions. Having emphasized several key points of departure and explored three broad areas of enquiry regarding global media sport, it is appropriate to anchor this review within the context of one specific case study. This examination of the initial phases in the emergence of American football as a global sport can act as a 'critical' test of the questions raised and the issues identified in these introductory comments.

Global Media–Sport Development in the Late Twentieth Century: the Example of American Football

As was noted in chapter 4, the origins of modern sport can be traced back to a European, and in particular, an English context. During the course of the eighteenth and nineteenth centuries, a sportization process unfolded that led to the codification of folk games. This process, marked as it was by a series of cultural struggles, subsequently involved the diffusion of modern versions of sport throughout the 'formal' and 'informal' British Empire. Hence, in former British colonies a range of sports such as cricket, rugby and soccer can be seen. In addition, British traders, diplomats and sailors brought their games along with them on their foreign travels. Many of today's leading clubs in a variety of sports were formed by the commingling of such servants of Empire with local indigenous elites. One such example of this global sport development includes the diffusion of rugby football to the USA. This sport form was to undergo a process of modification in the context of the elite universities of the former colony. But whereas at this early stage of global sport development the British were the dominant trendsetters – enjoying as they did high social, economic and political status – during the more recent phases of sportization and globalization North American sport forms have grown in ascendancy. These sport forms include basketball, baseball, ice hockey and American football. Here, the spread of American football to British society is viewed as symptomatic of broader processes of global media–sport development.

Prior to the early 1980s, American football was virtually unknown on the British cultural landscape. The game was infrequently reported and when it was, the report tended to be short and related to the annual end-of-season Super Bowl. In fact, a content analysis of *The Times* index for the five-year period prior to 1982, the year in which American football was first televised in Britain, revealed only seven brief reports. American football was also hardly played in England prior to that time except by US airforce personnel, and, even in this instance, games usually took place within the confines of their airbases. The same held true as far as spectatorship was concerned. When audiences did view the game prior to 1982, it was on closed-circuit television at cinemas in London with, for example, only some 2500 people, mainly American, in attendance (*The Times*, 27 January 1981). Radio coverage was also virtually non-existent except on the American Forces network (*Sunday Times*, 18 January 1987). But during 1982, the initial stages in the making of American football as a significant cultural form within the culture of sections of British society became evident. In tracing the main features of this process, several key elements have to be identified. These include the decision of Channel 4 to screen American football in a particular style and on a regular basis, the marketing strategy of the NFL and the involvement of Anheuser-Busch, the producers of Budweiser beer.

In 1982, the newly created Channel 4 began to screen American football on a regular basis. Why was this decision to screen 75 minutes per week of the regular season fixtures taken? The commissioning editor of Channel 4 Sport, Adrian Metcalfe, had been faced with both limited funds and limited airtime (Channel 4, 1987). The importing of American football and the coverage of British basketball appear to have been perceived as means to solve the problems faced. More crucially, however, it was not simply the decision to cover American football which was to prove important, but also the actual programme style and presentation which were of significance. This requires spelling out. The sports department of Channel 4 appears to have taken the decision that the traditional form of British sports coverage was no longer appropriate. Channel 4 decided to take the American television footage and commentary from the main networks, CBS, ABC and NBC, and then to use a British production company (Cheerleader Productions) to package the game via edited highlights, popularist presenters, rock-'n'-roll title music and colourful graphics. Derek Brandon, Cheerleader's executive producer, noted in this connection:

> The televising of sport in America is simply stunning. They make it fun, they make it stylish, and they make it a family occasion. These are the things that we've lost from British sport. If LWT had done American football . . . they'd have been back to the presenter in the blazer with the glass of water.
>
> (*Observer*, 5 October 1986)

This shift towards an American style of coverage with the emphasis on 'entertainment' and away from a British 'journalistic' style has also been commented on by Goldlust (1987), McKay and Rowe (1987) and McKay and Miller (1991) with reference to Australian television broadcasting. Before considering how this coverage of American football dovetailed with both the NFL and the Anheuser-Busch marketing strategies, it is perhaps best to give some indication of the growth in coverage and in viewing figures of the sport since 1982.

In 1982 American football, along with basketball, was the only sport shown by Channel 4, then a recent addition to British terrestrial broadcasting. Showing 75 minutes of edited highlights of the previous week's NFL action, this programme continued to occupy a central slot in the sport schedules of Channel 4 during the 1980s and early 1990s. In 1983 and 1984, it accounted for some 20 per cent of the sports broadcasting of the station. In 1985, despite diversification into other sports, American football still ranked in the top three of Channel 4's sport output (Channel 4, 1987). In fact, along with horse-racing and snooker, American football still made up over 50 per cent of the channel's sport output in 1985/86 and this, in turn, constituted 8 per cent of the total output of the station (Channel 4, 1987). During the period 1982 to 1986, the amount of time devoted to coverage of the regular season had remained the same, though this was complemented by increased live broadcasts of the play-off and Super Bowl games, the first live Super Bowl being broadcast in January 1983. In 1984, *The Times* felt it appropriate to publish the radio wavelengths of American broadcasts of live matches being played in the USA and claimed that 'several thousand' stayed up into the early hours to listen to them (*The Times*, 21 January 1984). During 1987, coverage of American football was further increased with an additional one-hour programme being broadcast on Tuesday evenings, and it made up 12 per cent of the total sport output of Channel 4 (Channel 4, 1987). But what were the numbers of people watching these programmes? Table 1 documents the growth in audiences watching American football between 1982 and 1990. As can be seen, in that period a substantial increase in audience numbers occurred.

Table 1   *Channel 4's American Football TV Audience Profile 1982/83–1989/90.*

Year	Average audience
1982/83	1.1 million
1983/84	1.5 million
1984/85	2.3 million
1985/86	3.1 million
1986/87	2.9 million
1987/88	3.7 million*
1988/89	3.32 million**
1989/90	2.39 million*

* 2 broadcasts per week
** 3 broadcasts per week

Source: 1982–8, AGB/BARB cited in NFL Merchandise Catalogue 1988; 1988–90, Channel 4 correspondence.

During 1987/88, figures as high as 4.7 million were achieved during weeks 11 and 12 of the regular NFL season and, for Super Bowl XXII, an audience high of 6.1 million was recorded (AGB/BARB, C4). These figures were, however, dwarfed by ratings in the USA. Analysis of the audience profile of viewers of American football appears to have been considered essential by Channel 4, NFL marketing and their existing and prospective clients. Based on market research conducted on their behalf, data are available for the crucial early development phase, that is seasons 1985/86 to 1987/88. It is sufficient at this point to note that the viewing audience had an affluent profile with a high proportion of AB (professional class) and C1 (lower middle and skilled working class) viewers evident. The audience also appeared to be disproportionately male and weighted towards the younger age groups.

This general picture of a rise in viewing figures and of a primarily young, male and affluent audience is borne out by other indices of the development of American football in Britain. Between 1982 and 1989, for example, there emerged a number of magazines devoted exclusively to the gridiron game, namely *Touchdown*, *Firstdown/Quarterback* and *GridIron*. *Touchdown* was reported to have sold some 25,000 copies per issue (*The Times*, 20 January 1984) and *GridIron* had sales of over 29,000 per issue in 1987 (Audit Bureau of Circulations, 1987). The *Daily Telegraph* published a weekly magazine, *The Daily Telegraph American Football Magazine*, with a readership peaking during 1988 at some 100,000. Marshall Cavendish, a specialist publisher of magazine collections, produced an eighteen-part series timed to coincide with the NFL season. The series was heavily advertised on television, including Channel 4, and part 1 achieved a sale in the region of 275,000 copies (Marshall Cavendish, 1989). The series sold, in total, in excess of two million copies (Connelly, 1987: p. 53).

Not surprisingly, the readership of this range of magazines appeared to be similar to that which watched American football on Channel 4. As part of the launch of the Marshall Cavendish series, a questionnaire was sent out with part 1, and analysis of its findings revealed that at least half of the respondents were in their teens, that the vast majority were male and that their social class origins tended towards the C1 and AB groupings (MIL Research Ltd, 1986: p. 2). Over 50 per cent of the respondents had purchased copies of magazines such as *Touchdown* and 91 per cent viewed American football on Channel 4 every week, though two-thirds had never attended a 'live game' (MIL Research Ltd, 1986: p. 13). Given data such as these, it is perhaps not surprising that a writer in the *Sunday Times* could claim in January 1987 that:

> Cheerleader have clearly found the advertisers' nirvana – a young, rich and enthusiastic audience ... It's almost as if the yuppies of the world were waiting for a spectator sport they could feel was theirs – something that was at its best when watched on the small screen in the warmth of their home.
>
> (*Sunday Times*, 18 January 1987)

In catering for this young, affluent and predominantly male group, American football *Yearbooks* have been published annually in

Britain since 1983, and other publishers such as Queen Anne Press produced a range of titles which were carried in most major book chains. This dissemination of American football literature is not confined, however, to journals and books. In 1987 the *Daily Telegraph* put together a series of eight guides to the game and distributed them free with the newspaper around the London area. Readership increased by between 5 per cent and 10 per cent each Friday it was distributed, and 30,000 readers outside the London area subscribed for special postal delivery of the magazines (Licensing Management International, 1989). Significantly, the *Daily Telegraph* not only underwrote the production costs of Cheerleader Productions' editing of American football for Channel 4, but the newspaper title was carried on caption when the programme broke for advertisements. While this example is revealing in terms of demonstrating the interweaving of media interests in the televising of American football, the underwriting of Cheerleader's production costs of American football is, in fact, nothing new. The production costs of the programmes broadcast in the first year of Channel 4's coverage of American football were underwritten by Anheuser-Busch. By 1993, however, Cheerleader Productions had lost out to a rival. During that year Trans World International (TWI) took control of Channel 4's NFL coverage. Having provided some indication of the growth in American football as a cultural phenomenon in Britain, it is perhaps appropriate at this stage to turn attention to how this development was dependent on the marketing strategies of Anheuser-Busch and the NFL.

Anheuser-Busch played a significant role in the development of American football in Britain in several key areas. The investment of £100,000 in the production costs of televising American football in Britain (*The Times*, 23 December 1985) was combined with direct advertising during slots in the programme. Significantly, Budweiser advertisements included American footballers on occasions. One notable example, where reality and fantasy arguably meshed, involved the meeting in a Western saloon of players of the Washington Redskins and the Dallas Cowboys! In 1986 the marketing strategy of Anheuser-Busch also involved them in establishing the Budweiser League. This league attempted to pull together several rival leagues which had mushroomed in the three years since the first Channel 4 broadcasts. It was only in the summer of 1983 that the first British American football team, the London Ravens, was formed, but the growth of others was rapid. In all, seventy-two teams joined the Budweiser League, in which Anheuser-Busch owned a 51 per cent share holding (*Budweiser League Yearbook*, 1987: p. 7). By 1987, the Budweiser League had expanded to

105 teams with the member clubs nominally owning the league. A rival British GridIron Football League was also formed in this period and, by 1988, it, too, had seventy-two teams. The main stumbling block to amalgamation of the various leagues appears to have been Anheuser-Busch's 51 per cent share of the Budweiser League. The European Football League, formed by clubs located in France, Germany, Spain and Scandinavia, refused to recognize the Budweiser League unless such ownership was dropped (*GridIron UK*, May 1986: p. 19). By late 1988, formal ownership had passed to the clubs but the involvement of Anheuser-Busch had not ceased, for the company had agreed to sponsor the Budweiser League for the following two seasons. Each season was planned to culminate in the playing of the Budweiser Bowl. In 1986, this involved an 18,000 sell-out crowd at Crystal Palace. By 1988, it was reported that there were 198 senior teams and 16,000 registered players in the UK (Algar, 1988: p. 58). In this situation, unification of the game was perceived to be crucial to further commercialization. Take the following comments made by a writer in *GridIron UK* in February 1987:

> ... the unification of the British game will help to make our American football more attractive to the sponsor ... Budweiser's own investment should help to convince other potential sponsors that British American football is a game worth backing.
>
> (*GridIron UK*, February 1987: p. 55)

The development of this league structure and of the Budweiser Bowl by Anheuser-Busch was combined with the development of the American Bowl at Wembley stadium. Held in the pre-season period of the NFL and played between two NFL teams, the first American Bowl was played in August 1986 between the Dallas Cowboys and the Chicago Bears. The event was sponsored by a combination of TWA, American Express and Budweiser (*The Times*, 11 April 1986). The 1986 game was a sell-out. Eighty thousand tickets were sold in seven days, with seat prices as high as £20. Television coverage ensured an even wider audience (Connelly, 1987: p. 54). Following the success of this venture, in December 1986 Anheuser-Busch announced that they were planning to increase their spending on American football in Britain over the next two years to more than £1.5 million (*The Times*, 20 December 1986). An indication of the success of this marketing strategy is that sales of Budweiser rose considerably in this period.

These developments also relate to and were reinforced by

the marketing strategy of the NFL. The NFL is not simply the administrative arm of the game of American football but is also a trade association which directs the operations of NFL Properties and NFL Films, the revenue-producing companies for American football. The activities of these companies in the home market centre on negotiating TV rights, retail licensing, publishing and corporate sponsor development. These companies have proved to be highly effective. Their products appear in over 40 per cent of US households, involving in the early 1980s a $250-million-a-year retail business. The publishing activities of the NFL involve a diverse range of magazines and books, and each year between thirty and forty business categories were selected and NFL promotion rights were granted which allowed the companies involved to promote, advertise and merchandise their own products endorsed with the NFL logo. It would appear, however, that the NFL became aware of limitations developing within their own market, especially with respect to TV revenues (Harris, 1987: p. 605). Sage has explored the NFL strategy by examining how they use their distinctive logo on a global stage (Sage, 1996). In this regard, the NFL were not unlike other US multinational companies who have sought to diversify their operations on a global scale (Gilpin, 1976). This trend was stressed by James Connelly when he addressed a British audience on the subject of 'Influencing your Customer' in 1987: 'the League now recognises that international marketing is the key area of future growth potential for the sport and has pledged its resources accordingly including the League Office, respective ball clubs, NFL Properties and NFL Films' (Connelly, 1987: p. 52).

But who exactly do the NFL regard as their customers? Three main groups are identified: the NFL fan/consumer, NFL licensees and NFL corporate clients. The marketing strategy for the UK was therefore clear. According to Connelly, the strategy was to 'create, develop and influence a whole new customer base in the UK' (Connelly, 1987: p. 46). In order to achieve this aim, the NFL sought to meet four main objectives. These were: to promote the game abroad on a long-term sustained basis; to create and then educate a new fan base; to establish and protect the NFL trademarks on a worldwide basis for commercial applications and to generate revenues (Connelly, 1987: p. 52). But how did the NFL achieve these goals in the UK in the 1980s and how were their efforts interrelated with the activities of Channel 4 and Anheuser-Busch? The first crucial step in the NFL strategy had been to achieve television and media coverage. Again Connelly addressed this issue when he argued:

... the key ... to building this marketing business is successful television placement. Once you are successfully able to place your
product on television with a strong programme package, and an
advantageous viewing hour, you can generate the initial awareness,
interest and exposure ... for your product. Once that has been
established you can then go in and develop the resulting licensing
businesses.

(Connelly, 1987: p. 52)

This strategy meshed with the programming policy of Channel 4.
That is, as was established earlier, Channel 4 sought to distance
themselves from the conventional style of British sports broadcasting. Taking their coverage from the main US networks, and with
the re-editing provided by Cheerleader Productions, a 'strong programme package' was achieved. In addition, given that the actual
programme was broadcast on a Sunday evening when the
BBC and ITV were then showing religious programmes, an
advantageous viewing hour was achieved. The fact that the programme was shown early in the evening also ensured that a potentially young audience could be attracted. The importance of the
initial screening of American football in 1982 was not overlooked
by either the television companies or the NFL. In 1984,
Andrew Croker, marketing director of Cheerleader Productions,
commented:

The high level of interest in the game is television led. The point is
that this is the best-covered sport in the world in terms of television
technology and cash. That makes it a very strong product, and one
that had very limited exposure here. And it is very much a television sport ... the packaging of the game into highlights tends to
allow the game to gain pace, in the way that soccer highlights lose
pace.

(*The Times*, 20 January 1984)

Significantly, Croker described American football as a television
sport. This did not happen by chance. Sewart (1987) has noted how
American football was regarded in its home market in the early
1970s as 'boring' and television ratings dropped to an all-time low.
The NFL Rules Committee responded with a series of rule changes
which were designed to speed up the action and increase the
potential for high-scoring games (Sewart, 1987: p. 172). The effect
of these rule changes was reinforced in Britain by the packaging by
Cheerleader, which Croker notes allowed the game to 'gain pace'.
The role of Channel 4 and Cheerleader was acknowledged by
Connelly in 1987 when he remarked:

> We were very fortunate in that ... there was a Channel 4 and a
> 'Cheerleader' production who put together a dynamically packaged
> programme at a good viewing hour ... that created the initial expo-
> sure and awareness of our sport. That has helped trigger all of the
> successes we have enjoyed in the resultant licensing areas.
>
> (Connelly, 1987: p. 53)

This strategy of promoting the game dovetailed with the attempt
to 'create and educate a fan base'. Here, the operations of the NFL
in other areas of the media reinforced the exposure received on
Channel 4. NFL Films and NFL Properties, working through a local
agent, Licensing Management International, reached publishing
agreements with a number of companies. As noted earlier, Marshall
Cavendish launched an eighteen-part magazine series devoted to
the game, timed to coincide with the 1986 coverage of American
football. NFL licences were agreed with other media organizations,
including Queen Anne Press, Mediawatch International and Lady-
bird Books. These companies produced publications such as *American Football Annual Yearbook*, *Who's Who in American Football?*,
Quarterback Magazine and *American Football Book*. Other licences
were granted to companies to produce American football fact
packs, calendars, stickers, diaries, posters, jigsaw puzzles, painting
by numbers games and playing cards (NFL Merchandise Catalogue, 1988: p. 23). The *Daily Telegraph*, which, as noted, gave away
free to its readers an American football magazine, received its
materials from NFL Films. Given the data cited earlier regarding
the extent of the consumption of these products, it would appear
that this part of the NFL marketing strategy had been achieved, but
this strategy had, as noted, other objectives.

The need which the NFL perceived to be essential in their operations was to establish and protect their trademark for commercial
applications on a worldwide basis. In Britain, this was to be
achieved through the operations of Licensing Management International. Beginning in 1983/84, this licensing operation has since
grown to a point where over seventy companies are involved. The
motivation behind this aspect of NFL strategy in Britain was not
only to increase profits in the short term. The concern appears also
to have been to increase awareness of the NFL logo in the
marketplace. Connelly said:

> If they [the corporate clients] ... by using an NFL theme promotion
> ... increase their sales and, at the same time, expose our trademarks
> in a quality promotional context, then we have achieved mutual
> objectives ...
>
> (Connelly, 1987: p. 49)

A diverse range of merchandise and companies was involved. The merchandise licensed under the NFL franchise included, but is by no means exhausted by, the following: children's clothing, replica NFL helmets, shirts, satin jackets, knitwear, underwear, nightwear, caps, coffee mugs, skateboards, roller-skates, bean bags, key rings, fun beds and seats, Easter eggs, watches and clocks! The companies involved range from specialist leisurewear manufacturers, e.g. Charterhouse Textiles Manufacturing, small sports retailers and outlets and larger and better-known British companies such as Marks and Spencer, Mothercare, Asda and British Home Stores. The scale of this merchandising operation was matched by the product endorsements which had been secured. These include products such as 'Marathon' (Snickers) chocolate bars, 'Wagon Wheel' biscuits and 'Leaf' bubble gum. An indication of the 'success' of these operations is that during the period of their promotion, sales of multipack Marathon bars went up by 40 per cent and Wagon Wheels by 30 per cent (Licensing Management International, 1989: p. 2). The NFL were clear why this occurred. Commenting on NFL operations in the USA, Connelly remarked: 'We allow them to trade on the equity of the NFL trademarks to enhance the sale of their products or services and/or to embellish their advertising or promotion programme' (Connelly, 1987: p. 47).

But why should this association with the NFL have proved so attractive and how did it apply to developments in Britain? In answering this it is necessary to keep in mind the audience profile of Channel 4 American football outlined earlier. In work conducted by Gallup Polls for the NFL, it was claimed that the NFL market was becoming 'younger and more affluent' (NFL Merchandising Catalogue, 1988: p. 3). This finding corresponds to the general profile of the television audience outlined earlier. More particularly, the findings of the market research showed that 38 per cent of all households with children between four and fifteen were interested in NFL football, and over 50 per cent watched it regularly on Channel 4; 33 per cent owned some NFL branded merchandise; 50 per cent of households with boys aged 10–15 were interested in the game (Social Surveys, Gallup Polls, 1988). Significantly, this market research also revealed that 77 per cent of the British households that viewed NFL football considered that products carrying the NFL shield would be of equal or higher quality than most products: 91 per cent of 16–25 year olds, 75 per cent of 25–44 year olds and 86 per cent of those in social class AB considered that products with the NFL shield were of equal or higher quality than most other products (Social Surveys, Gallup Polls, 1988). In fact, the licensing programme adopted reflected the audience profile reported by the market research (Licensing Management International, 1989: p. 1). This strategy is similar to the one adopted by the NFL in their home market. Regarding the USA, Connelly observed that 'We have worked within this licensing sector to target ourselves and market to a specific customer profile' (Connelly, 1987: p. 47).

It would appear, therefore, that the NFL strategy for their franchising and corporate client arrangements in Britain was to target specific groups identified as being interested in American football and this identification stemmed from the audience profile of Channel 4's programme. This strategy not only allowed for the possibility of greater profits to be generated in the short term but allowed for the NFL logo to penetrate deep into the cultural terrain of British society. This dissemination followed the cultural terrain which the products endorsed by the NFL then covered. An example of this process is the development of the biscuit, Wagon Wheels. Having reached agreement over NFL endorsement of their product, in autumn 1986, Burton Biscuits then arranged a media schedule which involved placing advertisements in a range of children's comics, including *Buster, Whizzer & Chips, Eagle* and *Roy of the Rovers*, with a combined circulation of 378,734. On this basis, perhaps it was no surprise that media commentators believed that an advertisers' nirvana had been found.

This penetration of the cultural terrain of British society is also evident in other areas. Linking with the marketing strategy of Anheuser-Busch, the American Bowl would not have been possible without NFL approval and co-operation. In fact, Licensing Management International appears to have played a significant part in arranging the sponsorship package which underpinned the 1986 American Bowl involving American Express, TWA and Budweiser (Connelly, 1987: p. 54). In addition, the NFL provide equipment and instructional advice for Budweiser League teams and allow limited use of the NFL logo on their jerseys. Channel 4 live coverage of Super Bowl XXI was complemented by the release of the official NFL programme, the only difference being that it carried British advertisements. In the three days prior to the screening of the game on Channel 4, over 150,000 copies were sold.

By adopting this strategy, the NFL also met their fourth objective. An indication of this can be gained from the fact that whilst in 1983/84 £125,000 worth of merchandised goods were sold at retail, by 1988/89 a figure of £24 million was forecast (Licensing Management International, 1989: p. 1). The success of this operation can also be gauged in other ways. In 1982, 60 per cent of NFL overseas business came from Canada and Mexico. By 1987, 80 per cent came from Europe, of which, as Connelly noted, 'the UK is by far our leading and most successful market' (Connelly, 1987: p. 53). Two points are of interest in this connection. One should not be surprised by the fact that the satellite broadcasts of Sky Television (Murdoch-owned) and Screensport to a wide range of European countries contained a significant proportion of American football and American sports coverage in general (*Guardian*, 1 February 1989). For a multinational company believing that 'international marketing is the key area of future growth', gaining a place on such satellite broadcasting was and remains essential. Indeed, according to Licensing Marketing International, NFL football is 'well established in the British high street as a family sport with good opportunities for growth in licensing, publishing and marketing programmes' (Licensing Management International, 1989: p. 3).

The success of these operations was such that in March 1989, Pete Rozelle, the NFL commissioner, proposed to the NFL Long Range Planning and Finance Committee that a 'Spring League' be established in Europe from 1990, involving NFL reserve team players and European teams (*Daily Telegraph*, 8 March 1989). This strategy was formally agreed by the NFL and a 'Spring League' operated in Europe from 1990 to 1992. But this World League of American Football has had mixed fortunes: during the 1990s it was, in fact, suspended for one season, questions being raised about its financial viability. Similarly, American football has retained a niche in television coverage but it has not become a central player.

By 1993, in British terrestrial channel coverage of sports, American football ranked seventh in total amount of hours devoted to it (*European TV Sports Databook*, 1995: p. 136). But the figure of around seventy-one hours was dwarfed by the coverage of association football that amounted to some 421 hours. Shown exclusively on Channel 4, American football coverage comprised some 17 per cent of total output during 1993 (*European TV Sports Databook*, 1995: p. 141). According to Mintel (1996: p. 68), American football amounted to 2.4 per cent of the overall total terrestrial television sport coverage. Though this was more than sports such as bowls and cycling, American football remained below association football, horse-racing, cricket, tennis, snooker, rugby, golf and track and field. In 1998, in an attempt to revitalize the game's flagging fortunes in Europe, the World League of American Football was scrapped and renamed the NFL Europe League (*Independent*, 3 April 1998: p. 30). Presumably, the sports officials were hoping that the 'NFL' tag would generate increased public interest through the implied closer connection with the superior American based version of the game. It is too early to tell if this goal will be achieved.

Conclusion: The Global Media–Sport Complex

What conclusions can we reach regarding the effects of the global media–sport complex on popular culture? Should media–sport products be seen as reflecting and reinforcing the general massification of society? Should media–sport products be associated with mediocrity and poor taste, and their consumers subject to external control and manipulation? Are consumers across the globe 'victims' prone to influence outside their consciousness and control? Do these media–sport influences reinforce more general Western values and/or a sports credo that celebrates achievement sport and perpetuates the gender, class and ethnic/race inequalities that exist across the planet? In answering these questions, the task is to maintain a radical critique of culture but to avoid both the cultural elitism of mass society theory and the 'blindness' of critical theory to the fact that the consumption of global media–sport products can involve the active appropriation of meanings and not just the passive surrender to the meanings imposed by powerful groups who seek to control and regulate the content and meaning of global sports. The impact of global sport – especially its American forms – is beginning to be assessed by scholars working within the sociology of sport (Andrews, 1997; Maguire & Possamai, in press). Drawing on broader research on popular culture the alleged effects of Americanization have been challenged by several writers, including Kaplan and Webster. Though written a decade ago, several of their arguments seemingly have not been heeded by those who seek to explain global sport. These arguments are worth restating.

First, the American culture thesis contains within it an undifferentiated and over-simplified view of popular culture. The receptivity of popular culture to global media sport is both active and knowledgeable. Though global media corporations and marketing companies package sport, these cultural products in and of themselves contain no 'fixed ideological message' (Webster, 1988: p. 179). These global products are reacted to differently by different national audiences. Indigenous people have a range of resources available to reinterpret, resist and recycle global sport products. Secondly, the impact of these products is not uniform but rather heterogeneous. This needs to be understood in two senses. While global media sport does contain a strong element of 'American' sports – the case study of American football demonstrated this – this does not exhaust the increasing varieties of global sports, folk games and recreations shown to and consumed by sections of different national audiences. Global media sport is clearly influenced by North American sports such as American football, basketball, baseball and ice hockey, but non-American achievement sports such as association football and non-achievement sports such as the martial arts are also part of the pattern of global media consumption.

Drawing on the work of Hebdige and Bigsby, two additional points can be made: rejecting a simple homogenizing view of the influences of American culture, Hebdige argues that 'American popular culture offers a rich iconography, a set of symbols, objects and artifacts which can be assembled and re-assembled by different groups in a literally limitless number of combinations' (Hebdige, 1982: p. 216). The work of Bigsby reinforces this. He argues that, in the process of cross-cultural diffusion, American culture 'suffers a sea-change', it 'assumes a new identity', and becomes, in effect, a 'superculture, a reservoir of shifting values' (Bigsby, 1975: p. 27). In arguing for the possibility of the emergence of a 'new identity', Bigsby is allowing for the capacity of individuals to reinterpret the American cultural product into something distinct. He further argues that Americanization is an 'emblematic' not a causal source of change. These arguments have provided a useful corrective to a too crude Americanization thesis, but this should not lead one to the conclusion that the consumer is sovereign and that there are no power differentials involved in the provision of global cultural forms. Again, the case study examining American football is instructive in this regard.

The analysis had to be steered carefully between two competing tendencies. While it is important to probe the existence of relatively autonomous transnational practices, the researcher should not be unaware that national and transnational media and marketing agencies, as well as sports organizations such as the NBA and the NFL, will attempt to manipulate and control such processes. It is also legitimate to note, though more particularly concerning specific sports, such as European basketball, that a combined process of commodification/Americanization has occurred, but has done so within *the context of broader globalization processes*. This can take several forms: the global migration of American sports personnel, the global spread of American sport forms and the global adoption of the marketing of sports along American lines. This is accelerated in both intended and unintended ways by the media–sport production complex. Though these forms have developed to varying degrees in different countries and continents, more usually they interweave in a mutually reinforcing manner. Research on the audience perception of these processes is required.

These observations can be borne out with reference to the case study examining the making of American football in Britain. Let me examine this more closely. In order to understand American-ization processes, of which this is a part, it is necessary to avoid 'today-centred' analyses which probe the issue in a non-relational manner. Instead, it is important to recognize that Anglo-American relations, in their totality, are deeply-rooted in the histories of these countries. In addition, there has always been a balance of power in this relationship, which, while early on it favoured the English, still allowed scope for the development of indigenous American cultural forms and for the exchange of cultural styles and values. In the early development of what Lipset has termed 'the First New Nation', the British, but more especially, the English, were dominant. This domination, however, was not com-plete. Significantly, as Lipset remarks, 'although colonial subjects, Americans were also Englishmen and were thus accustomed to the rights and privileges of Englishmen' (Lipset, 1964: p. 93). But despite these 'new Americans' shaking off their status as a colony, eighteenth- and nineteenth-century American intellectuals had not lost, according to Lipset, a sense of 'inferiority' relative to their European counterparts (Lipset, 1964: p. 71). The diffusion of Amer-ican ideas to Europe, in this period, demonstrates that there was a cultural exchange, albeit contoured by an uneven power ratio, which, at this stage, continued to favour the English.

Recognition of the role of American intellectuals and the exchange of cultural forms in the nineteenth century is particularly relevant for the case I am trying to argue. That is, it was in the late 1860s that the English game of rugby spread to American universi-ties. According to Riesman and Denney, it was Harvard and Yale which 'served as the culturally receptive importers of the English game' (Riesman & Denney, 1981: p. 681). While the details of their analysis need not concern us here, they note that, in the context of university sport, a distinctively American game emerged: Amer-ican football. It was this dissemination of English rugby to America that provided the antecedents for the game which appeared in British society in the 1980s. But despite Britain being, in the 1870s, relatively dominant, Americans still had the cultural power to remake the game of rugby in their own image. So, too, do Britons in the late twentieth century.

Though America has, during the course of the twentieth

century, become relatively more dominant in its relationship with Britain, and this has manifested itself in the spread of American cultural wares, this cultural exchange has not been all one way. In sport, we can observe that during the mid-1970s, the game of association football, arguably *the* world sport, became increasingly popular in the USA. A large number of Britons went there as players and coaches. Though not yet successful at a professional level, despite attempts by corporate business to 'package' the game for television (Sewart, 1987), soccer has become a significant participant sport at high-school and collegiate level. In the arts and the theatre, the British influence on sections of American culture is also evident. Developments since the 1994 World Cup would suggest that soccer will remain at the margins of American sport. That is, the soccer league established has failed to develop beyond the ethnic margins of American society.

What this indicates is that Anglo-American relations need to be understood in terms of interdependence and that the USA itself is caught up in a whole set of figurational power-balances. Anglo-American interdependence is contoured and shaped by power differentials, but these differentials are by no means fixed. Power needs to be understood as a structural characteristic of interdependencies, and attention needs to be focused on the potential for power-balances to move in different directions (Elias, 1978). That is, power refers to a capability which is not primarily the quality of an individual, but rather a structural property of all social relationships. It is both relational and processual. This conception of power is closely related to the problem of teasing out how unintended interdependencies can be used by human beings as a basis for intentional interventions in ongoing social processes (Bogner, 1986). People on both sides of the Atlantic have had, and continue to have, a fluctuating ability to interpret and change the cultural wares diffusing between their two countries. But they are, nevertheless, no less caught up in long-term unintended interdependency chains.

While the transfer of American football to British society cannot be reduced solely to an economic dimension, capital investment and entrepreneurial activity played an important role in this process. However, those who owned the TV and other companies involved and who produced the TV programmes were not in command of the overall figurational dynamics. Similarly, no one group had a monopoly over the making of American football in the USA itself. No matter how hard the NFL sought to further its marketing strategy, it too was caught up in figurational dynamics which they could not totally control. This is not to suggest that it, along with Channel 4 and Anheuser-Busch, has not been the most powerful player in seeking to create a British market for the consumption of its product. In this regard it has achieved not a little success. The consumers, too, are no less caught up in this unfolding figuration, but they do have the capacity, as Bigsby notes, to reinterpret the American cultural product into something distinct. British consumption will reflect local needs, interests and identities. In fact, as Hebdige observes, the receptivity of popular culture to American cultural wares is both active and heterogeneous. The idea about the 'homogenizing influence of American culture' is overstated and overlooks the possibility of the emergence of a 'new identity'.

Both existing and future global sports development and, as part of that, the media–sport complex, are and will be clearly affected by and interwoven with other global cultural flows. These flows are themselves characterized by both unplanned interdependency chains and conscious interventions by more or less powerful groups. Regarding the present chapter the mediascape cultural flow is of especial significance, and has served to illustrate the global nature of the processes involved. It was suggested that globalization is best understood as a balance and blend between homogenization and differentiation, integration and disintegration, unification and diversification. That is, these processes are interwoven and require substantive investigation as such. In seeking to understand global sport development, researchers must address two main substantive tasks. The nature and extent of the interdependencies involved in the media–sport complex must be traced. In turn, this network must be located within wider global developments. Debate over the adequacy of the concept of globalization will no doubt continue. Resistance to the concept may be rooted less in academic debate and more in an inability to emancipate oneself from thinking in terms of nation-states as *the* departure point for analysing and understanding the world (Robertson, 1990: p. 26). Indeed a general cultural insecurity appears to result from these globalization processes. Jameson refers to this when he writes of 'the incapacity of our minds, at least at present, to map the great global multinational and decentred communicational network in which we find ourselves caught as individual subjects' (Jameson, 1984: p. 84). Irrespective of how it is understood, future research on media sport development will have to be sensitive to issues of global cultural *continuity* and *change*. Likewise the debate within 'critical' theory on the media will persist. Whether a form of cultural studies, 'critical political economy' or a process-sociological perspective is adopted, attention will need to be paid to the areas identified in this chapter. Within the broader analysis regarding the global sport system, the ownership, control and production of media–sport cultural goods, the form and content of sport mediated texts and the mode of consumer consumption will all require examination.

8

Global Sport, Identity Politics and Patriot Games

If we are to conceptualize the problems of the globalization of cultural diversity and postmodernism it is vital that we consider the shifting power-balances and interdependencies that exist between nation states and civilizational blocs which increasingly bind them together in the emerging global order.

Mike Featherstone, *Consumer Culture and Postmodernism*, 1991

What are the connections between global sport, national identity and identity politics? Historically, international sports contests, as they developed in the late nineteenth century, became a form of patriot games in which particular views of national identities and habitus codes were constructed and represented. Close links can be traced between the rituals of national identity practices and these sports occasions, and sport remains an arena where processes of habitus/identity testing and formation are conducted. Sports represent different individuals, communities, regions and nations, and a key feature of the global sport process is that it is used by different groups – those which are more established, as well as emergent or outsider groups – to represent, maintain and/or challenge identities. But in the context of globalization the role sport plays in identity politics has grown more complex. This chapter seeks to explore this growing complexity.

Sport and the Construction of National Identity

National cultures contain competing discourses that are bound up with the actions of specific groups. Through these actions and discourses, people construct meanings which influence and organize both their own and others' actions and conceptions of themselves. The discourses promoted in and through sport by dominant groups construct identities by producing meanings about 'the nation' with which people can identify. These meanings are contained in the stories that are told about the nation. They are also evident in the memories that connect a nation's present with its past. Images are also actively constructed about the nation in social practices. In sum, aspects of national identity involve reference to an 'imagined community' (Anderson, 1983).

The role that sport plays in this regard has not gone unnoticed. In examining the 'invention of tradition' during the Victorian age, Hobsbawm observed that sport was 'one of the most significant of the new practices of our period'. The last three decades of the nineteenth century, Hobsbawm argued, 'mark a decisive transformation in the spread of old, the invention of new, and the institutionalization of most sports on a national and even an international stage' (Hobsbawm, 1983: p. 298). From this beginning, sport and national identities have been intertwined. This can be illustrated by the following examples. The crossover between sport and other aspects of national culture and identity was evident in the 1991 rugby union World Cup tournament. Take, for example, the France versus England match. During the pre-match dressing-room build-up the English players listened to a recording of Sir Laurence Olivier reciting the Agincourt speech from Shakespeare's *Henry V*. The message was clear: the English players were competing not perhaps for Harry but for God, England and St George! Another vivid example stems from media discourse surrounding the 1966 soccer World Cup final between England and (West) Germany. An editorial in an English newspaper concluded that 'if, perchance, on the morrow Germany should beat us at our national game, let us take comfort from the fact that twice we have beaten them at theirs' (cited in Michener, 1976: p. 427). A third example relates directly to the case study under investigation here. The 'bodyline' controversy in the Australia–England cricket test series of 1932–33 involved, at one level, the use of violent tactics by the English side. At a different level, these sporting acts became bound up with issues of national honour and identity. One consequence of this was a forging of a less colonial and more independent

Australian attitude to dealings with the 'British'. Similar processes have been at work in relation to Indian cricket (Appadurai, 1995). In each of these examples, a historical legacy was invoked, past glories emphasized and the task facing the players represented as maintaining a set of invented traditions.

In examining the issue of national identities two key questions therefore arise. How is the modern nation imagined and what representational strategies are deployed to construct common-sense views of national belonging? With regard to the specific concerns of this chapter, one further question must be addressed. What are the representations of 'England' – as opposed to 'Britain' – through which powerful established groups seek to win the identification and define the identities of British/English people? This representation of national culture is imagined through the telling and retelling of stories in history books, novels, plays, poems, the media and popular culture (Colls, 1986; Dodd, 1986). Shared experiences, sorrows, triumphs and disasters are recounted in compelling ways. It is these that give meaning to the notion of nation and national identity. British/English people learn, for example, that the battle of Waterloo was won on the playing fields of Eton!

Sport is well placed to contribute to this process of identity-formation and invention of traditions. Sometimes the nationhood of countries is viewed as indivisible from the fortunes of the national teams of specific sports. Uruguay and Wales, with soccer and rugby union respectively, are prime examples (Krotee, 1979; Williams, 1991). C. L. R. James's discussion of cricket in the Caribbean is another example of the interweaving of sport, identity and nationhood (James, 1963). It also highlights that a sport form can be used to support or undermine hegemonic social relations. This link between sport and national culture and identity can be extended. Specific sports are seen to embody all the qualities of national character. In the habitus of male upper-class Englishness, cricket *embodies* the qualities of fair play, valour, graceful conduct on and off the pitch and steadfastness in the face of adversity. The cricket is seen to represent what 'England' is and gives meaning to the identity of being 'English'. The sport fixes 'England' as a focus of identification in English emotions. Just as Englishness is represented as an indefinable matter of being, and beyond the powers of foreigners to comprehend, so too with the subtleties of cricket.

National culture and identity are also represented by an emphasis on origins, continuity, tradition and timelessness. The origins of English culture and identity, for example, are viewed as lost in the mists of time. English qualities become 'taken for granted'. This very same emphasis is evident in sport contests between nations. Here reference is made to the 'Auld enemies' (Scotland vs. England) and 'Ancient foes' (Australia vs. England). The latter play for a trophy, the Ashes, an urn that contains part of the wicket that was burned when England first lost to Australia. National institutions are also imbued with a sense of tradition. The pageantry that surrounds the English monarchy is one example. Yet, both with the monarchy and with sport, these traditions are not as 'old' as they claim to be. Indeed, both the monarchy and sport appear to be based on foundational myths. Myths of this type seek to locate the origins of the nation, the people and/or national character much further back in time and place than the evidence supports. These foundational myths spill over into sport. By so doing they also help to shore up the wider invention and representation of national culture and identity. Several examples spring to mind. Think of the Abner Doubleday myth that surrounds the origins of the 'American' national game of baseball. Consider too that Italians do not use the term *football* to describe that sport form. Instead, the term *calcio* is used to reinforce the invention of a tradition that suggests that the origins of modern football can be traced to Italy. One may also point to the myth surrounding the origins of rugby in England and the alleged involvement of William Webb Ellis.

Male sport then appears to play a crucial role in the construction and representation of national identity. The sport of rugby has been fruitfully examined in this light by a range of contributors in a collection edited by Nauright and Chandler (1996) and also in a paper by Maguire and Tuck (1998). In the English/British case, given the role that sport plays in personal and national identity-formation, defeats on the playing field become represented as a kind of litmus test for the nation's decline. Another consequence is the juxtapositioning of this present reality with some mythical golden political and sporting age of the past. Yet, in the context of globalization processes in general and the later phases in the sportization process in particular, the role that global sport plays in identity politics becomes more ambiguous. In examining the issue of British/English culture and identity the analysis in this chapter will probe what is happening to cultural identities and habitus codes more generally in late modernity. This examination gives rise to questions regarding the tension-balance between the local and the global. Central in this regard is the extent to which national culture and identities are undergoing processes of homogenization and/or heterogenization. Attention is also paid to the question of whether national cultures and identities are being weakened, strengthened or pluralized by globalization processes. Heine and Young (1997) have insightfully addressed similar issues in relation to Inuit culture and folk games. Irrespective of place, are such processes leading to a sense of crisis of identity and of dislocation? If so, can a defensive ethnic assertiveness and a retreat into nostalgic discourse and actions be traced to a culture at the core of the global system?

The 1880s witnessed not only a distinct phase of intense globalization and nationalistic expression, but also a burst of wilful nostalgia (Robertson, 1992). Sport development, as was noted in chapter 4, both reflected and reinforced these processes. In this chapter the identity politics evident in the more recent sportization phase is examined. In particular, *male* sporting and political disaster discourse in the British media during the early 1990s will be shown to illustrate the linkages being examined. The more recent acceleration in globalization has not only been 'dislocating' for the English but has also been combined with other elements. The more central of these include the failure of sections of English society to adjust to the loss of Empire and the concomitant failure to embrace the notion of European integration. In addition, both the nationalist assertiveness of the Celtic peoples who comprise the UK (outside England), and the changing social mores flowing from pluralization trends that are also linked to globalization processes, contribute to a sense of unease among the English. In periods of intense globalization one response that is evident in the political and sporting fields is a process of 'wilful nostalgia'. Such rhetoric was evident in speeches made by Conservative politicians during the 1990s. These dislocating factors engendered among sections of the English a sense of unease and a feeling that one does not belong in the new Europe being developed.

Such processes have prompted resistance by those within a national culture who still cling to more intense versions of the invented traditions that underpin their habitus and sense of identity. This may take various forms. Resistance both to pluralization processes and the integrative tendencies associated with globalization reflects the ability of the representatives of national cultures to be responsive to global flows. At its most intense, this adherence to the invented traditions associated with a national culture can lead to what has been termed 'ethnic cleansing'. In Japan, resistance has been evident in a hostile reaction to 'foreign' success in national Sumo competitions and to the dominance of American women in the Japanese national basketball league. The defensive 'little Englander' response to national decline in general, and sporting disasters in particular, especially in the more recent stages of the fifth sportization phase, also demonstrates these processes at work. Wilful nostalgia underpinned the identity politics in Britain in the early 1990s.

Tracing the sportization process between the third and the fifth phases, it is clear that English sporting success, increasingly an infrequent occurrence, restores, however superficially, a symbolic sense of stability and national pride. In contrast, increasing losses to former colonies in the latest phase of sportization processes, some of whom still regard victory over their former colonial overlords as a form of rite of passage, compounds the general sense of English dislocation. In probing what is happening to national cultures, identities and habitus codes more generally in late modernity, in particular whether they are being weakened, strengthened or pluralized by globalization processes, these long-term processes need to be borne in mind. Such an approach rests on a specific perspective on habitus codes and national character. Before turning attention to the case study that explores the issues outlined, a brief summary of the perspective that underpins this analysis is appropriate.

Sport, European Identity Politics, Habitus Codes and 'National Character'

In his studies on the Germans (1996), personal pronouns (1987/1991) and established/outsider relations (1994), Elias provided an important conceptual framework that, along with the work of Anderson (1983) and Hobsbawm & Ranger (1983), will be used to guide the observations made in this chapter regarding global sport and identity politics. In an insightful passage, Elias highlighted several specific issues that are of assistance in making sense of international sporting tournaments. He wrote:

> A striking example in our time is that of the we-image and we-ideal of once-powerful nations whose superiority in relation to others has declined ... The radiance of their collective life as a nation has gone; their power superiority in relation to other groups ... is irretrievably lost. Yet the dream of their special charisma is kept alive in a variety of ways – through the teaching of history, the old buildings, masterpieces of the nation in the time of its glory, or through new achievements which seemingly confirm the greatness of the past. For a time, the fantasy shield of their imagined charisma as a leading established group may give a declining nation the strength to carry on.... But the discrepancy between the actual and the imagined

position of one's group among others can also entail a mistaken assessment of one's resources and, as a consequence, suggest a group strategy in pursuit of a fantasy image of one's own greatness that may lead to self-destruction ... The dreams of nations ... are dangerous.

(Elias, 1994: p. xliii)

Considered in this light international sports contests involve 'patriot games' in which the 'special charisma' embodied in the view which nations have of themselves can be nurtured, refined and further developed. Success in such contests can both reinforce and reflect the 'fantasy shield' of peoples' 'imagined charisma'. However, these sporting dreams, while having potentially unifying effects internally, far from uniting nations, can, at one and the same time, be divisive, myth-forming and potentially dangerous. These 'dreams', 'fantasy images' and 'imagined charisma' not only connect with deeply rooted habitus codes, but are also reflected in and reinforced by powerful media representations of political and cultural events.

Using this framework to examine English newspaper coverage of Euro 96, Maguire and Poulton (in press) identified several main findings. First, media coverage of Euro 96 served to 'divide' sections of the English from the nations of continental Europe, ironically within the unifying context of football. Second, English media coverage reflected a number of social currents that were evident in domestic politics at the time. These social currents include: an anti-Europeanism, particularly with regard to the so-called 'Beef War', the prospective single currency and the perceived 'interference' by Brussels in internal British concerns; a latent anti-German sentiment reflecting long-standing rivalry; and, with a general election imminent, the desire of the then Conservative British government and its allies in the right-wing press to foster what was termed a 'feel-good factor'. Third, the identity politics evident in the media discourse underpinning coverage of Euro 96 reflected more deep-seated British, probably mainly English, concerns regarding national decline and rapid social change. As a result, such media discourse tended towards two interwoven themes: nostalgia and ethnic assertiveness/defensiveness (Maguire & Poulton, in press). Similar sentiments, as will be shown, also surface with regard to sporting and political disasters.

The sense of nostalgia was particularly evident in the build-up to and in the early part of the Euro 96 tournament. Ethnic assertiveness/defensiveness became more evident as the tournament developed and as the English team encountered a series of old European foes, specifically Scotland, Holland, Spain and Germany. Media discourse of this kind can be understood as part of an active construction of 'fantasy group charisma', that is based on both the 'invention of traditions' and, at a deeper and more enduring level, the habitus codes that underpin the 'national character' of European nations. This requires further explanation. Commenting in the light of recent attempts to construct a 'European' identity on the greater potency of identification with the nation, Elias observed:

> Think, for example, of the difference in the emotional charge between the statements: 'I am an Englishman', 'I am a Frenchman', 'I am a German' and the statement: 'I am an English, French or German European'. All references to the individual European nation-states have a strong emotive value to the people involved whether positive, negative or ambivalent. Statements like 'I am a European, a Latin American, an Asian' are emotively weak by comparison.
>
> (Elias, 1987/1991: p. 226)

Underpinning these observations is a range of empirically based figurational concepts that assist in making sense of global sport and national identity politics. These include: Elias's developmental account of European history, social development and national identity; his use of concepts such as established and outsiders; his use of pronoun pairs (I/we, us/them) as a way of drawing attention to the emotionally charged character of relationships and identifications; the coupling of the concept of national habitus codes with the idea of multilayered identities, and the placing of both identity politics (and the role that sport plays in this regard) within the context of globalization processes. One of the problems that Elias sought to address in his study of established and outsider figurations was:

> how and why human beings perceive one another as belonging to the same group and include one another within the group boundaries which they establish in saying 'we' in their reciprocal communications, while at the same time excluding other human beings whom they perceive as belonging to another group and to whom they collectively refer as 'they'.
>
> (Elias, 1994a: p. xxxvii)

In his introduction to *The Established and the Outsiders*, Elias made the connection between these issues of identity and national character, but it was in his work on the Germans where these links were most fully substantiated. In this latter study, Elias investigated the deeply embodied aspects of German habitus, personality, social structure and conduct and how these features (the I/we-image of the Germans) emerged out of the nation's history and pattern of social development. The fortunes of the nation became sedimented, internalized and fused as part of the 'second nature' (the habitus) of its citizens, whose actions made and remade the national habitus anew. The 'image' of the nation is also constitutive of a person's self-image. These observations run counter to conventional notions of the individual, the nation and 'national character' – which conceptualize them as if they are separate entities. Yet, as Elias observes:

> The concept of identification makes it appear that the individual is here and the nation is there; it implies that the 'individual' and 'nation' are two different entities separated in space. Since nations consist of individuals and individuals who live in the more developed twentieth century state-societies belong, in the majority of cases, unambiguously to a nation, a conceptionalization which evokes the picture of two different entities separated in space, like mother and child, does not fit the facts.
>
> (Elias, 1996: p. 152)

In fact, the emotional bonds of individuals with the nations they form with each other can have, as one of their levels, 'sleeping memories' which tend to crystallize and become organized around common symbols – national sports teams being one example. These symbols and sleeping memories usually go unnoticed, yet they powerfully reinforce the notion of I/we-relations and form the focal point of a common belief system. Examining these habitus codes allows investigation of why, for example, European integration at the level of political institutions is running ahead of the degree of identification that many, perhaps the majority, of the citizens of the European nation-states feel towards the notion of being 'European'. Writing in this connection, Elias observed:

> The deeply rooted nature of the distinctive national characteristics and the consciousness of national we-identity closely bound up with them can serve as a graphic example of the degree to which the social habitus of the individual provides a soil in which personal, individual differences can flourish. The individuality of the particular Englishman, Dutchman, Swede or German represents, in a sense, the personal elaboration of a common social, and in this case national, habitus.
>
> (Elias, 1994a: p. 210)

Such observations should not be taken as implying that these emotional bonds and I/we-images are permanently fixed and go unchallenged. In all nations there are, to blend aspects of Elias's conceptualization with that of Raymond Williams, 'dominant', 'emergent' and 'residual' habitus codes (Williams, 1977). There is a blend of habitus codes that is related to the twin processes of diminishing contrasts and increasing varieties, between homogenizing and heterogenizing tendencies. The interplay between these tendencies varies in intensity and scope over time and place. For Elias, the layer of social identity/habitus code forming 'national character' is 'like [a] language, both hard and tough, but also flexible and far from immutable' (Elias, 1987/1991: p. 209). In a sense, then, when examining national characteristics we are dealing with the interconnected ways of knowing that have been termed by Giddens (1986: pp. 41–4) 'practical consciousness' and 'discursive consciousness'. The level of 'practical consciousness' (everyday actions that are intuitively performed) is more taken for granted, yet finds expression in and is influenced by the two-way traffic conducted with the 'discursive consciousness' (actions that are based on cognitively based decision-making) of an individual. While the concepts of invented traditions and imagined communities are also fruitful in exploring European identity politics, such concepts appear to be dealing only with the level of 'discursive consciousness', to ignore the level of 'practical consciousness' and to overlook the interplay between the two.

There is no standardized, immutable, genetically inherited national character. Yet the habitus codes, embodied feelings and discursive practices of the individuals who constitute a nation play a powerful role both in the foundation of cultural relations and in the construction and maintenance of national identities. National cultures can be said to provide one of the main sources of self-identity. As Elias stated:

> In the present day world, nations ... appear to have become the dominant and most powerful of all ... supra-individual influences on people's feelings of meaning and value ... They [individual people] are coming to recognise more and more clearly the functions of nations or national groups as the guarantors, guardians, embodiments or symbols of a great part of that which they perceive as of lasting value in their individual existence.
>
> (Elias, 1996: p. 352)

In a word, people in complex nation-states, have multiple identities that are many-layered – local, regional, national, global. These layers form a flexible lattice work of the habitus of a person. Individuals do not only have an 'ego-image' and an 'ego-ideal', but also a 'we-image' and a 'we-ideal'. The image of this 'we' 'forms an integral part of the personality organisation of the individual who ... uses the pronouns "I" and "we" with reference to him- or herself' (Elias, 1996: p. 153). As Elias explained in an earlier text:

> The I-we identity ... forms an integral part of the social habitus of a person, and as such is open to individualization. This identity represents the answer to the question 'Who am I?', both as a social and as an individual being.
>
> (Elias, 1987/1991: p. 183)

One of the most potent I/we-identities of an individual member of a modern nation-state is that associated with that individual's nation. These stronger identifications stem from the fact that nation-states are social survival groups. The 'traits' of national group identity, what is conventionally termed 'national character', are a layer of the social habitus built very deeply and firmly in the personality structure of an individual (Elias, 1987/1991: p. 209). The problem of national character for Elias is thus:

> a habitus problem par excellence. The idea that the individual bears in himself or herself the habitus of a group, and that it is this habitus that he or she individualizes to a greater or lesser extent, can be somewhat more precisely defined ... the social habitus ... in more complex societies ... has many layers. Someone may, for example, have the peculiarities of a Liverpool-English or a Black Forest-German European. It depends on the number of interlocking planes in his (*sic*) society how many layers are interwoven in the social habitus of a person.
>
> (Elias, 1987/1991: p. 183)

Through discursive practices and practical actions, both of which have an often unacknowledged affective component, our I/we-identity is constructed. The familiar, the taken-for-granted, the daily unnoticed actions bind us to a particular I/we-identity – a process that has occurred through childhood and continues through adult life. The deepening and consolidation of an I/we-feeling is also a double-bind – a cognition/sentiment which, while it enables us to 'share' things in common with others who are like 'us', also acts to separate 'us' from 'them' – the 'outsiders'. The group dynamics observable in this connection are of particular relevance for an understanding of what has recently come to be conceptualized as 'national identity politics'. For nation-states 'were born in wars and for wars, between established and outsider groups' (Elias, 1987/1991: p. 201). Indeed, inter-national civilizing processes are also marked by elimination struggles between groups. For Elias, this helps to explain the importance of national identity to contemporary peoples:

> Here we find the explanation why, among the various layers of we-identity, the state level of integration today carries special weight and a special emotional charge. The integration plane of the state, more than any other layer of we-identity, has in the consciousness of most members the function of a survival unit, a protection unit on which depends their physical and social security in the conflicts of human groups and in cases of physical catastrophe.
>
> (Elias, 1987/1991: p. 208)

From what has been argued so far, it can be seen that national habitus codes can be understood as one of the most embracing and significant of the members of a modern nation-state's multilayered I/we-identities. The I/we habitus code gives the person a sense of individual self, but also of her/his we-group identity. When such a person is confronted with 'outsiders', such codes tend to harden and become more sharply defined. While the process of national habitus/character-formation is framed, constructed and represented by and through discursive practices (such as the production and consumption of media sport discourses), these practices themselves are interwoven with activities occurring at the level of 'practical consciousness'. While the former involve a set of consciously created images, histories, symbols and invented traditions which have endured for greater and lesser periods of time and which confer meaning on what is involved in being psychologically and socially part of the 'imagined community' of the nation, the latter entail unnoticed activities, deeply rooted memories, that are part of the group's collectively shared embodied experiences and stocks of knowledge.

The fantasy shield and imagined group charisma of European nations are based on such practices and actions. Yet, currently, the citizens of these nations are being confronted with the twin, interlocking processes of Europeanization and globalization. It has already been noted how the citizens of European countries tend to have stronger and more emotive I/we identifications with their nations rather than with the we-identity notion of themselves as Europeans. A question that arises, as noted at the outset, is whether as a result of processes of Europeanization and globalization, I/we national identities are being strengthened, weakened or

pluralized. Internal political/cultural processes are also leading to
the questioning of more dominant national habitus codes in European states such as Great Britain, Italy and Spain, where demands
for Scottish and Basque independence are matched by attempts by
the Northern League to separate from the rest of Italy.

Viewed in processual terms, this is not surprising. While the
nation-state-based we-identity of the European individual in our
day is almost 'taken-for-granted', Elias also notes that 'one does
not always remember clearly enough that the role of the state as a
frame of reference for the we-identity of the great majority of all
members of a state, i.e. the state's role as nation-state, is of relatively recent origin' (Elias, 1987/1991: p. 206). Tracing this process
back to the shift between absolutist and multi-party states, Elias
notes that it has only been in the course of the twentieth century
that a more complete integration of citizens in European countries
in their nation-states has occurred. During the twentieth century:

> the manipulation of feelings in relation to state and nation, govern-
> ment and political system, is a widespread technique in social
> praxis. In all nation states the institutions of public education are
> dedicated to an extreme degree to deepening and consolidating a
> we-feeling based exclusively on the national tradition ... If we are
> looking for examples of the reality-congruence of the habitus
> concept, we could hardly find a more cogent example than the per-
> sistent way in which the national habitus of the European nation-
> states impedes their closer political union.
>
> (Elias, 1994a: p. 210)

Just as it takes several generations for the collective group memories and habitus codes of individuals' fantasy beliefs of former
greatness and superiority to dissipate, so it may be that the citizens
of present-day nation-states are but the first generation who are
voluntarily taking the first step towards European I/we group
identification within a 'United States of Europe'. Perhaps it will be
only the descendants of present-day citizens who will feel an emotionally stronger I/we European identity than their ancestors currently feel towards the various nation-states of Europe. On the
other hand, the twin processes of Europeanization and globalization may prompt, and, in fact, may already be prompting,
ethnically assertive and defensive forms of nationalism. Euro-
peanization/globalization may be being viewed by individuals as
a form of dislocation. As Hall has observed, 'when the era of
nation-states in globalization begins to decline, one can see a
regression to a very defensive and highly dangerous form of
national identity which is driven by a very aggressive form

of racism' (Hall, 1991: p. 26). As a consequence of such processes, individuals living within such nation-states may feel a sense of heterophobia, 'a phenomenon of unease, anxiety, discomfort and a sense of loss of control commonly experienced when confronted by the unknown' (Cohen, 1994: p. 194), and they may seek refuge in 'wilful nostalgia' and assert a more ethnically cleansed I/we-identity and habitus code. These are issues that require further investigation. At this stage it is appropriate to examine in greater detail how globalization processes are impacting on both European and British/English national identity politics.

Globalization, English Identity Politics and 'Wilful Nostalgia'

Nostalgia as a concept has a long history in Western traditions. The person so afflicted is seen not to feel comfortable in their time/space, with their world. As Turner remarks, 'for the nostalgic, the world is alien' (1987: p. 149). The same can be said for sections of the English today. Closely linked to nostalgia is a sense of melancholy – a longing for a time, a place or, sometimes, a person. These embodied feelings can affect us in different ways. Some individuals, and people in some societies, may be more nostalgia-prone than others. Four main dimensions of nostalgic discourse have been identified (Turner, 1987), and each is evident in the discourses underpinning media reporting of sporting and political disasters in British society in the early 1990s. The first includes a sense of historical decline or loss, a departure from some mythical golden age of belonging, evident, for example, in the problems created by the loss of the British Empire. Second, there is a sense of the absence or loss of personal wholeness and moral certainty. In this regard, the pluralization of morals, the questioning of religious certainty and the emergence of multiculturalism affect British society in a variety of ways. The third involves a concomitant sense of loss of individual freedom, autonomy and personal authenticity. The perceived threats posed by European integration to national sovereignty and the liberties of the 'free-born' English are to the fore in this discourse exemplified by Prime Minister Major's address to the Conservative Party conference in 1992:

> I will never, come hell or high water, let our distinctive British identity be lost in a federal Europe . . . And if there are those who have in mind to haul down the union jack and fly high the star-spangled

banner of a United States of Europe, I say to them: you misjudge the
temper of the British people.

(Guardian, 10 October 1992: p. 2)

The fourth dimension links this nostalgic discourse with the perceived and actual loss of rural life, traditional stability and cultural
integration. This is vividly encapsulated in speeches by John Major
which evoke a specific aspect of the British past and emphasize the
'essentials' of Englishness. During the same party conference,
Major had concluded his speech with an assurance that Britain
would survive, fifty years hence, in its unamendable essentials. It
would remain, as the *Guardian* noted some six months later, 'the
country of long shadows on county [cricket] grounds, warm beer,
invincible green suburbs, dog lovers and pools fillers' (*Guardian*, 23
April 1993: p. 1).

Such rhetoric overlooks the contested, gendered nature of being
British and collapses the notion of being a Briton with being
English. The discourse evident in some English sport forms (e.g.,
cricket) reinforces such sentiments. Yet, in other sports (e.g., rugby
union) the contentious nature of identity is only too evident. In this
respect, Britain appears to be a culture that is particularly prone to
intermittent nostalgic crises. While these insights are fruitful, there
is also a need to explore the sociogenesis of nostalgia in a broader
manner that explores the circumstances that both generate periodic
bouts of nostalgia and which are currently engendering a sense of
dislocation in the English, which may also connect with eighteen
years of Conservative rule. A developmental account is needed
that places the processes of national habitus/identity on a broader
canvas. During the 'take-off' phase of globalization, corresponding
with the third phase in sportization processes, a tide of embodied
nostalgia swept across established and emergent Western nations.
The interwoven processes that globalization entails set in motion a
form of cultural politics that found expression in wilful nostalgia.
Britannia was seen to rule the waves.

In this period there was a clear connection between nation-
state formation, cultural identity politics and the global diffusion
of sport. Since the late 1960s, humanity has experienced, to a
greater or lesser extent, another major phase of globalization.
There is a connection between this and the fifth phase of sportization. The accelerating speed and changing form of globalization has led to an exacerbation of the tendencies, in some
cultures more than others, towards the construction and
representation of nostalgia. This is evident in the discourse
underpinning commentary on English sporting and political

disasters. In the new global figuration, English*men* were and are being beaten at their 'own' games. Their refuge is nostalgia, their last bastion patriotism.

This more recent phase of globalization also involves the reconstruction and problematization of the four key reference points of globalization identified by Robertson (1992: p. 27). With regard to each reference point, Britain and its citizens provide an ideal typical exemplar of the processes at work. At the level of the British nation, for example, problems of heterogeneity and diversity have arisen. Internal and external pressures have developed that are leading some to seek to reconstruct collective identities along pluralistic lines. Closely connected to this is the process by which individuals have become subject to competing ethnic, cultural and religious reference points. The system of international interdependency chains in which Britain is located has also become more fluid, multipolar and dynamic. European, Commonwealth and United Nations networks are undergoing processes of rapid change. The loss of positions of power in sporting politics (e.g., in FIFA and the IOC) coincides with decline in global political terms. The idea of humankind has also become more contested and open to critical scrutiny. Perhaps it is less surprising to observe that, in some societies, nostalgic resistance to globalization processes has grown more intense. In the identity politics of modern Britain, the fragile male 'little Englander' wrestles with more fluid, pluralistic and less male-defined global identities. In the male versions of sports such as cricket, rugby union and soccer this struggle is most evident. How were these themes and issues played out in English identity politics during the 1990s?

Sporting Disasters, English National Malaise and the Identity Politics of Wilful Nostalgia during the 1990s

By examining links between nostalgia, globalization and the dislocating elements within British society, aspects of the perspective on which the present book is based can be extended. The case study presented here links political and sporting discourses evident in the British media during the 1990s with each other. It focuses on a sense of national angst, malaise and a longing for some mythical golden age and what might be termed *Heimat*. Underpinning the construction and representation of national identities of those countries in relative decline is a sense of nostalgia that is engendered, represented and embodied. The question concerns how people who compose societies remember (Connerton, 1989)? A dominant way in the modern world is through embodied male sport habitus/identity practices.

Writing in July 1993, a *Guardian* correspondent observed that 'our streets are no longer safe, we're giving up power to Brussels, we can't even win at cricket anymore. Whatever happened to the English?' (*Guardian*, 28 July 1993: p. 2). This observation links a set of sociocultural and political problems that had been perceived as besetting Britain especially over the past year or so. Though contoured by short-term dynamics, they were also part of the long-term dislocating trends that are evident in British society at large. They include but are no means exhausted by the following: economic decline and the attendant problems of mass unemployment; the loss of Empire and the failure fully to embrace the notion of European integration; the ongoing tensions associated with the aspirations of the various nations and peoples that compose the United Kingdom; and the changing social mores and the seemingly inexorable rise of crime and the perceived increase in violence. Short-term calamities, such as the effective devaluation of the pound sterling in 1993 on what was dubbed 'Black Wednesday', became portrayed as symptomatic of decline and how these dislocating trends can be judged.

During the 1990s media reporting of these issues was incessant. The general tenor of the reports centred on a sense of pessimism, a lack of national cohesion and direction and a longing for a time when things 'worked' and people felt more secure. It will have to suffice in this context to cite an extract from an editorial in the *Daily Telegraph* to illustrate the issues involved:

> A mental state of pessimistic fatalism has the country in its grip. The sense of national despondency is not purely political or economic ... but spans almost the entire range of human experience. It is a crisis of national will, a moral crisis.
>
> (*Daily Telegraph*, 22 February 1993: p. 18)

Discourse of this kind was repeatedly linked to a series of sporting disasters. Four days after the above report, an editorial in the *Guardian* illustrated the links that the media were making. It is worth quoting at some length:

> The grief-stricken tributes of the past two days to the former England football captain Bobby Moore represent something more than a general mourning for a great sporting hero.... Detectable within them is another kind of mourning: for a world as it seems looking back, when things sometimes used to go right ... Wherever you look, people seem to be saying, things are steadily getting

worse. Our streets are less safe than they were 30 years ago, our world reputation less glowing, our monarchy less revered, our sportsmen less sporting, our educational system less educational. The word of an English gentleman is no longer his bond in the way it was when England conquered the world. What this evidence really describes is a nation ill at ease with itself, fed up with the present and fretful about the future. That made the pictures of Moore yesterday ... especially poignant. They belonged to an age, as it seems in retrospect, when we still seemed to win. The reverse of our present predicament – losing on the economy, losing on jobs, losing on law and order – even losing to India: unshaven despondent Gooch, in brutal contrast to clean-cut triumphant Moore.

(*Guardian*, 26 February 1993: p. 20)

Several issues are raised in this editorial. In particular, defeats by the men's English cricket team in India and Sri Lanka and the death of an Englishman Bobby Moore, captain of the 1966 World Cup winning soccer team, were connected to broader social ills. In addition, reporting dwelt on notions of 'England's agony' and 'England's sadness'. Another reporter, writing in the *Independent*, was not slow to highlight this tendency:

That word again. The death of Bobby Moore, *England's* hero. Golden-haired, a gentle giant, a great *Englishman*. Sport, where Britain supports different national teams, has become one of the few areas where an uncomplicated celebration of Englishness is permissible. It is only a mild exaggeration to call England the submerged nation.... So England becomes a country that exists on the sports field, but not elsewhere.

(*Independent*, 26 February 1993: p. 19)

Reinforcing this type of media discourse was specially commissioned polling research. A Gallup poll confirmed, as one newspaper noted, that 'the nation's morale (was) approaching a crisis' (*Daily Telegraph*, 22 February 1993). A 'mood of moral despondency' was said to have 'gripped the country' (*Daily Telegraph*, 23 February 1993: p. 16). Clearly the litany of sporting disasters that was in part being referred to requires closer examination. During late 1992 and early 1993, the male English cricket team lost heavily to India and Sri Lanka. The magnitude of the defeat was perceived to be great. In India a record 3–0 series defeat was inflicted on the English and, for the first time ever, Sri Lanka defeated the former colonial power. One newspaper suggested that the latter defeat was 'another day of English shame' (*Daily Mirror*, 18 March 1993: pp. 46–7). The defeats were bad enough, but complaints also

surfaced in the media that the players were not acting like gentlemen. Poor dress sense, unshaven appearance, bad manners and a
lack of sporting attitude were all emphasized. An editorial in the
Independent illustrates the sentiments expressed:

> Ultimately, the quality that most sharply differentiates cricket from
> other sports is its elegance and capacity to give aesthetic pleasure.
> Take that away and the game is greatly diminished. If the England
> team cannot win, they should at least behave in a way that does not
> bring them – and this country – into disrepute.
>
> (*Independent*, 12 March 1993: p. 24)

This discourse was not confined to media personnel. Male Labour
Party politicians were not hesitant to enter the fray. The former
deputy leader, Roy Hattersley, observed:

> I suspect that we lost gracefully at cricket because we won so regu-
> larly at almost everything else. There were occasional setbacks but
> we always overcame them. The Zulus overran us at Isandhlwana
> but in the replay at Rourke's Drift, we forced an honourable
> draw.... Losing at cricket was a setback which could be greeted
> with a joke about ashes and urns and an obituary notice in the
> *Times*. But not now ... The reaction to Sri Lanka's victory bore all
> the marks of hysteria borne out of lost confidence.
>
> (*Guardian*, 15 March 1993: p. 21)

Such defeats, then, were viewed as 'England's considerable fall
from Grace' (*Independent*, 23 March 1993: p. 21). Terms such as
humiliation, disgrace, shame, unparalleled ineptitude, calamity,
ultimate ignominy were all used to conjure up the scale of the
debacle. The press, composed mostly of English reporters, urged
the team to salvage some honour, do their duty and, if not, do the
'decent thing', meaning in this case, resign! Take the following
comments:

> The England cricket team – failing, morally shifty, globally insignifi-
> cant, distracted by irrelevant attention to demeanour, run by dis-
> credited leaders insolently continuing in office – may not be a credit
> to the nation, but is a perfect reflection of it.
>
> (*Independent*, 23 March 1993: p. 21)

This fall from grace and the sense of angst dovetailed well with
the rhetoric surrounding the death of Bobby Moore. Again the discourse centred around a sense of loss and regret that times had
changed for the worse. Britain was no longer at ease with itself.

Moore was juxtaposed with the sports stars of the present and represented as a 'heroic symbol of a golden age'. Such sentiments concerning the sense of unease that sections of the English felt were also to resurface following the death of Diana, Princess of Wales in 1997. The connection with Moore can be best shown by observations made in the *Observer*:

> Amid the coarsening of spirit that has been manifest in this country over the past couple of decades, there is a measure of reassurance in finding so much of the nation so deeply affected by the death of Bobby Moore ... There was a pervasive sense of loss, an unforced emotion that suggested many had been taken unawares by the depth of their feelings.
>
> (*Observer*, 28 March 1993: p. 23)

Reference to Moore and soccer is connected to a series of 'disasters' in that sport that confirms the above discussion. Defeat in a World Cup qualifying match in Oslo proved to be a painful experience for the English. Media reporting dwelt on the 'country's day of sporting shame' (*Daily Mirror*, 3 June 1993: p. 1). In the rhetoric of the tabloids, the defeat was viewed simply as the 'end of the world' (*Daily Star*, 3 June 1993: p. 1). The Oslo 'debacle' was represented as a 'symptom of a deeper crisis' and the media launched into a critical review of the perceived malaise in English soccer. One newspaper posed the following question:

> Where are our heroes now? The national disillusion about English football and cricket goes beyond disappointment at humiliating defeat. The heart of the matter is the failure of England's sporting stars to inspire, either by their talent or their behaviour.
>
> (*Independent*, 12 June 1993: p. 16)

These sporting disasters were also linked to the defeats that the sports-loving cricket buff, Prime Minister John Major, was experiencing. Ironically, Major himself stressed the link between sport and national identity when he commented that 'People like sport and they enjoy it. It is part of our national psychology ... I think we have undervalued sport and the place it has in our national life' (*Daily Telegraph*, 23 August 1993: p. 34). Cartoons depicted a hapless Major trying to deal with an assorted range of issues. In one cartoon Major is keeping goal in a soccer match with shots raining in on him. The soccer balls were meant to signify the political problems besetting his administration. Following the Norwegian defeat, the *Sun* explicitly made this linkage when commenting on the general state of sport and politics:

Did you wake up this morning with pride in your heart? With the feeling that it is good to be British? You probably didn't. And that's a crying shame. For the one thing this country has never lacked spirit ... What has gone wrong is that we lack someone to inspire us, to bring out the best in us. Whether it is football, cricket or politics, we seem to be on a losing run. Graham Taylor manages a football team that doesn't want to play for him. Ted Dexter runs a cricket team so uninspired it probably wouldn't survive on a village green. John Major is not only failing to lead the country ... He also heads a Tory party more divided than at any time for twenty years. Why is Britain playing below form, why are our heads down? Because we are not being led. The British people are a great crew. What we need now is a great skipper.

(*Sun*, 11 June 1993: p. 40)

Other parallels were also made between the fortunes of the Prime Minister and the manager of the England soccer team. The *Independent* (11 June 1993: p. 1) treated it as a front page lead in which the fortunes and fate of the respective leaders were discussed. Such sentiments also found expression in editorials. In a general account of the perceived mess the country was in and the supposed lack of leadership, the *Daily Telegraph* concluded:

The morale of the British people is at a low ebb. A range of unrelated misfortunes ... coalesce to create a sense of national failure: lost football and cricket matches, strife in the schools system, recession, impotence in the face of horror in Bosnia, terrorist attacks and crime on the streets at home.... Underlying the mood of gloom there is the indisputable fact that the government has not been conducted with much skill or conviction in recent months.

(*Daily Telegraph*, 11 June 1993: p. 22)

Reinforcing this imagery were cartoons questioning the competency of the nation's leaders. John Major was depicted in a cricket context with headlines asking 'Follow what Leader' and being given 'Out' by public opinion. Trivial incidents like the erosion of coastal land that led to the fall of a hotel into the sea were depicted as symbolising the fall of Britain in general (*Daily Mail*, 12 June 1993: p. 9). Right-wing political commentators linked the issues of the experience of the hotel with the general cultural malaise. During the same period in which this political commentary was being expressed, English sporting disasters continued apace. The Australians were busy thrashing the male English cricket team. The success of the women's national cricket team in the World Cup competition being held in England at the same time was largely overlooked, and certainly not represented as relevant to the fortunes of national identity. This was a male-defined affair.

This angst about the fortunes of the cricket team spread to a general examination of the state of British sport and the leadership provided. A writer in the *Guardian* claimed that 'a lack of character has caused England's current dismal standing in modern sport' (*Guardian*, 23 June 1993: p. 15). The *Observer*, in an article entitled 'Sport in Crisis', again linked the failure of political with sporting leadership. The cartoon accompanying the report vividly displayed this linkage, depicting an assortment of sporting and political leaders. The writer concluded:

> Sport has always been a source of pride to Britain. We gave the world most of its greatest games and many of those we did not invent, we codified and regulated. The story of sport in the past half-century is symptomatic of the state of the nation. We are not as influential as we once were and when things go wrong rarely does anyone do the decent thing ... There is little honour and a lot of greed ... Why has our sport turned so sour in this summer of discontent?
>
> (*Observer*, 27 June 1993: p. 41)

This sense of decline, crisis, despondency and malaise was compounded by defeats for the English soccer team against the USA and, in late 1993, against the Netherlands. A series of vitriolic headlines called for the manager to be sacked and again declared that defeat against the USA was a national disgrace, humiliation and a stain on the national honour (*Guardian*, 11 June 1993: p. 20; *Daily Express*, 11 June 1993: p. 8; *Daily Star*, 11 June 1993: p. 44; *Daily Mirror*, 11 June 1993: p. 42; *Daily Telegraph*, 11 June 1993: p. 40). Defeat was again represented as indicative of the nation's decline. Some commentators were swift in alluding to the ills of the nation that sporting disasters reveal. The following commentary in the *Daily Mail* highlights both the reaction to the defeat by the USA and the more general issues that have been raised by this case study:

> We lose to America in football; to Brussels in European policy; to Japan in industry; to secularism in the church; our economic policy has been a disaster. When the time comes to choose successors to these leaders I expect we shall be looking for birds of a brighter feather.
>
> (*Daily Mail*, 12 June 1993: p. 9)

Media representation of defeats in the male versions of soccer, rugby and cricket were thus represented as something of greater significance than sport and both as reinforcing and reflecting a range of emotions said to be at play in the nation as a whole. This range of sporting disasters was paralleling the perceived decline in the nation at large. Discussing this 'crisis of self-confidence', former *Times* editor William Rees-Mogg returned to the nostalgia theme when he concluded:

> The lack of confidence eats into our national life. The British who are about 1% of the world's population ran the world for about 100 years, from the defeat of Napoleon to the outbreak of the First World War. That was an exceptional episode. Before then we were one of several powers; since then we have again been one of several powers. Before we ran the world we produced Shakespeare, who is the world's greatest poet and Isaac Newton, who may be the world's greatest scientist. We also gave birth to the United States. Even nowadays Britain is one of the pleasantest and fairest countries in the world to live in. We play a not unworthy part in world trade, world communication and world defence. But it would be good for our national morale if our cricketers recovered their belief in themselves.
>
> (*The Times*, 12 August 1993: p. 16)

In the autumn of 1993, John Major again gave his annual address to the Conservative Party conference. Two dominant themes of the speech were an advocacy of 'Back to Basics' and an assertive Englishness. 'Back to Basics' became both a slogan and a set of policies that emphasized a return to the values of an earlier England. This nostalgic longing for what was presumed to be a past golden age dovetailed well with a patriotic fervour that emphasized the virtues of Englishness and pillorying of foreigners. In a series of speeches cabinet ministers expanded on these themes. The education minister argued that each school should 'fly the flag'. Another minister, Michael Portillo, mapped out what he termed 'the new British disease'. This, he identified, as 'the self-destructive sickness of national cynicism'. He concluded:

> A country which places no value on its national characteristics cannot be stable or prosperous for long. Self-doubt gnaws away at the sinews of our institutions and weakens the nation. An elite that raises up heroes merely for the enjoyment of pulling them down is indeed sick ... Our mission must be to rebuild national self-confidence and self-belief. We need to assert the value and quality of the British way of life and of British institutions.
>
> (*Observer*, 16 January 1994: p. 22)

Significantly, some sections of the British press reinforced these sentiments. *The Times*, for example, noted that 'the current mood of national self-doubt cannot be addressed without a comprehensive debate on Britishness itself' (*The Times*, 18 January 1994: p. 19). Such self-doubt was not confined to national identity. Several newspapers continued to juxtapose the varying fortunes of English sports stars with the ill-fated premiership of John Major. The success of ice stars Torvill and Dean in the European Championships was contrasted vividly with the problems – political, economic and social – besetting Major's administration in early 1994 (*Independent*, 11 January 1994: p. 9). The poor form of the male English national rugby team was also linked to the performance of Major. The *Daily Telegraph* captured this in headline form, linking Major's inability to catch a rugby ball with his own 'annus horribilis', echoing the ongoing traumas of the monarchy (*Daily Telegraph*, 11 February 1994: p. 12).

Concerned by the perceived decline of English, as well as British, sporting performances, especially in 'traditional' sports, Major sought to improve participation rates, identify talent and nurture elite athletes. These sentiments found expression in the government report *Sport: Raising The Game*, published within a year of the sporting disasters just outlined. The significance of sport for national identity was not overlooked by Major. Writing in the foreword to the report he observed:

> Sport is a central part of Britain's national heritage. We invented the majority of the world's great sports. And most of those we did not invent, we codified and helped to popularise throughout the world. It could be argued that nineteenth century Britain was the cradle of a leisure revolution every bit as significant as the agricultural and industrial revolutions we launched in the century before. Sport is a binding force between generations and across borders. But, by a miraculous paradox, it is at the same time one of the defining characteristics of nationhood and of local pride. We should cherish it for both those reasons.
>
> (*Sport: Raising The Game*, 1995: p. 2)

Such sentiments clearly underpinned the successful campaign to host the Euro 96 soccer championships. One of the *Daily Telegraph*'s political correspondents noted when the tournament started:

> Mr Major is clearly hoping that a repeat of England's 1966 victory could kick-start the feel-good factor. He predicted that when he meets his European partners at the Florence summit this month the most animated discussions will probably be about football despite the beef stand off. He quipped: 'The Italians may have the European

presidency but we have home advantage. We made it count in 1966. Let's hope that football comes home in glory this summer'.

(Daily Telegraph, 8 June 1996: p. 5)

Echoing its political correspondent, one of the sports reporters for the same newspaper (8 June 1996: p. 30) observed that 'England's opportunity to restore pride begins today at 3pm sharp'. As Maguire and Poulton (in press) have noted, a range of patriot games was on display during the tournament, especially in matches involving England's 'old enemies': Scotland, Spain and Germany. But against Germany the English were again to be defeated and the defeat hurt. Reaction in the tabloid press dove-tailed well with the broadsheet editorials prior to the game. In somewhat emotive language, an editorial in the *Daily Mail* again made the link between sporting success and economic decline:

> Only a game? The ramifications of this national calamity extend far beyond the sports field. Take economics, for instance. For years, prophets of economic decline like the Observer editor Will Hutton have been contrasting British economic decline with the post-war German economic miracle ... But last night's display of footballing Vorsprung durch Technik seemed to confirm the Huttonite view. If we can't even beat them at footie, what chance have we of beating them at manufacturing. No matter how unfounded, such feelings of economic inferiority have political implications too. When historians look back on John Major's defeat at the coming election, I suspect that many will cite last night as the moment when any outside chance of a Tory comeback flickered and died.
>
> *(Daily Mail,* 27 June 1996: p. 8)

Gaining what the editor felt was some solace from the defeat, the *Daily Mail* continued by arguing that the English had been defeated at their game, not at Germany's. What the *Daily Mail* concluded is worthy of quoting at some length:

> We must regard last night's defeat as another sort of victory – not a moral victory, but a historical victory. For surely we British have achieved nothing more admirable this century than teaching the Germans how to beat us at our own game. It was in 1863 – 133 years ago – that the Football Association was born. At that time, Germany did not even exist as a united state. And although the game had caught on in Imperial Germany by the time of World War I – so much so that on Christmas Day, 1914, British and German soldiers played football together in 'No-Man's Land' – it continued to be regarded as an English import ... Nor is football the only thing we have taught the Germans this century. We have – after two great

conflagrations – taught them economic liberalism and parliamentary democracy too. Not bad going. True, no teacher likes it when his brilliant pupil gets the better of him. But there is surely some satisfaction in seeing how well the pupil has been taught.

(*Daily Mail*, 27 June 1996: p. 8)

The somewhat condescending tone of this editorial was matched by a similar article in the *Daily Express*. One of its reporters, Cosmo Forbes, acknowledged that 'defeat is bitter' but that the nation had to find a way of coping. Ironically, given the defeat but not the agenda the paper was setting, the writer concluded:

It is the example of Germany which can instruct us in how to handle, and not handle, defeat. Germany, after all, has failed catastrophically in the real world and not on the sporting field, twice this century. It has crashed to two overwhelming defeats in wars, in which we have been among the victors ... Of course, their defeats were in every way of greater significance than the loss of a mere football match, but the lesson is clear. You can brood on defeat and that will corrupt and diminish you, or you can learn from it, then put the past behind you and look to the future.

(*Daily Express*, 27 June 1996: p. 8)

English media coverage of Euro 96 thus served more to 'divide' than to 'unite' the nations of Europe and reflected the social currents that were evident in British politics at the time, possibly reinforcing anti-European sentiments (Maguire & Poulton, in press). Such sentiments were, of course, also a reflection of the Thatcher/Major years. But these Tory prime ministers, along with the peculiar brand of 'little-Englandism' that marked their premierships, have now been defeated. It is too early to tell if the 'modernization' of British society espoused by Tony Blair and New Labour, with their programme of constitutional change including a degree of devolution to Scotland and Wales, will have a significant impact on the fantasy shield of the 'English' and their perceived group charisma relative to the other constitutive nations of the United Kingdom. Similarly, the likely effect this has on sport – and vice versa – is yet unclear, though the New Labour administration has established a national academy for elite sport along similar lines to that proposed by John Major.

During Euro 96, 'old foes' provided convenient excuses to buttress deeply laden habitus codes about the fragile I/we-identities of sections of the English. The identity politics evident in media discourse underpinning Euro 96 coverage reflected more deep-seated British concerns regarding national decline, the fragmentation of the British Isles and European integration. Failure in such competitions and also in the Olympic Games leaves the English with the scant consolation of success in the Commonwealth Games. Media discourse during the 1990s has tended towards two interwoven themes: nostalgia and ethnic assertiveness/defensiveness. Sport media discourse of this kind performs the function that Elias detected regarding national identity politics and socialization practices more broadly. That is, such sport media discourse reinforced invented traditions but also national habitus codes. As such, it acted as a 'drag' on further European integration. International team sports seemingly bind people to dominant I/we national identities, and the incipient European identity remains at an 'emergent' stage.

Conclusion: National Identities and Global Processes

Though national identities are not as monolithic as they are sometimes represented, and they appear currently to be in a state of rapid flux, they have tended to win out in recent years over other sources of cultural identity. Nevertheless, national identities also appear to be undergoing a process of dislocation. This dislocation is arguably connected to globalization processes. Here, as noted at the outset, it is important to raise the question of to what extent national cultures and identities are weakened, strengthened or pluralized by globalization processes? From the available evidence it would appear that a balancing or blending of these tendencies is involved. That is, a series of 'double-bind' or seemingly contradictory processes is at work. At various points, in different places, local cultures or identities (such as Englishness) are strengthened, show resistance or increase in variety. In the Euro 96 case study a defensive English reaction was being strengthened. At other points, in the same and/or in different places, the contrasts between cultures diminish. Such a view on the issue depends on the adoption of a very long-term perspective. It also requires tracing the lengthening chains of interdependencies that, today, characterize global culture. Further, the use of the concepts of diminishing contrasts and increasing varieties attunes the researcher to thinking relationally and developmentally. As was argued in chapter 2, the concepts of diminishing contrasts and increasing varieties, the idea of the commingling of Western and non-Western cultures, the subsequent emergence of new amalgams and the ongoing attempts by established groups to integrate outsider people(s) as workers and/or consumers, all shed important light onto the debate regarding national cultures, identities and globalization.

How then can the media discourse surrounding the English sporting disasters and the position of English/British identity be best understood? It was suggested at the outset that a dislocation of identity faces the 'British' and the 'British nation-state'. Several interlocking elements have contributed to this. The development of Empire, for example, resulted in a diverse commingling of 'British' national culture and identity with other cultures. While the spread of British 'civilization' – including its sport forms – ensured that contrasts were diminished, the process of cultural interchange, though unequal, was not all one way. Even as British sport forms were spreading through the Empire, some 'native sports', such as polo, were diffusing back to the mother country. This process continues today: the emergence of revamped versions of British sport forms, including American football, is an example of these processes at work. Further, while the spread of sport is evidence of the success of the British at penetrating other cultures, over time people from former colonies have not only won their independence, but they now beat the British/English at 'their own games'.

This diffusion, reconstruction and representation of cultural forms has been combined with a movement of people. Citizens of the colonies of the Empire had long visited the mother country. Despite the demise of the Empire, and the crisis of identity that this itself presented, this movement of people has continued. More recently, citizens of Britain's former colonies not only visited but stayed and made Britain their 'home'. A diverse range of ethnic groups drawn from former colonial possessions now lives in Britain. This ethnic settlement is not confined to former colonials. Since World War II Italians, Poles and Greeks have settled in Britain. This phenomenon is nothing new. The British Isles have long been settled by peoples from other lands. In the English version of their own history these elements are overlooked.

One consequence of these processes is that old certainties regarding British identity have been called into question. These are, however, not the only processes at work. The reassertion of Irish, Scottish and Welsh national culture and identity has combined with a crisis within the 'British' royal family. Moves towards European integration also raise fears over a loss of 'sovereignty'. Globalization processes of the kind described only exacerbate the sense of crisis and dislocation. Victories in sport over former colonial subjects such as the Australians at cricket restores, however briefly and superficially, a symbolic sense of stability. The same may be true of English sporting success more generally. In contrast, losing at sport to former colonies, whose people may regard their first victory over the British/English as a form of rite of passage, compounds the general sense of dislocation. The 1990s defeat of the English cricket team by Sri Lanka is a case in point.

Resistance to such processes can take various forms. In Britain over the past decade a revamped Englishness, with an emphasis on a Little Englander mentality has resurfaced in a more intense form. This strong defensive reaction to globalization processes, to European integration, to the pluralization of national culture and the assertiveness of the 'Celtic fringe' manifests itself in several areas. The public response to the Falklands 'adventure' was one of its more extreme forms. Here, the Empire was militarily striking back. The defensive reaction also manifests itself within the British state, particularly with regard to changes to the constitution. The jingoism associated with (rare) English sporting success at the highest levels of male sport is another manifestation of this revamped aggressive Englishness. Sport then plays a contradictory role in globalization processes and national identity formation. Sport development has been and continues to be contoured by the interlocking processes of diminishing contrasts and increasing varieties. The emergence of modern sport from its European, and particularly British, heartland was, as noted, closely tied to globalization processes. Its standardization, organizational development and global diffusion both reflected and reinforced the global processes that were being powered by the West. During the twentieth century sport was to become a 'global idiom'.

In certain respects sports also act as 'anchors of meaning' at a time when national cultures and identities are experiencing the effects of global time–space compression. Victory over Australia provides the English with a secure status point. The association of sport with a specific place and season also provides a sense of *Heimat*, a sense of invented 'permanence'. Think of Wimbledon, Super Bowl Sunday, the US Masters at Augusta and, for the English, test cricket against Australia. These sports occasions are counterpoints to change. As was noted earlier, the formation of sport was closely connected to the invention of traditions that attempt to bind the past and present together. Yet, paradoxically, as chapter 7 demonstrated, the media–sport production complex also erodes this sense of stability. Through satellite broadcasting the consumer can cross spaces and be at any sport venue across the globe. It also brings new varieties of sport subcultures to national cultures. New identities can be forged. Some British people now identify with, and want to be, famous American sports stars, such as basketball player Michael Jordan.

Though sport has reinforced and reflected a diminishing of contrasts between nations, the close association of sport with national cultures, identities and habitus codes also means that moves towards the integration of regions at a political level are undermined by the role of sport. This is evident at a British and a European level. As noted, some Scots 'live to beat the English'. It is not overstating the case to suggest that the jubilation expressed by those groups over the Danish 'No' in their national referendum on the Maastricht Agreement regarding European integration was uncannily paralleled in the joy expressed over the Danish victory in the 1992 European Nations soccer championships in which they defeated the favourites, Germany. Sport, being inherently competitive and based on a hierarchical valuing of worth, binds people to the dominant invented traditions and habitus codes associated with the nation.

Yet, there may be also the first signs of countervailing trends. The tentative emergence of a European sports identity is a case in point. The incipient stages of this are evident in the formation of 'European' teams to play the USA in the men's Ryder Cup and women's Solheim Cup golf competitions. Sage (1993) has insightfully assessed the impact that this European unification process is having on American sports. He observes that while few, if any, European coaches or sports scientists have been recruited in the USA, the recruitment of European athletes in a range of professional sports such as ice hockey and basketball is developing at a fair pace. Although Sage (1993: p. 28) rightfully observed that in 1993 European athletes had 'made a minimal impact in intercollegiate sports', between 1992–93 and 1997–98 the number of foreign, mostly European, players doubled in college basketball – from 135 in 1992–93 to 268 by the 1997–98 season (*Sports Illustrated*, 26 January 1998: p. 61). The 1992 athletics World Cup competition held in Havana, Cuba, also had teams representing six 'geographical' areas, of which Europe was one. The degree to which the athletes felt any strong sense of identification with these areas is debatable but, as yet, is also unexplored. EU officials have also raised the idea of a common European team for the Olympics and also have endorsed a Formula One Grand Prix of Europe. Yet, as the research on the media coverage of Euro 96 demonstrated, such discourse reinforced both invented traditions and also national habitus codes and can have a more powerful effect than policy emerging out of Brussels.

Media coverage of this kind acts as a 'drag' on further European integration. International team sports bind people to dominant I/we national identities, and the incipient European identity remains at an 'emergent' stage. By studying media discourse, aspects of the processes through which national habitus/character construction is framed, constructed and represented by and through discursive practices become more evident. These themselves were interwoven with the activities of spectators and supporters that were occurring at the level of 'practical consciousness', entailing unnoticed activities that reflect deeply rooted memories. These are part of the group's collectively shared stock of knowledge. The fantasy shields and imagined group charisma of European nations are based on such practices and actions. Euro 96 thus served to reinforce the stronger emotive I/we identification of European citizens with their nation rather than with the we-identity notion that they are also Europeans. Despite broader processes of Europeanization and globalization, dominant I/we national identities are arguably strengthened in sporting tournaments of this nature. In considering national institutions of public education, Elias concluded: 'we could hardly find a more cogent example than the persistent way in which the national habitus of the European nation states impedes their closer political union' (Elias, 1994a: p. 210). Given what has been shown, he could well have addressed such comments both to the media sport discourse of the kind evident during Euro 96 and that which accompanied English sporting 'disasters' throughout the 1990s. As with European integration more generally, the sport process occupies contested terrain in which the defensive response of *strengthened* ethnic identities may yet win out over broader *pluralizing* global flows. It is, perhaps, too early to tell.

Conclusion:
Diminishing Contrasts, Increasing Varieties – Towards a Global Sport Culture or the Globalization of Sports?

> The reader of these pages should not look for detailed docu-
> mentation of every word. In treating of the general problems
> of culture one is constantly obliged to undertake predatory
> incursions into provinces not sufficiently explored by the
> raider himself. To fill in all the gaps in my knowledge before-
> hand was out of the question for me. I had to write now, or
> not at all. And I wanted to write.
>
> Johan Huizinga, *Homo Ludens*, 1949

In common with Huizinga I set out on this task of exploring global
sport without having a full knowledge of the conceptual and
empirical terrain I would have to travel. I still have to fill in the
gaps in my knowledge and, if anything, have become more aware
of the size of the task I set myself and the limitations that remain. I
began this task, as I paraphrased Weber (1920/1992: p. 13), as 'a
product of modern European civilization' and sought to address
several key questions. In pointing out that the sportization of the
planet seemingly knows no bounds, I asked in the Introduction

how this present global sport formation has emerged out of the past. What are the main 'structured processes' involved? What functions, meanings and significance has the existing global sport system in people's lives across the world? What possible tendencies can be detected as we approach the end of the twentieth century? These were the questions I set myself and I have tried to address them by applying and refining aspects of a figurational/process-sociological perspective. It is appropriate both to summarize what answers have been provided to these initial questions and in so doing, to state some key points of departure that I can leave readers with should they choose to try to fill in the knowledge gaps that remain.

Modern sport began first to develop in the context of eighteenth-century English society. Fusing together the five-phase globalization schema employed by Robertson and the sportization thesis outlined by Elias and Dunning, the argument presented in chapter 4 linked the world-wide diffusion of sport to the take-off phase of globalization between 1870 and 1914. During this period the distinctive characteristics of modern achievement sport reflected its European, and, in particular, its English origins. In noting this source for the diffusion process, several points need stressing.

Though the genesis of modern sport may lie in the West, the approach adopted does not preclude the possibility of earlier, non-occidental linkages and influences on developments in Europe. One possible source might have been the Arab world. Yet, as Mazrui observes, 'One aspect of ancient Greece that the Arabs did little to promote or transmit . . . was the field of sports and athletics – the legacy of the Olympic games. Islamic civilization was too earnest to incorporate a subculture of leisure' (Mazrui, 1987: p. 217). While the Arab influence may not have been great, even at the height of European power – in the take-off phase of globalization – sports such as polo and badminton diffused from the colonies back to the core 'mother' country. The outdoor version of badminton, though Western in origin, was developed by British officers in Poona, India.

The honour code of these officers and the notions of fair play they promoted and embodied also illustrate another key point. Though emphasis has been placed on the initial sportization phase which emerged during the eighteenth century, earlier influences on the development of English notions of sport, such as the European code of chivalry, should not be overlooked (Maguire, 1986). In developing a model of global sport attention should therefore be paid to earlier and non-occidental influences on the changes that occurred in eighteenth-century England. Modern achievement sport began to diffuse out of its Anglo-European core in the late nineteenth and early twentieth centuries. However, English/British predominance was not to last. During the fourth sportization phase American influence over the context, organization, content and ideology of achievement sport increased significantly. English models of sport and Czech, Danish, German and Swedish models of gymnastics began to be replaced by American versions that reflected the values of the 'new world' (Quanz, 1991). American success on the sports field was matched by the diffusion of sports such as baseball, basketball and volleyball. This American ability to develop their own sports, and to redefine the meaning of sports training, performance and consumption, not only reflected the changing balance of political, economic and cultural power in the world, but also demonstrates how the diffusion of achievement sport was actively interpreted by occidental and non-occidental people. This is not always recognized in studies of global sport.

American football and baseball have their antecedents in English games that accompanied the European migrants who crossed the Atlantic. Exponents of the developing American culture proved adept at adapting and reinterpreting these sports and although their subsequent diffusion is seen by some as 'proof' of Americanization, they are overlooking these European roots. Bearing this in mind it is necessary to recognize that, over the long term, globalization processes are multidirectional, not unidirectional. In this regard the findings presented here concur with the argument put forward by Alan Scott when he observed:

> No matter how determined the attempt to transmit homogenous and uniform cultural material, actors are too knowing and culture too complex for any process of cultural exchange – no matter how unequal – to be exclusively one-way. One implication here may be that it is the complexity of culture itself rather than the greater flexibility of globalization as compared to so-called 'Americanization' that explains the eclecticism of cultural exchange; such eclecticism being the normal condition of cultural interaction irrespective of the ways in which inequalities of power mould those interactions.
>
> (Scott, 1997: p. 19)

Non-Western peoples did not just embrace these Anglo-European and American sport cultures unwittingly. Fellow occidentals such as the French and the Germans resisted the import of English sports. Ironically, the French now use soccer, in the form of the French Cup, to maintain links between their former colonies

(Outre-Mer) and metropolitan France. As noted earlier, referring to Western imperialism Said has rightly indicated how the 'coming of the white man brought forth some sort of resistance' (Said, 1993: p. xii). Sport diffusion was no exception. To state this is not simply to emphasize the contested nature of the inter-civilizational dimension of globalization processes. What also needs stressing – and requires further exploration than this book has allowed – are the local responses to these global processes and the linkages with and the influences that non-occidental people have had on each other and on Westerners in the context of global sport. Discussing Indian cricket, Appadurai highlights some of the dimensions involved:

> Part of the decolonization of cricket is the corrosion of the myth of the Commonwealth, the loose fraternity of nations united by their previous status as parts of the British Empire . . . the Commonwealth that is constituted by cricket today is not an orderly community of former colonies held together by common adherence to a Victorian and colonial code. It is an agonistic reality in which a variety of postcolonial pathologies (and dreams) are played out on the landscape of a common colonial heritage. No longer an instrument for socializing black and brown men into the public etiquette of empire, it is now an instrument for mobilizing national sentiment in the service of transnational spectacles and commoditization.
>
> (Appadurai, 1995: p. 42)

In order to further knowledge of the influences that non-occidental people have had on each other, detailed case studies of regional sport competitions such as association football's African Cup, and multi-sport tournaments such as the Asian Games, could be explored in future research, along with more in-depth study of the historical linkages and networks involved. The recent success in world athletics of non-Western women such as Algeria's Hassiba Boulmerka, a Muslim, and the Syrian Christian Ghada Shouaa, not only illustrates diversity within the sport world but also how the study of such involvement can provide glimpses of broader global processes. Case studies of this kind would also cast light on the most recent sportization phase. While undoubtedly Western and particularly American control of global sport remains strong, since the 1960s non-occidental influence in the sports world has increased. This is not confined to success on the sports field *per se* but holds with respect to sports administration, too. The balance of power in the global sport figuration still favours the West and representatives of transnational corporations, but such control is not complete or without contestation.

Studies outlined in previous chapters confirm how a complex

political economy structures sports. But cultural and social factors also contour and shape the global sport figuration, and as such monocausal explanations and perspectives fail to capture the complexity of these processes. Indeed, contemporary global sport is marked not only by the narrowing of sport cultures but achievement sport itself is being challenged even within the West. As was argued earlier, a diversification of achievement sport is evident: activities such as snowboarding and a range of extreme sports have emerged that challenge the dominant achievement sport ideology. Martial arts have also spread to the West and groups within such societies have revived residual folk games. Such trends bear out Hannerz's observation that global processes are characterized by the 'organization of diversity rather than by a replication of uniformity' (Hannerz, 1990: p. 237).

Despite these new varieties of sport cultures, a series of structured processes indicate that a reduction in the contrasts between sport cultures has also occurred. The early signs of a global sport monoculture – evident in the emergence of sports science, administrative and marketing systems and also through the spread of the Olympic movement – are reinforced by the way in which the global sport figuration is structured along the flows of people, finance, technology, mediated images and ideologies. The case studies contained in Part II reveal the multicausal and multidirectional dynamics involved. Western societies and the elites of transnational corporations have so far had greater influence in these processes and the balance of power clearly favours these groups. Yet, these global flows are also marked by a series of what Appadurai termed 'disjunctures'. The interweaving of the flows produces, over the long term, outcomes that were neither planned nor intended by the more and less powerful groups involved. To argue this is not to overlook or downplay the shorter-term impact that issues of political economy have on sports such as association football and which has been so well captured by researchers such as Sugden and Tomlinson (1998a). These disjunctures need as much exploration as the intended plans and actions of what Sklair (1991) has labelled the transnational capitalist class, or indeed representatives of different nation-states. Over the very long term these disjunctures and a myriad of inter-civilizational linkages have had a powerful impact on the global sport process. Global flows, as Appadurai notes, 'follow increasingly non-isomorphic paths' (Appadurai, 1990: p. 301).

The global processes under investigation here may have led to the diminishing of contrasts between cultures but also the increasing variety of cultures that has emerged has fostered forms of cosmopolitan consciousness. Hand in hand with this, however, go questions concerning nationhood. As Richard Kilminster has observed:

> Globalization both fosters forms of cosmopolitan consciousness *and* stimulates feelings and expressions of ethnicity. It is not surprising, therefore, that the dominant contemporary sociological conception of globalization is of a Janus-faced process of global incorporation and local resistance.
>
> (Kilminster, 1997: p. 280)

Evidence that global sport fosters both cosmopolitan consciousness and stimulates feelings and expressions of ethnicity was provided and highlighted by the studies of elite labour migration and the patriot games that underpin international sport. The interconnected processes of globalization and further European integration have fostered in sections of the English both a defensive ethnic reassertiveness but also a deep sense of nostalgia. International sport appears to reawaken sleeping memories, to promote traditional national habitus codes and to engender a series of I/we–us/them tensions. The members of nation-states remain active participants in shaping and determining aspects of the scope and reach of globalization processes: they are not passive victims of processes that lie outside their control. Yet global sport also projects images of otherness – other people and other places – and in doing so may contribute to a cosmopolitan consciousness that can lead to identification with global commodified sports idols such as Michael Jordan and Martina Hingis, but also lead to an awareness of the environmental impact of the sports industry and the need to develop sustainable sports. The 'greening' of sport has yet to gather momentum but may be forged as part of these broader globalization processes.

The complexity of global sport lies not only in terms of how sports are used in different societies but also how these sports are read and interpreted. This observation applies both to those who participate in and/or who consume sport via the media–sport complex. Global sport provides some people with opportunities to experience moments of 'exciting significance' in their daily local lives. For global sport has proved to be, as Galtung remarked, a most powerful cultural transfer mechanism, and 'carrier of deep culture and structure' that carries a 'message of western social cosmology' (Galtung, 1982: pp. 136–7). Yet, local reinterpretation of the significance that this social cosmology has in people's lives also needs to form part of an analysis of global sport. The dynamics of global sport interchange are characterized by tendencies towards both the diminishing of contrasts, emulation, equalization and imitation but also by tendencies towards increasing varieties, differentiation, individuality and practices that distinguish established groups from outsiders (Featherstone, 1991b).

Globalization is accordingly best understood as a balance and blend between diminishing contrasts and increasing varieties, a commingling of cultures and attempts by more established groups to control and regulate access to global flows. Global sport development can be understood in the same terms: that is, in the late twentieth century we are witnessing the globalization of sports and the increasing diversification of sport cultures. Yet, if the double-bind tendencies of diminishing contrasts and increasing varieties are uncoupled from each other, then support for arguments emphasizing either cultural homogenization or a global cultural pastiche is possible. Homogenization theorists who claim that national cultural identities are weakened by the processes of globalization are correct to point out that aspects of globalization are *powered* by Western notions of 'civilization'.

The sports industries do provide a staple diet of Western products, and the cult of consumerism is spreading around the globe. In some respects, the media–sport production complex also ensures that the marketing of the *same* sport forms, products and images does occur. 'Local' people do not freely choose which cultural products are consumed. There is a political economy at work regulating global flows. But an over-emphasis on the marketing of sameness leads the analyst to overlook the celebration by global marketing strategies of difference and individuality. That is, the cultural industries constantly seek out new varieties of ethnic wares. These ethnic wares are targeted at specific 'niches' within a local culture. This targeting can lead to a strengthening of 'local' ethnic identities. The spread of the South Asian 'sport' of kabbadi and Japanese Sumo wrestling to Britain are examples, the latter sport being promoted by Channel 4 television in the UK. It is also important to note that the members of 'indigenous' cultures are responsive and active in the interpretation of the global flow of people, ideas, images and technologies. There is also reason to suggest that those national cultures and identities most affected by these processes appear to be those at the 'centre', not the 'periphery' of the global system. Globalization processes are also unevenly distributed within central regions. Given this, there is reason to doubt, as has been argued at various points in this book, the more strident claims made by advocates of the homogenization thesis.

The globalization/sportization trends I have tried to capture in this book are also evident in the development of specific sports. The diffusion of cricket demonstrates the attempts by the English to infuse this sport with their colonial image but also shows how indigenous people developed the game in their own image. The globalization of cricket followed the lines of the British Empire. Its development reflected the inequalities evident within and between the outsider colonies and the established mother country. Yet, its postcolonial development came to indicate the processes of functional democratization, the inter-civilizational struggles and the changing balance of power that accompanied imperial breakdown. This has been documented both with regard to West Indies cricket (James, 1963; Beckles & Stoddart, 1995) and also Australia (Stoddart, 1979, 1988). Referring to the decolonization of Indian cricket Appadurai has captured elements of the multiple dynamics involved in these inter-civilizational struggles:

> The indigenization of a sport like cricket has many dimensions: it has something to do with the way the sport is managed, patronized, and publicized; it has something to do with the class background of Indian players and thus with their capability to mimic Victorian elite values; it has something to do with the dialectic between team spirit and national sentiment, which is inherent in the sport and is implicitly corrosive of the bonds of empire; it has something to do with the way in which a reservoir of talent is created and nurtured outside the urban elites, so that the sport can become internally sustaining; it has something to do with the ways in which media and language help to unyoke cricket from its 'Englishness'; and it has something to do with the construction of a postcolonial male spectatorship that can charge cricket with the power of bodily competition and virile nationalism. These processes interacted with one another to indigenize cricket in India.
>
> (Appadurai, 1995: pp. 24–5)

Inter-civilizational processes then are double-edged weapons. Though varying degrees of domination and colonization were achieved by the West, the more powerful became dependent on the 'colonized'. This happens through processes of differentiation, integration and what Elias calls 'functional democratization'. In turn, the seepage downwards of high-status civilized conduct, and the resurgence of indigenous customs, leads to a decrease in the power of occidentals. In this scenario, according to Wouters (1990), inequalities decrease and an informalization process, at a global level, gathers momentum. In the sports world, former colonial masters are beaten at their own games, and the formal patrician attitude that characterized, for example, tours to the cricket grounds of the former empire, has waned in favour of off-field informal interaction and an assertive, independent attitude (Maguire & Stead, 1996).

Such observations raise three interrelated issues that need attention as I draw this text to a close. Throughout this text I have sought to identify common ground with other sociological approaches but also to map out the distinctive contribution that a process-sociological perspective can make to the study of sport in particular and globalization processes more generally. At the heart of this perspective lie questions of power, elimination struggles and civilizational hegemony. In hindsight, figurational sociologists would have been better served if they had used terms such as power-geometry, civilizational offensives and also coupled more explicitly civilizing with decivilizing processes. Despite this oversight, such issues lie at the heart of the figurational project when examining sport processes. The local–global struggle for relative ascendancy in power networks is also located within the unintended and unforeseen consequences of earlier intended actions: it is these unintended consequences that provide the seedbed in which future power struggles are played out. In emphasizing the need to explore *both* the intended and the unintended dynamics of local–global processes I am also conscious that some observers may see this as ignoring the short-term economic relations that contour and shape such processes. Nothing could be further from the truth. Looking at the empirical studies that underpin this text, the political economy that influences the global sport figuration has been given due prominence. Yet, as noted in chapter 2, monocausal and unidirectional analyses simply do not capture what can be observed in the study of local–global processes: multidirectional and multicausal processes involving cultural, economic, social and political strands make up the human tapestry of life. To argue this does not lead the researcher to abandon the task of examining the inequalities that characterize local–global interchange. Unlike some elements of postmodern writings on sport, process sociologists still believe that the task of a sociologist entails being both a hunter or destroyer of myths and the provider of relatively adequate reality-congruent knowledge. What better form of empowerment is there than to provide citizens with such knowledge?

It is true that process sociologists are more circumspect with regard to predicting the future: as my Marxist colleagues rightly point out, human history is there to be made. Yet, given recent events in state socialist societies, a degree of circumspection is also needed. I cannot pretend to argue, given our present state of knowledge regarding humankind, that we have all the answers; work of this kind is, hopefully, a symptom of a beginning. Thus when Mao was asked about the consequence of the French Revolution for humankind, he replied tersely, 'It's too early to tell.'

Yet, process sociologists share in common with Marxist, cultural studies and feminist colleagues a critical perspective. This manifests itself in different ways among this disparate group of scholars. In teaching the sociology of sport, process sociologists see their task as a 'subversive activity' and share the consciousness-raising role that others promote. In doing research, process sociologists give relative primacy to the search for understanding but they are not only involved in what they study they, in a *verstehen* sense, have to be involved. Yet, they also, at one and the same time, by what they term a detour via relative detachment, seek to avoid 'going native' and generate knowledge that they then have a responsibility to disseminate in a critical manner. Each of these areas relates to questions concerning involvement/detachment, observation/theory formation, the sociology of knowledge and a theory of sciences. Yet, process sociologists are also citizens, concerned parents and partners, who like others, get some things right and other things wrong. My hope is that this text has contributed in some small way to a more realistic and as such, more emancipatory perspective on modern sport. Let me draw these final remarks to a close.

While the contrasts between cultures may have diminished, there has also occurred an increase in the varieties of cultural identities available. This is hardly surprising if one bears in mind the Eliasian idea of a commingling of cultures. These commingling processes involve the movement of people and with them of styles, images, commodities and consumer identities. Global flows are also patterned not by one but by several competing processes that include Africanization, Americanization, Europeanization, Orientalization and Hispanicization. While this cultural exchange to date has been patterned by unequal power-relations, the very commingling of these global flows *may* be the first sign of what Hall (1992) termed the decentring of the West. Further studies of the global sport process may indicate whether this process will gather momentum in the next century. Or perhaps such studies might reveal that the long rise of the West will continue?

Bibliography

Algar, R. (1988): 'American football', *Leisure Management* 8, pp. 58–60.

Anderson, B. (1983): *Imagined Communities: reflections on the origin and spread of nationalism.* Verso: London.

Andrews, D. (1997): 'The (trans)national basketball association: American commodity-sign culture and global–local conjuncturalism', in Cvetkovich, A. & Kellner, D. (eds), *Articulating the Global and the Local: globalization and cultural studies.* Westview Press: Boulder, Colo., pp. 72–101.

Andrews, D., Carrington, B., Mazur, Z. & Jackson, S. (1996): 'Jordan-scapes: a preliminary analysis of the global popular', *Sociology of Sport Journal* 13, pp. 428–57.

Appadurai, A. (1990): 'Disjuncture and difference in the global cultural economy', *Theory, Culture & Society* 7, pp. 295–310.

Appadurai, A. (1995): 'Playing with modernity: the decolonization of Indian cricket', in Breckenridge, C. A. (ed.), *Consuming Modernity: public culture in a South Asian world.* University of Minnesota Press: Minneapolis, pp. 23–48.

Arbena, J. (ed.) (1988): *Sport and Society in Latin America: diffusion, dependency and the rise of mass culture.* Greenwood Press: Westport, CT.

Arbena, J. (1993): 'Sport and nationalism in Latin America, 1880–1970: the paradox of promoting and performing "European" sports', *History of European Ideas* 16, pp. 837–44.

Arnason, J. (1990): 'Nationalism, globalization and modernity', *Theory, Culture & Society* 7, pp. 207–36.

Avedon, E. & Sutton-Smith, B. (eds) (1971): *The Study of Games.* John Wiley & Sons: New York.

Baker, W. (1982): *Sports in the Western World.* Rowman & Littlefield: Totowa, NJ.

Baker, W. & Mangan, J. A. (eds) (1987): *Sport in Africa: essays in social history*. Africana: New York.
Bale, J. (1985): 'Toward a geography of international sport'. Occasional Paper 8, Department of Geography, University of Loughborough.
Bale, J. (1994): *Landscapes of Modern Sport*. Leicester University Press: Leicester.
Bale, J. & Maguire, J. (eds) (1994): *The Global Sports Arena: athletic talent migration in an interdependent world*. Frank Cass: London.
Bale, J. & Sang, J. (1996): *Kenyan Running: movement culture, geography and global change*. Frank Cass: London.
Barnett, S. (1990): *Games and Sets: the changing face of sport on television*. British Film Institute Publishing: London.
Beamish, R. (1982): 'Sport and the logic of capitalism', in Cantelon, H. & Gruneau, R. (eds) *Sport, Culture and the Modern State*. University of Toronto Press: Toronto, pp. 141–97.
Beamish, R. (1988): 'The political economy of professional sport', in Harvey, J. & Cantelon, H. (eds) *Not Just a Game: essays in Canadian sport sociology*. University of Ottawa Press: Ottawa, pp. 141–58.
Beckles, H. McD. & Stoddart, B. (eds) (1995): *Liberation Cricket: West Indies cricket culture*. Manchester University Press: Manchester.
Beyer, P. (1994): *Religion and Globalization*. Sage: London.
Bigsby, C. (ed.) (1975): *Superculture: American popular culture and Europe*. Elek Books: London.
Blomstrom, M. & Hettne, B. (1984): *Development Theory in Transition*. Zed Books: London.
Bogner, A. (1986): 'The structure of social processes: a commentary on the sociology of Norbert Elias', *Sociology* 20, pp. 387–411.
Bourdieu, P. (1984): *Distinction. A social critique of the judgement of taste*. Routledge: London.
Bromberger, C. (1994): 'Foreign footballers, cultural dreams and community identity in some north-western Mediterranean cities', in Bale, J. & Maguire, J. (eds) *The Global Sports Arena: athletic talent migration in an interdependent world*. Frank Cass: London, pp. 171–82.
Brookes, B. & Madden, P. (1995): *The Globe-trotting Sports Shoe*. Christian Aid: London.
Bryant, J. (1989): 'Viewers' enjoyment of televised sports violence', in Wenner, L. (ed.) *Media, Sports and Society*. Sage: Newbury Park, Calif., pp. 270–89.
Budweiser League Yearbook (1990): Budweiser: London.
Burkitt, I. (1991): 'Social selves: theories of the social formation of personality', *Current Sociology* 39, pp. 1–225.
Cantelon, H. & Gruneau, R. (1988): 'The production of sport for television', in Harvey, J. & Cantelon, H. (eds) *Not Just a Game: essays in Canadian sport sociology*. University of Ottawa Press: Ottawa, pp. 177–93.
Cantelon, H. & Hollands, R. (eds) (1988): *Leisure, Sport and Working Class Cultures*. Garamond Press: Toronto.
Cashman, R. (1988): 'Cricket and colonialism: colonial hegemony and indigenous subversion?' in Mangan, J. A. (ed.) *Pleasure, Profit and Pros-*

elytism: British culture and sport at home and abroad 1700–1914. Frank Cass: London, pp. 258–72.

Chase Dunn, C. (1989): *Global Formation: structures of the world economy*. Blackwell: Oxford.

Chernushenko, D. (1994): *Greening our Games: running sports events and facilities that won't cost the earth*. Centurion Publishing: Ottawa.

Clignet, R. & Stark, M. (1974): 'Modernization and the game of soccer' in Cameroun, *International Review of Sport Sociology* 9, pp. 81–98.

Cohen, R. (1994): *Frontiers of Identity: the British and the others*. Longman: London.

Colls, R. (1986): 'Englishness and the political culture', in Colls, R. & Dodd, P., *Englishness, Politics and Culture 1880–1920*. Croom Helm: London, pp. 29–61.

Connelly, J. (1987): 'Influencing your customer recreation management'. The Sports Council's national seminar and exhibition, Harrogate, March, pp. 46–58.

Connerton, P. (1989): *How Societies Remember*. Cambridge University Press: Cambridge.

Coubertin, P. de (1892): Paper presented at the Union des Sports Athlétiques, Sorbonne, November 25, np.

Council of Europe (1992): *European Sports Charter*. 7th Conference of European Sports Ministers, Rhodes, Greece.

Critcher, C. (1992): 'Is there anything on the box? Leisure studies and media studies', *Leisure Studies* 11, pp. 97–122.

Daddario, G. (1994): ' "Chilly scenes" of the 1992 winter games: the mass media and the marginalisation of female athletes', *Sociology of Sport Journal* 7, pp. 22–43.

Deacon, J. (1995): 'Hockey's reversal of fortune', *Macleans Magazine* 9 October, pp. 62–6.

Dezalay, Y. (1990): 'The big bang and the law: the internationalization and restructuration of the legal system', *Theory, Culture & Society* 7, pp. 279–98.

Dickens, P. (1992): *Global Shift: the internationalization of economic activity*. Paul Chapman: London (2nd edn).

Dodd, P. (1986): 'Englishness and national culture', in Colls, R. & Dodd, P., *Englishness, Politics and Culture 1880–1920*. Croom Helm: London, pp. 1–28.

Donaghu, M. & Barff, R. (1990): 'Nike just did it: international subcontracting and flexibility in athletic footwear production', *Regional Studies* 24, pp. 537–52.

Donnelly, P. (1996): 'The local and the global: globalization in the sociology of sport', *Journal of Sport and Social Issues* 20, pp. 239–57.

Drackett, P. (1987): *Flashing Blades: the story of British ice hockey*. Crowood Press: Marlborough, UK.

Duncan, M. C. & Brummett, B. (1989): 'Types and sources of spectating pleasure in televised sports', *Sociology of Sport Journal* 6, pp. 195–211.

Duncan, M. C. & Hasbrook, C. (1988): 'Denial of power in televised women's sport', *Sociology of Sport Journal* 5, pp. 1–21.

Dunning, E. (1975): 'Theoretical perspectives on sport: a developmental critique', in Parker, S., Ventris, N., Haworth, J. & Smith, M. (eds) *Sport and Leisure in Contemporary Society*. Symposium of Papers: Polytechnic of Central London, January 1975, pp. 16–27.

Dunning, E. (1986): 'The dynamics of modern sport: notes on achievement-striving and the social significance of sport', in Elias, N. & Dunning, E., *Quest for Excitement: sport and leisure in the civilizing process*. Blackwell: Oxford, pp. 205–23.

Dunning, E. (1992a): 'Culture, "civilization" and the sociology of sport', *Innovation* 5, pp. 7–18.

Dunning, E. (1992b): 'Sport and European integration'. Unpublished paper delivered at the Conference *Macht und Ohnmacht im neuen Europa*, Vienna, May, pp. 29–30.

Dunning, E. (1992c): 'Uber die Dynamik des Sportkonsums: eine figurative Analyse', in Horak, R. & Penz, O. (eds) *Sport: Kult & Kommerz*. Verlag für Gesellschaftskritik: Vienna, pp. 203–22.

Dunning, E. (in press): *Sport Matters*. Routledge: London.

Dunning. E. & Maguire, J. (1996): 'Aspects of sport, violence and gender relations: some process-sociological notes', in *International Review for the Sociology of Sport* 31, pp. 295–321.

Dunning, E. & Sheard, K. (1979): *Barbarians, Gentlemen and Players: a sociological study of the development of rugby football*. Martin Robertson: Oxford.

Duquin, M. (1989): 'Fashion and fitness images in women's magazine advertisements', *Arena Review* 13, pp. 97–109.

Dyer, K. F. (1982): *Catching up the Men: women in sport*. Junction Books: London.

Eichberg, H. (1984): 'Olympic sport: neocolonism and alternatives', *International Review for the Sociology of Sport* 19, pp. 97–105.

Eisenberg, C. (1990): 'The middle class and competition: some considerations of the beginnings of modern sport in England and Germany', *International Journal of the History of Sport* 7, pp. 265–82.

Elias, N. (1939/1994): *The Civilising Process*. Blackwell: Oxford.

Elias, N. (1970): 'The genesis of sport as a sociological problem', in Dunning, E. (ed.) *The Sociology of Sport*. Frank Cass: London, pp. 88–115.

Elias, N. (1978): *What is Sociology?* Hutchinson: London.

Elias, N. (1983): *The Court Society*. Blackwell: Oxford.

Elias, N. (1986): Introduction in Elias, N. & Dunning, E., *Quest for Excitement: sport and leisure in the civilizing process*. Blackwell: Oxford, pp. 19–62.

Elias, N. (1987): *Involvement and Detachment*. Blackwell: Oxford.

Elias, N. (1987/1991): *The Society of Individuals*. Blackwell: Oxford.

Elias, N. (1994a): 'A theoretical essay on established and outsider relations', in Elias, N. & Scotson, J. (1965/1994) *The Established and the Outsiders*. Frank Cass: London, pp. xv–lii.

Elias, N. (1994b): *Mozart: portrait of a genius*. Polity Press: Cambridge.

Elias, N. (1996): *The Germans*. Polity Press: Cambridge.

Elias, N. & Dunning, E. (1986): *Quest for Excitement: sport and leisure in the civilizing process*. Blackwell: Oxford.

Elias, N. & Scotson, J. L. (1965/1994): *The Established and the Outsiders: a sociological enquiry into community problems*. Frank Cass: London.

Emanuel, S. (1992): 'Culture in space: the European cultural channel', *Media, Culture & Society* 14, pp. 281–99.

Ensor, R. C. K. (1936): *England 1870–1914. The Oxford history of England*. Clarendon Press: Oxford.

European TV Sports Databook (1995): Kagan World Media: London.

Featherstone, M. (1990): 'Global culture: an introduction', *Theory, Culture & Society*.7, pp. 1–14.

Featherstone, M. (1991a): 'Local and global cultures', *Vrijetijd en Samenleving* 3/4, pp. 43–58.

Featherstone, M. (1991b): *Consumer Culture and Postmodernism*. Sage: London.

Featherstone, M. (1995): *Undoing Culture: globalization, postmodernism and identity*. Sage: London.

Featherstone, M. & Lash, S. (1995): 'Globalization, modernity and the spatialization of social theory: an introduction', in Featherstone, M., Lash, S. & Robertson, R. (eds) *Global Modernities*. Sage: London, pp. 1–24.

Featherstone, M., Lash, S. & Robertson, R. (eds) (1995): *Global Modernities*. Sage: London.

Fiske, J. (1989): *Reading the Popular*. Unwin Hyman: London.

Frank, G. (1967): *Capitalism and Under-development in Latin America*. Monthly Review Press: New York.

Friedman, J. (1994): *Cultural Identity and Global Process*. Sage: London.

Gallup Polls Social Surveys: Textile Market Studies, May 1988.

Galtung, J. (1982): 'Sport as carrier of deep culture and structure', *Current Research on Peace and Violence* 5, pp. 133–43.

Galtung, J. (1991): 'The sport system as a metaphor for the world system', in Landry, F., Landry, M. & Yerles, M. (eds) *Sport ... the third millennium*. University of Laval Press: Quebec, pp. 147–56.

Gan, S., Tuggle, C., Mitrook, M., Coussement, S. & Zilmann, D. (1997): 'The thrill of the game: who enjoys it and who doesn't?' *Journal of Sport and Social Issues* 21, pp. 53–64.

Gantz, W. (1981): 'An exploration of viewing motives and behaviours associated with television sports', *Journal of Broadcasting* 25, pp. 263–75.

Gantz, W. & Wenner, L. (1995): 'Fanship and the television sports viewing experience', *Sociology of Sport Journal* 12, pp. 56–74.

Giddens, A. (1986): *The Constitution of Society*. Polity Press: Cambridge.

Giddens, A. (1990): *The Consequences of Modernity*. Polity Press: Cambridge.

Gillett, J., White, P. & Young, K. (1995): 'The prime minister of Saturday night: Don Cherry, the CBC, and the cultural production of intolerance', in Holmes, H. & Taras, D. (eds) *Seeing Ourselves: media, power, & policy in Canada*, Harcourt Brace: Toronto (2nd edn), pp. 59–72.

Gilpin, R. (1976): *US Power and the Multinational Corporation: the political economy of foreign direct investment*. Macmillan: London.

Gilpin, R. (1987): *The Political Economy of International Relations*. Princeton University Press: Princeton.

Goksøyr, M. (1996): 'Phases and functions of nationalism: Norway's utilization of international sport in the late nineteenth and early twentieth centuries', in Mangan, J. A. (ed.) *Tribal Identities: nationalism, Europe, sport*. Frank Cass: London, pp. 125–46.

Goldberg, A. & Wagg, S. (1991): 'It's not a knockout: English football and globalization', in Williams, J. & Wagg, S. (eds) *British Football and Social Change: getting into Europe*. Leicester University Press: Leicester, pp. 239–53.

Golding, P. & Harris, P. (eds) (1996): *Beyond Cultural Imperialism: globalization, communication and the new international order*. Sage: London.

Golding, P. & Murdock, G. (1991): 'Culture, communications and political economy', in Curran, J. & Gurevitch, M. (eds) *Mass Media and Society*. Edward Arnold: London, pp. 15–32.

Goldlust, J. (1987): *Playing for Keeps: sport, the media and society*. Longman: Melbourne.

Goodger, J. (1986): 'Pluralism, transmission and change in sport', *Quest* 3, pp. 135–47.

Gorn, E. J. & Goldstein, W. (1993): *A Brief History of American Sports*. Hill & Wang: New York.

Goudsblom, J. (1977): *Sociology in the Balance*. Blackwell: Oxford.

Goudsblom, J. & Mennell, S. (eds) (1998): *The Norbert Elias Reader*. Blackwell: Oxford.

Gruneau, R. (1988): 'Modernization or hegemony: two views on sport and social development', in Harvey, J. & Cantelon, H. (eds) *Not Just a Game*. University of Ottawa Press: Ottawa, pp. 9–32.

Gruneau, R. (1989a): 'Television, the Olympics and the question of ideology', in Jackson, R. & McPhail, T. (eds) *The Olympic Movement and the Mass Media: past, present and future issues*. Hurford Enterprises: Calgary, pp. 23–34.

Gruneau, R. (1989b): 'Making spectacle: a case study in television sports production', in Wenner, L. (ed.) *Media, Sports and Society*. Sage: Newbury Park, Calif., pp. 134–56.

Gruneau, R. & Whitson, D. (1993): *Hockey Night in Canada*. Garamond Press: Toronto.

Gruneau, R., Whitson, D. & Cantelon, H. (1988): 'Methods and media: studying the sports/television discourse', *Society and Leisure* 11, pp. 265–81.

Grupe, O. (1991): 'The sport culture and the sportization of culture: identity, legitimacy, sense, and nonsense of modern sport as a cultural phenomenon', in Landry, F., Landry, M. & Yerles, M. (eds) *Sport ... The Third Millennium*. Proceedings of the International Symposium, Quebec City, Canada. 21–25 May 1990, pp. 135–45.

Guttmann, A. (1991): 'Sports diffusion: a response to Maguire and the Americanization commentaries', *Sociology of Sport Journal* 8, pp. 185–90.

Guttmann, A. (1993): 'The diffusion of sports and the problem of cultural imperialism', in Dunning, E. G., Maguire, J. A. & Pearton, R. (eds) *The*

Sports Process: a comparative and developmental approach. Human Kinetics: Champaign, Ill., pp. 125–38.

Guttmann, A. (1994): *Games and Empires: modern sports and cultural imperialism.* Columbia University Press: New York.

Hadfield, D. (1992): *Playing Away: Australians in British rugby league.* The Kingswood Press: London.

Hall, S. (1991): 'The local and the global: globalization and ethnicity', in King, A. D. (ed.) *Culture, Globalization and the World-system.* Macmillan: London, pp. 19–39.

Hall, S. (1992): 'The question of cultural identity', in Hall, S., Held, D. & McGrew, T. (eds) *Modernity and its Futures.* Polity Press: Cambridge, pp. 274–316.

Hall, S., Held, D. & McGrew, T. (eds) (1992): *Modernity and its Futures.* Polity Press: Cambridge.

Hannerz, U. (1990): 'Cosmopolitans and locals in world culture', *Theory, Culture and Society* 7, pp. 237–51.

Hargreaves, Jennifer (1994): *Sporting Females: critical issues in the history and sociology of women's sports.* Routledge: London.

Hargreaves, John (1986): *Sport, Power and Culture.* Polity Press: Cambridge.

Harris, D. (1987): *The League: inside the NFL.* Bantam Books: New York.

Harris, J. & Park, R. (eds) (1983): *Play, Games and Sports in Cultural Contexts.* Human Kinetics: Champaign, Ill.

Harvey, D. (1989): *The Condition of Postmodernity.* Blackwell: Oxford.

Harvey, J. & Houle, F. (1994): 'Sport, world economy, global culture and new social movements', *Sociology of Sport Journal* 11, pp. 337–55.

Harvey, J., Rail, G. & Thibault, L. (1996): 'Globalization and sport: sketching a theoretical model for empirical analyses', *Journal of Sport and Social Issues* 20, pp. 258–77.

Hebdige, D. (1982): 'Towards a cartography of taste 1935–1962', in Waites, B., Bennett, T. & Martin, G. (eds) *Popular Culture: past and present.* Croom Helm: London.

Heine, M. K. & Young, K. (1997): 'Colliding identities in Arctic Canadian sports and games', *Sociological Focus* 30, pp. 357–72.

Heinilä, K. (1970): 'Notes on the inter-group conflicts in international sport', in Luschen, G. (ed.) *The Cross-cultural Analysis of Sport and Games.* Stipes Publishing Co.: Champaign, Ill., pp. 174–82.

Hellspong, M. (1989): 'Traditional sports on the island of Gotland', *Scandinavian Journal of Sports Science* 11, pp. 29–34.

Henry, N., Pinch, S. & Russell, S. (1996): 'In pole position? Untraded interdependencies, new industrial spaces and the British motor sport industry', *Area* 28, pp. 25–36.

Hettne, B. (1990): *Development Theory and the Three Worlds.* Longman: London.

Hoberman, J. (1984): *Sport and Political Ideology.* University of Texas Press: Austin.

Hoberman, J. (1997): *Darwin's Athletes: how sport has damaged Black America and preserved the myth of race.* Houghton Mifflin: Boston, Mass.

Hobsbawm, E. (1983): 'Mass-producing traditions: Europe, 1870–1914', in Hobsbawm, E. & Ranger, T. (eds) *The Invention of Tradition*. Cambridge University Press: Cambridge, pp. 263–307.

Hochschild, A. (1983): *The Managed Heart*. University of California Press: London.

Horne, J. & Jary, D. (1987): 'The figurational sociology of sport and leisure of Elias and Dunning: an exposition and a critique', in Horne, J., Jary, D. & Tomlinson, A. (eds) *Sport, Leisure and Social Relations*. Routledge & Kegan Paul: London, pp. 86–112.

Houlihan, B. (1994): 'Homogenization, Americanization, and creolization of sport: varieties of globalization', *Sociology of Sport Journal* 11, pp. 356–75.

Huizinga, J. (1949/1970): *Homo Ludens: a study of the play element in culture*. Temple Smith: London.

Hutchins, B. & Phillips, M. (1997): 'Selling permissible violence: the commodification of Australian rugby league 1970–1995', *International Review for the Sociology of Sport* 32, pp. 161–76.

Ikegami, E. (1995): *The Taming of the Samurai: honorific individualism and the making of modern Japan*. Harvard University Press: Boston, Mass.

Jackson, R. & McPhail, T. (eds) (1989): *The Olympic Movement and the Mass Media: past, present and future issues*. Hurford Enterprises: Calgary.

James, C. L. R. (1963): *Beyond a Boundary*. Stanley Paul: London.

Jameson, F. (1984): 'Postmodernism or the cultural logic of late capitalism', *New Left Review* 146, pp. 53–92.

Jarvie, G. & Maguire, J. (1994): *Sport and Leisure in Social Thought*. Routledge: London.

Jhally, S. (1984): 'The spectacle of accumulation: material and cultural factors in the evolution of the sports/media complex', *Insurgent Sociologist* 3, pp. 41–57.

Jhally, S. (1989): 'Cultural studies and the sports/media complex', in Wenner, L. (ed.) *Media, Sports & Society*. Sage: Newbury Park, Calif., pp. 70–96.

Jobling, I. (1986): 'The lion, the eagle and the kangaroo: politics and proposals for a British empire team at the 1916 Berlin Olympics', in Redmond, G. (ed.) *Sport and Politics*. Human Kinetics: Champaign, Ill., pp. 99–108.

Johnson, R. J., Taylor, P. J. & Watts, M. J. (1995): *Geographies of Global Change: remapping the world in the late twentieth century*. Blackwell: Oxford.

Jokl, E. & Simon, E. (eds) (1964): *International Research in Sport and Physical Education*. Charles Thomas: Springfield, Ill.

Kagan World Media (1995): Paul Kagan Associates: London.

Kaplan, C. (1986): 'The culture crossover', *New Socialist* 43, pp. 38–40.

Katz, D. (1994): *Just Do It: the Nike spirit in the corporate world*. Random House: New York.

Kidd, B. (1981): 'Sport, dependency and the Canadian state', in Hart, M. & Birrell, S. (eds) *Sport in the Sociocultural Process*. Wm. C. Brown: Dubuque, Ia, pp. 707–21.

Kidd, B. (1988): 'The elite athlete', in Harvey, J. & Cantelon, H. (eds) *Not Just a Game*. University of Ottawa Press: Ottawa.

Kidd, B. (1991): 'How do we find our own voices in the "New World Order"? A commentary on Americanization', *Sociology of Sport Journal* 8, pp. 178–84.

Kilminster, R. (1997): 'Globalization as an emergent concept', in Scott, A. (ed.) *The Limits of Globalization: cases and arguments*. Routledge: London, pp. 257–83.

King, A. D. (ed.) (1991): *Culture, Globalization and the World-system: contemporary conditions for the representation of identity*. Macmillan: London.

Klatell, D. A. & Marcus, N. (1988): *Sports for Sale: television, money and the fans*. Oxford University Press: New York.

Klein, A. M. (1989): 'Baseball in the Dominican Republic', *Sociology of Sport Journal* 6, pp. 95–112.

Klein, A. M. (1991): *Sugarball. The American game, the Dominican dream*. Yale University Press: New Haven, Conn.

Klein, A. M. (1997): *Baseball on the Border: a tale of two Laredos*. Princeton University Press: Princeton, NJ.

Korsgaard, O. (1989): 'Fighting for life: from Ling and Grundtvig to Nordic visions of body culture', *Scandinavian Journal of Sports Science* 11, pp. 3–7.

Korzeniewicz, M. (1994): 'Commodity chains and marketing strategies: Nike and the global athletic footwear industry', in Gereffi, G. & Korzeniewicz, M. (eds) *Commodity Chains and Global Capitalism*. Greenwood Press: Westport, Conn., pp. 247–65.

Krotee, M. (1979): 'The rise and demise of sport: a reflection of Uruguayan society', *Annals of the American Academy of Political and Social Science* 445, pp. 141–54.

Larrain, J. (1989): *Theories of Development*. Polity Press: Cambridge.

Larson, J. F. & Park, H. (1993): *Global Television and the Politics of the Seoul Olympics*. Westview Press: Boulder, Colo.

Lawrence, G. & Rowe, D. (1986): 'The corporate pitch: televised cricket under capitalism', in Lawrence, G. & Rowe, D. (eds) *Power Play: the commercialization of Australian sport*. Hale & Iremonger: Sydney, pp. 166–78.

Licensing Management International, private correspondence (1989).

Lipset, S. (1964): *The First New Nation*. Heinemann: London.

Lyons, T. (1994): 'A global version of the name game', *Hoop – the Official NBA Program Magazine* XX, pp. 22–32.

MacAloon, J. (1988): 'Festival, ritual and television', in Jackson, R. & McPhail, T. (eds) *The Olympic Movement and the Mass Media: past, present and future issues*. Hurford Enterprises: Calgary, pp. 21–40.

MacAloon, J. (1991): 'The turn of two centuries: sport and the politics of intercultural relations', in Landry, F., Landry, M. & Yerles, M. (eds) *Sport ... the Third Millennium*. Proceedings of the International Symposium, Quebec City, Canada, 21–25 May 1990, Les Presses de L'Université Laval: Sainte-Foy, pp. 31–44.

MacGregor, R. (1993): *Road Games: a year in the life of the NHL*. MacFarlane, Walker and Ross: Toronto.

McGrew, A. (1992): 'A global society?' in Hall, S., Held, D. & McGrew, T. (eds) *Modernity and its Futures*. Polity Press: Cambridge, pp. 61–116.

McKay, J. (1995): ' "Just Do It": corporate slogans and the political economy of "enlightened racism" ', *Discourse: Studies in the Cultural Politics of Education* 16, pp. 191–201.

McKay, J. & Miller, T. (1991): 'From old boys to men and women of the corporation: the Americanization and commodification of Australian sport', *Sociology of Sport Journal* 8, pp. 86–94.

McKay, J. & Rowe, D. (1987): 'Ideology, the media and Australian sport', *Sociology of Sport Journal* 4, pp. 258–73.

McKay, J. & Rowe, D. (1997): 'Field of soaps: Rupert v. Kerry as masculine melodrama', *Social Text* 15, pp. 69–83.

McKay, J., Lawrence, G., Miller, T. & Rowe, D. (1993): 'Globalisation and Australian sport', *Sport Science Review* 2, pp. 10–28.

Macleans Magazine, 22 January 1996.

MacNeil, M. (1988): 'Active women, media representations and ideology', in Harvey, J. & Cantelon, H. (eds) *Not Just a Game: essays in Canadian sport sociology*. University of Ottawa Press: Ottawa, pp. 195–211.

Maguire, J. (1986): 'Images of manliness and competing ways of living in Late Victorian and Edwardian England', *British Journal of Sport History* 3, pp. 265–87.

Maguire, J. (1988): 'The commercialization of English elite basketball 1972–1988', *International Review for the Sociology of Sport* 23, pp. 305–24.

Maguire, J. (1990): 'More than a sporting "touchdown". The making of American football in Britain 1982–1989', *Sociology of Sport Journal* 7, pp. 213–37.

Maguire, J. (1991): 'The media sport production complex: the emergence of American sports in European culture', *European Journal of Communication* 6, pp. 315–36.

Maguire, J. (1993a): 'American football, British society and global sport development', in Dunning, E., Maguire, J. & Pearton, R., *The Sports Process*. Human Kinetics: Champaign, Ill., pp. 207–30.

Maguire, J. (1993b): 'Bodies, sportscultures and societies: a critical review of some theories in the sociology of the body', *International Review for the Sociology of Sport* 28, pp. 33–52.

Maguire, J. (1993c): 'Globalization, sport and national identities: the empires strike back?' *Society & Leisure* 16, pp. 293–322.

Maguire, J. (1993d): 'Hired corporate guns? Elite sport migrants in the global arena', *Vrijetijd en Samenleving* 10, pp. 19–30.

Maguire, J. (1993e): 'Globalization, sport development, and the media/sport production complex', *Sports Sciences Review* 2, pp. 29–47.

Maguire, J. (1994): 'Sport, identity politics and globalization: diminishing contrasts and increasing varieties', *Sociology of Sport Journal* 11, pp. 398–427.

Maguire, J. (1995a): 'Sport, the stadium and metropolitan life', in Bale, J. &

Moen, O. (eds) *The Stadium and the City*. Keele University Press: Keele, pp. 45–58.

Maguire, J. (1995b): 'Sportization processes: emergence, diffusion and globalization', *Swiss Journal of Sociology* 21, pp. 577–95.

Maguire, J. (1996): 'Blade runners: Canadian migrants and global ice-hockey trails', *Journal of Sport and Social Issues* 20, pp. 335–60.

Maguire, J. & Mansfield, L. (1998): 'Nobody's perfect: women, aerobics and the body beautiful', *Sociology of Sport Journal* 15, pp. 109–37.

Maguire, J. & Possamai, C. (in press): 'Rugby league, global sport and local identities', in Nauright, J., Maguire, J. Phillips, M., White, P. & Schimmel, K., *The Local and the Global*. Leicester University Press: Leicester.

Maguire, J. & Poulton, E. (in press): 'European identity politics in Euro 96: invented traditions and national habitus codes', *International Review for the Sociology of Sport*.

Maguire, J. & Roberts, S. (1998): 'Less weight, more gain?: pain/injury/diet issues in elite British female gymnastics'. Paper presented at the 14th International Sociological Association *World Congress of Sociology*. Montreal, Canada.

Maguire, J. & Stead, D. (1996): 'Far pavilions?: cricket migrants, foreign sojourn and contested identities', *International Review for the Sociology of Sport* 31, pp. 1–24.

Maguire, J. & Stead, D. (1997): 'Border crossings: soccer labour migration and the European union', *International Review for the Sociology of Sport* 32, pp. 59–73.

Maguire, J. & Stead, D. (1998): 'Cricket's global "finishing school": the migration of overseas cricketers into English county cricket', *European Physical Education Review* 4, pp. 54–69.

Maguire, J. & Tuck, J. (1998): 'Barbarians, gentlemen, players and patriots: rugby union and national identity in Britain since 1945', *Immigrants and Minorities* 17, pp. 103–26.

Mandell, R. (1984): *Sport: a cultural history*. Columbia University Press: New York.

Mandle, J. & Mandle, J. (1988): *Grass Roots Commitment: basketball and society in Trinidad and Tobago*. Caribbean Books: Parkesburg, Ia.

Mangan, J. A. (1986): *The Games Ethic and Imperialism*. Viking Press: London.

Mangan, J. A. (ed.) (1988): *Pleasure, Profit and Proselytism: British culture and sport at home and abroad 1700–1914*. Frank Cass: London.

Mason, T. (1995): *Passion of the People? football in South America*. Verso: London.

Massey, D. (1993): 'Power geometry and a progressive sense of place', in Bird, J., Curtis, B. Putman, T., Robertson, G. & Tickner, L. (eds) *Mapping Futures: local cultures, global change*. Routledge: London, pp. 59–69.

Massey, D. (1994): *Space, Place and Gender*. Polity Press: Cambridge.

Mattelart, A. (1977): *Multi-national Corporations and the Control of Culture: the ideological apparatuses of imperialism*. Harvester: Hassocks.

Mazrui, A. (1976): *A World Federation of Cultures: an African perspective*. The Free Press: New York.

Mazrui, A. (1987): 'Africa's triple heritage of play: reflections on the gender gap', in Baker, W. & Mangan, J. A. (eds) *Sport in Africa: essays in social history*. Africana: New York, pp. 217–28.

Meinander, H. (1992): 'Towards a bourgeois manhood: Nordic views and visions of physical education for boys, 1860–1930', *International Journal of the History of Sport* 9, pp. 337–55.

Mennell, S. (1985): *All Manners of Food: eating and taste in England and France from the middle ages to the present*. Blackwell: Oxford.

Mennell, S. (1990): 'The globalization of human society as a very long-term social process: Elias's theory', *Theory, Culture & Society* 7, pp. 359–73.

Mennell, S. (1992): *Norbert Elias: an introduction*. Blackwell: Oxford.

Mennell, S. (1994): 'The formation of we-images: a process theory', in Calhoun, C. (ed.) *Social Theory and the Politics of Identity*. Blackwell: Oxford, pp. 175–97.

Mennell, S. & Goudsblom, J. (eds) (1998): *Norbert Elias on Civilization, Power, and Knowledge*. University of Chicago Press: London.

Messner, M. (1990): 'When bodies are weapons: masculinity and violence in sport', *International Review for the Sociology of Sport* 25, pp. 203–18.

Michener, J. (1976): *Sports in America*. Random House: New York.

MIL Research Ltd (1986): American football national launch. Report prepared for Marshall Cavendish, December.

Mintel (1996): *Special Report, Sport*. Mintel Marketing Intelligence: London.

Murray, B. (1994): *Football: a history of the world game*. Scolar Press: Aldershot.

Nauright, J. & Chandler, J. L. (eds) (1996): *Making Men: rugby and masculine identity*. Frank Cass: London.

Nederveen Pieterse, J. (1995): 'Globalization as hybridization', in Featherstone, M., Lash, S. & Robertson, R. (eds) *Global Modernities*. Sage: London, pp. 45–68.

Nelson, B., Roberts, D. & Veit, W. (eds) (1992): *The Idea of Europe: problems of national and transnational identity*. Berg Press: Oxford.

NFL Merchandising Catalogue (1988). NFL: London.

Official International Handbook for the Sporting Goods Industry (1998): Pillet SA: Martigny, Switzerland.

Panorama Ansett Magazine (1997): POL Corporate Publishing: Redfern, NSW, Australia.

Pfister, G., Niewerth, T. & Steins, G. (eds) (1993): *Games of the World: between tradition and modernity*. Proceedings of the 2nd ISHPES Congress, Berlin. Academia Verlag: Sankt Augustin, pp. 367–73.

Pooley, J. C. (1981): 'Ethnic soccer clubs in Milwaukee: a study in assimilation', in Hart, M. & Birrell, S. (eds) *Sport in the Sociocultural Process*. Wm. C. Brown: Dubuque, Ia, pp. 430–47.

Quanz, D. (1991): 'The impact of North-American sport on European sport and the Olympic movement', in Landry, F., Landry, M. & Yerles, M. (eds) *Sport . . . the Third Millennium*. Proceedings of the International

Symposium, Quebec City, Canada, 21–25 May 1990. Les Presses de L'Université Laval: Sainte-Foy, pp. 117–32.

Rail, G. (1990): 'Physical contact in women's basketball: a first interpretation', *International Review for the Sociology of Sport* 25, pp. 269–87.

Real, M. (1989a): *Super Media: a cultural studies approach*. Sage: Newbury Park, Calif.

Real, M. (1989b): 'Super bowl football versus world cup soccer: a cultural-structural comparison', in Wenner, L. (ed.) *Media, Sports and Society*. Sage: Newbury Park, Calif., pp. 180–203.

Riesman, D. & Denney, R. (1981): 'Football in America: a study in cultural diffusion', in Hart, M. & Birrell, S. (eds) *Sport in the Sociocultural Process*. Brown: Ia, pp. 678–93.

Roberts, S. (ed.) (1994): *The Ice Hockey Annual 1994–1995*. Caldra House: Hove.

Robertson, R. (1990a): 'After nostalgia: wilful nostalgia and the phases of globalization', in Turner, B. S. (ed.) *Theories of Modernity and Postmodernity*. Sage: London, pp. 45–61.

Robertson, R. (1990b): 'Mapping the global condition: globalization as the central concept', *Theory, Culture & Society* 7, pp. 15–30.

Robertson, R. (1992): *Globalization: social theory and global culture*. Sage: London.

Robertson, R. (1995): 'Globalization: time–space and homogeneity–heterogeneity', in Featherstone, M., Lash, S. & Robertson, R. (eds) *Global Modernities*. Sage: London, pp. 25–44.

Robins, K. (1991): 'Tradition and translation: national culture in its global context', in Corner, J. & Harvey, S. (eds) *Enterprise and Heritage: cross-currents of national culture*. Routledge: London.

Rollin, R. (ed.) (1989): *The Americanization of the Global Village*. Bowling Green University Press: Bowling Green, Ohio.

Rosenau, J. (1980): *The Study of Global Interdependence*. Francis Pinter: London.

Roudometof, V. & Robertson, R. (1995): 'Globalization, world-system theory, and the comparative study of civilizations: issues of theoretical logic in world-historical sociology', in Sanderson, S. K. (ed.) *Civilizations and World Systems*. Alta Mira: Walnut Creek, Calif., pp. 273–300.

Rowe, D. (1995): *Popular Cultures: rock music, sport, and the politics of pleasure*. Sage: London.

Rowe, D. (1996): 'The global love-match: sport and television', *Media, Culture & Society* 18, pp. 565–82.

Rowe, D., Lawrence, G., Miller, T. & McKay, J. (1994): 'Global sport? core concern and peripheral vision', *Media, Culture & Society* 16, pp. 661–75.

Ryan, J. (1995): *Little Girls in Pretty Boxes: the making and breaking of elite gymnasts and figure skaters*. Doubleday: New York.

Sabo, D. (1993): 'Sociology of sport and new world disorder', *Sport Science Review* 2, pp. 1–9.

Sage, G. (1990): *Power and Ideology in American Sport*. Human Kinetics: Champaign, Ill.

Sage, G. (1993): 'The impact of European unification on American sports', *Journal of Comparative Physical Education and Sport* 15, pp. 21–9.

Sage, G. (1995): 'Deindustrialization and the American sporting goods industry', in Wilcox, R. C. (ed.) *Sport in the Global Village*. Fitness Information Technology, Inc.: Morgantown, W.Va, pp. 39–51.

Sage, G. (1996): 'Patriotic images and capitalist profit: contradictions of professional team sports licensed merchandise', *Sociology of Sport Journal* 13, pp. 1–11.

Said, E. (1993): *Culture and Imperialism*. Chatto & Windus: London.

Sanderson, S. (ed.) (1995): *Civilizations and World Systems: studying world-historical change*. Alta Mira: Walnut Creek, Calif.

Schiller, H. (1969): *Mass Communication and American Empire*. Beacon Press: Boston, Mass.

Scott, A. (ed.) (1997): *The Limits of Globalization: cases and arguments*. Routledge: London.

Seppanen, P. (1970): 'The role of competitive sports in different societies'. Paper presented at the 7th World Congress of Sociology, Varna, Bulgaria, September.

Seward, A. K. (1986): 'An attempt to perpetuate a cultural identity through traditional games in the face of the influence of western sports in Papua New Guinea', in Mangan, J. A. & Small, R. B. (eds) *Sport, Culture & Society*. Spon: London, pp. 33–8.

Sewart, J. (1987): 'The commodification of sport', *International Review for the Sociology of Sport* 22, pp. 171–92.

Sheard, K. (1997): 'Aspects of boxing in the western "civilising process" ', *International Review for the Sociology of Sport* 32, pp. 31–58.

Sklair, L. (1991): *Sociology of the Global System*. Harvester: London.

Snyder, E. & Spreitzer, E. (1984): 'Baseball in Japan', in Eitzen, S. (ed.) *Sports in Contemporary Society*. St. Martin's Press: New York, pp. 46–50.

Sport: Raising The Game (1995): London: Department of National Heritage.

Stiven, A. B. (1936): *Englands Einfluss auf den Deutschen Wortschatz*. B. Sporn: Zeulenroda.

Stoddart, B. (1979): 'Cricket's imperial crisis: the 1932–33 MCC tour of Australia', in Cashman, R. & McKernan, M. (eds) *Sport in History*. University of Queensland Press: St Lucia, pp. 124–47.

Stoddart, B. (1988): 'Sport, cultural imperialism, and colonial response in the British empire', *Society for Comparative Study of Society and History*, pp. 649–73.

Stoddart, B. (1989): 'Sport in the social construct of the lesser developed world: a commentary', *Sociology of Sport Journal* 6, pp. 125–35.

Stokvis, R. (1989): 'The international and national expansion of sports', in Wagner, E. (ed.) *Sport in Asia and Africa: a comparative handbook*. Greenwood Press: Westport, CT, pp. 13–24.

Sugden, J. & Tomlinson, A. (1998a): *FIFA and the Contest for World Football: who rules the people's game?* Polity Press: Cambridge.

Sugden, J. & Tomlinson, A. (1998b): 'Power and resistance in the governance of world football: theorizing FIFA's transnational impact', *Journal of Sport & Social Issues* 22, pp. 299–316.

Thompson, J. B. (1995): *The Media and Modernity: a social theory of the media*. Polity Press: Cambridge.

Tomlinson, A. & Whannel, G. (1984): *Five Ring Circus: money, power and politics at the Olympic games*. Pluto Press: London.

Tomlinson, J. (1991): *Cultural Imperialism*. Pinter Publishers: London.

Tomlinson, J. (1996): 'Olympic spectacle: opening ceremonies and some paradoxes of globalization', *Media, Culture & Society* 18, pp. 583–602.

Trujillo, N. (1991): 'Hegemonic masculinity on the mound: media representations of Nolan Ryan and American sports culture', *Critical Studies in Mass Communication* 8, pp. 290–308.

Tunstall, J. (1977): *The Media are American*. Constable: London.

Turner, B. (1987): 'A note on nostalgia', *Theory, Culture & Society* 4, pp. 147–56.

Turner, G. (1990): *British Cultural Studies: an introduction*. Unwin Hyman: London.

Valentine, J. (1997): 'Global sport and Canadian content: the *Sports Illustrated* Canada controversy', *Journal of Sport and Social Issues* 21, pp. 239–59.

Vamplew, W. & Stoddart, B. (eds) (1994): *Sport in Australia: a social history*. Cambridge University Press: Cambridge.

Van Bottenburg, M. (1992): 'The popularity of sports in continental Europe', *The Netherlands Journal of Social Sciences* 28, pp. 3–30.

Van der Poel, H. (1991): 'Media policy in Europe: compromising between nationalism and markets', *Leisure Studies* 10, pp. 187–201.

Van Krieken, R. (1998): *Norbert Elias*. Routledge: London.

Wagner, E. (ed.) (1989): *Sport in Asia and Africa: a comparative handbook*. Greenwood Press: Westport, Conn.

Wagner, E. (1990): 'Sport in Africa and Asia: Americanization or mundialization?' *Sociology of Sport Journal* 7, pp. 399–402.

Wallerstein, I. (1974): *The Modern World System*. Academic Press: New York.

Waters, M. (1995): *Globalization*. Routledge: London.

Weber, M. (1920/1992): *The Protestant Ethic and the Spirit of Capitalism*. Routledge: London.

Webster, D. (1988): *Looka Yonder! the imaginary America of populist culture*. Routledge: London.

Wenner, L. (1989): 'Media, sports and society: the research agenda', in Wenner, L. (ed.). *Media, Sports and Society*. Sage: Newbury Park, Calif., pp. 13–48.

Wenner, L. & Gantz, W. (1989): 'The audience experience with sports on television', in Wenner, L. (ed.) *Media, Sports and Society*. Sage: Newbury Park, Calif., pp. 241–69.

Whannel, G. (1989): 'History is being made: television sport and the selective tradition', in Jackson, R. & McPhail, T. (eds) *The Olympic Movement and the Mass Media: past, present and future issues*. Hurford Enterprises: Calgary, pp. 13–22.

Whannel, G. (1992a): *Fields in Vision: television sport and cultural transformation*. Routledge: London.

Whannel, G. (1992b): 'Profiting by the presence of ideals: sponsorship and Olympism'. Paper presented at the *British Olympic Academy*, May, University of Manchester, pp. 1–8.

Wilcox, R. C. (ed.) (1995): *Sport in the Global Village*. Fitness Information Technology, Inc: Morgantown, W.Va.

Williams, C., Lawrence, G. & Rowe, D. (1986): 'Patriarchy, media and sport', in Lawrence, G. & Rowe, D. (eds) *Power Play: the commercialization of Australian sport*. Hale & Iremonger: Sydney, pp. 215–29.

Williams, G. (1991): *1905 and All That: essays on rugby football, sport and Welsh society*. Gomer Press: Dyfed.

Williams, R. (1977): *Marxism and Literature*. Oxford University Press: Oxford.

Wilson, B. (1997): ' "Good blacks" and "bad blacks": media constructions of African-American athletes in Canadian basketball', *International Review for the Sociology of Sport* 32, pp. 177–89.

Wilson, J. (1994): *Playing by the Rules: sport, society, and the state*. Wayne University Press: Detroit.

Wisden Cricketers' Almanack (1950): John Wisden & Co: Guildford.

Wolfe, J. (1991): 'The global and the specific: reconciling conflicting theories of culture', in King, A. D. (ed.) *Culture, Globalization and the World-system*. Macmillan: London, pp. 161–73.

Wouters, C. (1990): 'Social stratification and informalization in global perspective', *Theory, Culture & Society* 7, pp. 69–90.

Yearley, S. (1996): *Sociology, Environmentalism, Globalization*. Sage: London.

Young, K., White, P. & McTeer, W. (1994): 'Body talk: male athletes reflect on sport, injury, and pain', *Sociology of Sport Journal* 11, pp. 175–94.

Index